WITHDRAWN
UTSA Libraries

KEMAL ATATURK

A RECENT PORTRAIT OF KEMAL ATATURK

KEMAL ATATURK

A Biography

HANNS FROEMBGEN

Translated from the German by
KENNETH KIRKNESS

With 21 *Illustrations*

BOOKS FOR LIBRARIES PRESS
FREEPORT, NEW YORK

First Published 1935
Reprinted 1971

INTERNATIONAL STANDARD BOOK NUMBER:
0-8369-6612-0

LIBRARY OF CONGRESS CATALOG CARD NUMBER:
70-175697

PRINTED IN THE UNITED STATES OF AMERICA
BY
NEW WORLD BOOK MANUFACTURING CO., INC.
HALLANDALE, FLORIDA 33009

CONTENTS

PART ONE. THE SOLDIER

CHAPTER		PAGE
I.	GALLIPOLI	11
II.	SALONIKA	36
III.	SYRIA	72

PART TWO. THE REBEL

IV.	CONSTANTINOPLE	89
V.	ERZERUM	100
VI.	ANATOLIA	108
VII.	PARIS	121
VIII.	SIVAS	124
IX.	ANGORA	136
X.	SÈVRES	148

PART THREE. THE VICTOR

XI.	SAKARIA	167
XII.	DUMLU PUNAR	186
XIII.	LAUSANNE	198
XIV.	MOSUL	218
XV.	ALHAMBRA	246
XVI.	FATHER OF THE TURKS	256

LIST OF ILLUSTRATIONS

A Recent Portrait of Kemal Ataturk	*Frontispiece*
Istanbul	16
The Anglo-French Fleet in the Dardanelles, March 18th, 1915	32
Talaat Pasha	48
Enver Pasha	48
General Liman von Sanders (1855–1929)	64
A War-time Portrait of Kemal Ataturk	64
Zubeide Hanum, Mother of Kemal Ataturk	80
Kemal Ataturk	80
A Peasant Woman of Anatolia	96
Angora	112
July 14th, 1920. General Gouraud, Commander-in-Chief of the French Army in Syria, marches into Beyruth	128
General Ismet Ineunu	160
Mohammed VI, Sultan of Turkey, 1861–1926	160
Kemal Ataturk with his Wife, Latifeh Hanoum	176
Angora	192
Kemal Ataturk attends a School Hour	208
The Girls' High School in Ankara	224
A Small Section of the Schoolchildren of Istanbul	248
Harem Ladies of Anatolia in outdoor Costume before the Abolition of the Veil	248
Modern Turkey is Athletic	272

PART ONE

THE SOLDIER.

CHAPTER I

GALLIPOLI

CONSTANTINOPLE on 17 March, 1915.
In Pera, where the hoarse cries of haggling Armenians, Levantines, Greeks and Jews echoed day and night, a rumour passed from mouth to mouth:

" They are coming !—The *Inglis !* The English ! "

No one dared to say it aloud, but grinning lips whispered it into ears which eagerly received the message.

When a Turkish gendarme came into view, the groups scattered, and the solitary individuals who still remained hugged the shady side of the street, smiled humbly, and lowered their heads. When the gendarme passed, the humble smile transformed itself into a poisonous grimace.

Ah, you dog ! In a few days' time we'll slit your throat. In a few days' time, when the English march into Constantinople, when Pera is beflagged and flood-lit, when the women smother the English sailors in perfume, when flowers rain down from the balconies. . . .

Already all windows in the main streets had been let at sinful prices to those who were anxious to witness the entry of the victors.

Assembled outside the Straits, near the Ægean Islands, were the united British and French Fleets, consisting of dreadnoughts, armoured cruisers, destroyers, torpedo-boats and submarines. In Pera people spoke of a fantastic force numbering a thousand ships and a hundred thousand men. . . .

For some time past spies had been secretly spreading information that the obsolete, tumbledown Dardanelles forts were without munitions. The Germans were said to be taking shells from the fortress of Bosporus to Chanak, the principal fort in the Dardanelles, while the Bosporus was being left completely defenceless. If the Russians attacked from the Black Sea, and if both sides attacked at the same time—the British from the west, from the Mediterranean, the Russians from the east. . . .

Pera trembled with impatience, joy and hatred, and the street scene was, if such a thing were possible, livelier than usual. Spies and traitors were active everywhere, and invisible threads connected

Pera with the Gallipoli positions and, beyond them, the enemy fleets lying in the shelter of the Ægean Islands.

This under-current of excitement was not confined to Pera. It had spread over the whole of Constantinople. The old Imperial City at the Golden Horn seemed to realize that the eyes of the whole world were upon her, and that a decision of the Great War was to be forced at her gates.

How impertinent the Levantines had become ! Now they were quite openly stating that special trains had been got in readiness to take his Majesty Sultan Mohammed V and his Court to Asia Minor, that the outer forts had been completely demolished by shell-fire and that Constantinople was to be evacuated. . . .

Turks had disappeared from the streets. In the cafés and bazaars there remained a few old men, solemnly and anxiously sipping their coffee. All the others, on orders from the military authorities, had made themselves scarce. Constantinople had been transformed overnigiht into an armed camp. The foreign element, spying and foretellng evil, alone remained visible.

At the Ministry of War there was a big conference. His Excellency the Vice-Commander-in-Chief, Enver Pasha, was receiving the Head of the German Military Mission, General Liman von Sanders ; behind closed doors negotiations were being pursued and plans discussed.

Dependable news had been received. During the last few days the *Queen Elizabeth*, England's mightiest ship, had been lying off the Dardanelles. The whole world impatiently waited to be told of the effect of her 16-inch guns, which were mounted in her at the Southampton Docks.

The decisive action was expected hourly. The forts had just enough munitions to last them for a single day's fighting. They were short of everything. Moreover, there was no communication with Germany, from whom war supplies could have been obtained. A hundred and eighty ancient guns, vintage 1879, faced the Anglo-French Fleet, equipped with the most up-to-date artillery, which was approaching in overwhelming force.

The fall of Constantinople, the capital of the Ottoman Empire, Germany's ally, would at a single blow have altered the entire war situation to the disadvantage of the Central Powers, and it was evident that the British, with their well-known tenacity, would leave no stone unturned to reach this goal.

The faces of those in the Turkish Ministry of War bore anxious expressions.

Sleep was not easy in Constantinople that night.

Some distance away, along the Narrows, beyond the Sea of Marmora, all was silent. Long and slender, the Gallipoli Peninsula gradually lost itself in the black expanse of the Ægean Sea. Away on the other side Asia approached to within a few kilometres. The silhouettes of the forts, like giant tombs, rose from the dark strip between sky and water which represented the other shore.

The soldiers, light sleepers, were ready for their call. The black shadows of the sentries were reflected in the rippling waves.

Suddenly the day broke, casting light over the sea and its shores and flooding the world with colour.

It was early spring in the Dardanelles.

Over on the Asiatic side, behind Fort Kum Kale, lay the ruins of Troy, the oldest memorial of the struggle for the Straits which separate Asia from Europe.

On the walls of Nagara stood two officers, field-glasses held to their eyes, scrutinizing the glittering sea. They were Colonel Wehrle, who had charge of the fortifications, and Colonel Jevad, the Dardanelles Commandant.

" Is the weather too fine for our English friends ? " asked one of them.

" Can't see anything suspicious . . ." the other replied.

The German glanced at his watch.

" It's getting on for eleven. In Europe it is the time for paying calls."

" Very impolite of them to keep us waiting so long."

The Turk smiled and looked out over the sea towards the horizon. Small waves playfully lapped the seashore.

Suddenly the German whistled softly. The Turk quickly picked up his glasses and turned them towards the horizon, and whispered :
" Allah ! "

A minute cloud of smoke could be distinguished in the distance above the dancing waves. Quickly it developed into a dense wall of black-grey cloud. Heavy, dark shadows fell across the sea.

The sun disappeared behind an impenetrable smoke-screen. The arrows of the Persian Army, which crossed from here to Greece, are said once to have similarly obscured the light. England's Fleet was steaming from Tenedos and Imbros. The frightened sea divided to allow the armoured giants of battleships to pass. Leading the way was the speedy pack of torpedo-boats, destroyers, mine-sweepers and pinnaces. Behind them followed the big fellows. Ten battleships, a French squadron and two British squadrons. Hydroplanes circled above the Kum Kale Fort, which had been demolished in February, and light cruisers reconnoitred the coasts.

With uncanny rapidity the advance developed. In this battle 318 of the latest guns were to be used against 180 aged pieces, ripe for the museum.

The Fleet now arrived at the entrance to the Narrows. Level with Troy, within sight of the ruined Fort Kum Kale, a "roundabout" was formed affording to all ships the maximum fire scope.

Flags of smoke fluttered wildly, spreading themselves like giant cloths, screening the sky.

Suddenly there came sounds of music ! The ships' bands had paraded on deck, and their marches echoed across the water. As in an opera, the Fleet advanced into battle with martial music, triumphantly. . . .

But listen ! . . .

Sounds of music came from the land, too, but a different kind of music. The muffled sounds of drums. Turkish kettledrums sounding the alarm. And from Chanak, on the other side, the subdued notes of the bugles could be heard.

Then thunder shook the world. It burst forth from the mouths of the guns. The iron roundabout began to open fire. The reports of the guns eclipsed all other sounds ; and the bursts were frightful. Under blows from the *Queen Elizabeth's* 16-inch guns the earth writhed.

The forts swallowed the rain of iron in silence, for the Fleet was still beyond range of the Turkish guns, and the strictest account had to be taken of every shell fired.

Great ribbons of flame illuminated the opposite shore—burning villages.

At noon signs of life were no longer visible in the outer works.

But fountains of earth continued to ascend skywards, and walls continued to crumble.

Victory was assured. France was eager to be first at the finishing post. Rather surprisingly, the French passed the British lines and steamed full speed into the inner Dardanelles, in the direction of Fort Chanak.

Gaulois led the way, casting up a great wash as she progressed, ploughing her way towards the Sea of Marmora, *en route* for Constantinople.

They were now within range of the Turkish guns, which at once opened fire. The armoured giants trembled under the first hits. Shell-fire from the battered forts continued without interruption. In all cases the Turkish gunners had managed to hold out under the murderous bombardment. The works were destroyed, but the soldiers were still living beneath the ruins to serve the guns which were still capable of firing, for, luckily, the Briton had exhausted most of his energy upon skilfully mounted dummy batteries.

The French continued to advance deeper into the inner Narrows, and failed to observe the vivid flames which suddenly shot forth from the battleship *Inflexible*, which only a short while before, near the Falkland Islands, had run down the valiant Spee. The giant ship took a serious list. A howitzer shell had found its way through the deck and reached the magazine. With difficulty the *Inflexible* limped from the scene.

Two o'clock in the afternoon. The French had advanced ten kilometres into the Dardanelles, and commenced to pound the main defences at Chanak. In the meanwhile, the British hurled salvo after salvo at the Peninsula of Gallipoli. A new line of battleships now arrived and took the position formerly occupied by the French.

The break-through had succeeded. There remained one more obstacle—Fort Hamidie—and then Chanak!

A hurricane of iron swept the fort away, transforming it into a huge burial ground. The earth opened up and swallowed the ruins.

The *Gaulois* continued on her course. The way was free. Pennants fluttered, cannons roared. The ruins that were Fort

Hamidie had just been passed. Four French battleships had broken through to the Dardanelles. *En avant!* . . .

Then, suddenly, to the horror and dismay of the French, their misfortune became apparent.

From the heap of ruins, Fort Hamidie, there came deadly fire. Shot after shot.

With superhuman strength, the occupants of Fort Hamidie, most of them severely wounded, dug their way out of the wreckage and fought a way back to the light. With blood coursing over them, the gunners ran to the few guns that were still serviceable and—with more than one foot in the grave—did their duty, to save Constantinople, to save the Sultan.

The *Gaulois* was hit, put out of action, and listed. Helpless, she drifted with the current and ran aground at Tenedos in the Ægean Sea.

The British steamed ahead at full speed. But they were too late to avert a catastrophe.

The *Bouvet* foundered and in a few minutes she sank, 600 of her crew of 660 perishing with her.

Fort Hamidie continued to fire shot after shot. The dying gunners were delivering deadly blows.

The *Suffren*, the French flagship, sprang a leak, and appealed for help, maintaining herself above the surface with the utmost difficulty

The French squadron was destroyed.

The British were now on the scene and poured concentrated fire on Fort Hamidie, finally bringing the ruins to silence.

Four o'clock in the afternoon. The British Commander-in-Chief wirelessed a message of victory to the Admiralty.

A little later, the *Queen Elizabeth*, the pride of the British Fleet, went about and, severely hit, fled from the scene of battle.

Fort Hamidie was now firing spasmodically—every round was precious—but she was still scoring telling hits. The other forts were in no wise inclined to lag behind her. The battle reached its peak.

A Turkish shell struck the armoured turret of the *Irresistible* and carried it away. Hardly had the British curses died away when a fearful detonation rent the air. The *Irresistible* had struck a mine.

The *Ocean* rushed forward to her assistance, but in a short

ISTANBUL
The street of steps showing the Tower of Galata.

time collapsed under Turkish howitzer fire and, together with the *Irresistible*, began to drift, relentlessly pursued by the Turkish artillery. Level with Troy, at the entrance of the Dardanelles, the *Ocean* met her fate and foundered. The *Irresistible*, sorely stricken, was taken in tow.

The Commander-in-Chief, Admiral de Robeck, witnessed these misfortunes. He had no need to wait for them to be reported to him. The thunder and noise of battle in the Straits increased to a frenzied pitch. At any moment one expected the heavens to break asunder.

He glanced at his staff-officers. Their features, grey and grim, betrayed emotions of excitement, tension, intense anxiety, fear.

Who would have imagined such a resistance possible? The enemy's fire continued to increase.

" Break off the battle ! "
" Hold out ! "
" Return to the harbour of Mudros ! "
" Fight on, sir, for God and England's sake ! "

The Admiral hesitated, cast a glance at the sky, then at his watch. . . .

" Withdraw ! To Mudros ! "

Dry and hard were his words. The great roar of the coastal batteries continued unabated.

The huge ships turned and sought refuge in the Ægean Sea, from whose waters night would presently rise, to cover the scene of battle in a dark mantle of silence.

From the ruins, dust and smoke along the shores a hoarse, guttural cheer was raised.

Constantinople and the Straits were for the present saved. Torchlight processions marched through the streets of the capital. In the mosques foreheads touched the ground in a prayer of thanksgiving. The muezzin's cry from the minaret echoed louder :

" Allah is great ! There is no god but Allah ! This day He has shown us His blessing. Come to Allah ! "

A more serious view of the events was taken by the men at the Ministry of War. While endless torchlight processions were filling the streets with lights and noise, the pashas were conferring. They knew that only the beginning had been seen.

Spies, agents and confidential men reported that British officers and authorized agents in Greek ports were chartering every vessel they could lay their hands on, from the most unseaworthy fishing boat to thousand-ton freighters. Money was pouring in—good, honest English pounds. An unprecedented prosperity reigned along the Greek coasts. Patched-up craft fetched unheard-of prices. The harbours thrived as never before. Was war a good or an evil thing? They left that problem to others, and continued selling. . . .

The Briton had no time to waste upon negotiations. He paid without question, and bought up everything that was offered to him—ships, provisions and articles of equipment—for an army is a hungry monster, and the Tommies were not accustomed to experiencing want.

Intelligence ! It was not sold once, but many times. First to the English, then to the Turks, then once more (in a new guise) to the English. The French, too, had from time to time their own little, delicate interests, which again were a source of profit.

English and Turkish pounds waged a bitter struggle round the " smiling " Greek soul.

An endless procession of troop-transports ploughed deep furrows in the disturbed waters of the Ægean. The ships came from Gibraltar, from England, Northern France, from Marseilles, from the South, from Egypt, from India, from Australia. In the mighty depôts at Malta there was feverish activity. Mountains of supplies and equipment were unstacked and loaded into the ships—in addition to munitions and war materials of the latest kind, of which the Anatolian soldier had not even heard.

Forward against Constantinople ! Forward to the Straits !

The British were no longer willing to tremble for India's sake and no longer prepared to leave their armies as helpless victims of the German cannons in Northern France; they wanted more than anything to establish communication with the Russian ally, supply him with munitions and instruments of war, and transform him into a really dangerous opponent of the Central Powers. In London there was a man who visualized the bold way by which England could achieve a quick victory : Winston Churchill, the First Lord of the Admiralty. If God were with him, he would discover the right men to bring his daring plan to fruition.

GALLIPOLI

Under General Sir Ian Hamilton's command were one hundred thousand men—Scots, New Zealanders, Australians, Gurkhas—the finest troops at England's disposal. In their ranks was an enthusiasm that had not been known since the days of Nelson. Gallipoli ! It was the greatest war adventure that had come England's way for many decades. Who would miss such a chance ? The flower of Britain's youth rushed to join the Dardanelles Army, the great Expeditionary Corps that was assembling off the Greek islands.

Time passed, precious time. English military bureaucracy, a superabundance of men and materials. . . .

Already four weeks had passed since the naval battle. In the Turkish War Ministry nerves were getting frayed. How much longer did the enemy need for his preparations and plans ?

It was a lucky thing that he needed so long ! Each day was of inestimable value to the defender. In all haste, the Vth Army was formed. No less a soldier than Marshal Liman von Sanders, the Head of the German Military Mission, was appointed its commanding officer. Here, too, we have the same picture. The best men had one ambition : to be transferred to the Vth Army.

Their strength was rather less than half that of the enemy. It was impossible, therefore, to guard the whole coastline, and the only thing to do was to mass troops at points where a landing attempt might be expected. The long strips of coast between these points were watched only by small formations of the military and by gendarmes.

The Briton had a clear picture of what was happening, had maps showing the minutest details, and an intelligence service which functioned perfectly.

On 25 April people were surprised by the sound of gunfire. The Briton was manœuvring up and down the coast with the object of causing confusion on the other side. Torpedo-boats, as though possessed, darted here and there, firing whenever the slightest target presented itself. This continued all through the day. Lucky was the man who possessed strong nerves !

For the present Liman von Sanders had to content himself with relying on the training which he had given to his army and divisional commanders. At the decisive moment everything depended on the right man giving the right orders quickly.

19

Night came. At the southern end of Gallipoli, near Sedd-el-Bahr, the Briton had disembarked and set foot on land. There a battle had been raging for several hours. What was happening on other sectors of the front was still not clear.

In the vicinity of Cape Ariburnu, under cover of the darkness, a giant flotilla of boats neared the unguarded coast. A landing was difficult, especially as the strong current began to carry the boats slightly to the north. Soon it would be dawn. On shore nothing stirred, though several pairs of eyes kept a constant watch on the black surface of the sea.

As quietly as possible the boats worked their way towards the shore, and before it was yet light a party of Australians set foot on Gallipoli. The Turkish sentinels were noiselessly liquidated, only a few gendarmes succeeded in escaping. They took to their heels and disappeared into the darkness.

A little way inland rose the heights of Ariburnu. It was known that they were not defended, and it was essential that they should be seized without loss of time. Their possession meant victory half gained, for from there the whole Peninsula could be commanded. From there the Turks could be shot to pieces in their trenches without being able to do very much in their own defence. The heights of Ariburnu were of first-class importance.

They drew nearer and nearer to their goal and the first men of the Anzac Corps were commencing to climb the slopes, when they suddenly and noiselessly collapsed under Turkish bayonets. Immediately there was confusion. In the uncertain light of dawn Turkish fezes could be seen rising over the crest. With fixed bayonets, and bending low, the Anatolian infantry advanced at the double, and in the next few moments the full force of their attack struck the British. There was a brief and vicious hand-to-hand skirmish, in the course of which the English were defeated and forced to retreat to the beaches. There fresh troops were still being landed. Fearful confusion broke out. Fugitives and landing parties collided and got in each other's way. Then the Turkish artillery opened fire, and wrought fearful havoc among the masses of men assembled on the unsheltered beaches. What had happened? What was the solution of the mystery? The secret of this gruesome surprise? . . .

Liman von Sanders gave instructions for the time of calm before the storm to be employed by the troops in practice manœuvres to prepare them for their task of repulsing the enemy invasion, and none showed greater zeal in carrying out this order than the young commander of the 19th Turkish Division, to whose sector of the front the Ariburnu area belonged.

He was a sharp-spoken, rather unapproachable gentleman, with a completely un-Turkish conception of military service: he was as severe and as demanding as any German officer of the Military Mission. He was a harsh disciplinarian, and had all the officers and men under his command on tip-toe. It went hard with the man who was found guilty of the slightest breach of discipline or neglect of duty. But no one—not even in the Arab regiments—in the 19th Division was ever convicted of those offences. The young lieutenant-colonel had only recently taken over the command. He had come from Sofia, where he held the post of Military Attaché, had set to work with fierce energy and in a few weeks transformed his men into soldiers who would not hesitate to face the *Sheitan* himself, if the *Kumandan* were at their head.

Also on this night, instead of sleep and rest, there was a field exercise—on the heights of Ariburnu. A battery of artillery accompanied the infantry on this manœuvre. When he was asked whether ball ammunition was to be issued to the men, he replied briefly: Yes. Some extra sense must have warned him of the coming danger.

Practising modern war tactics, the soldiers slowly advanced towards the heights. Presently they were close to them. In the chilly atmosphere which immediately precedes daybreak, the men shivered. It was at this time that they noticed the Turkish gendarmes breathlessly running towards them.

" *Inglis! Inglis!* "

Immediately the *Kumandan's* voice echoed over their heads:
" Forward against the enemy! "

What was formerly an exercise was now the real thing. The troops ascended the slope at the double. Every minute was costly. The Australians were scaling the other side of the mountain. Soon the sounds of fighting, quiet at first, gradually swelled into a furious crescendo.

The *Kumandan* himself remained with the battery of artillery, shouting orders and encouraging the gunners. . . .

The thunder of the guns echoed over the Peninsula and the sea, the sounds gradually losing themselves in the bays, coves, valleys and ravines. The battle speedily developed, and the invaders, taken by surprise, were driven back to the sea.

The Anatolians rushed after them, eager to make a thorough job of their work. But, at the moment they occupied the beach, the first salvo from the British naval batteries burst forth, and an iron screen of death parted the two adversaries.

Against the ships' heavy artillery the Turks, with their small calibre guns, were unable to make any headway. The *Kumandan* cursed to himself. He had to leave the British in occupation of the beaches, for to send his men through that screen of death was more than he could dream of attempting.

But that did not minimize the victory. The enemy's attempt to make a successful landing at the most vulnerable spot on Gallipoli had been frustrated, brilliantly frustrated, thanks to the masterly generalship of the Officer Commanding the 19th Turkish Division, Lieutenant-Colonel Mustafa Kemal.

At once his name became known in the streets, cafés, the bazaars and drawing-rooms of Constantinople. With Eastern extravagance the Turks named him the Saviour of Constantinople; and the Commander-in-Chief, Liman von Sanders, realized better than any that they had in him a soldier in a million.

We must not forget the Anatolian soldiers, whose leader he was. In the loneliness of his uneventful peasant existence, the Anatolian in remote Asia Minor was by nature a philosopher and deep thinker. The world, as he knew it, consisted of a plot of land and a strip of sky bordered by a high wall of jagged mountains. At night the stars shone powerfully in this strip of sky. Time then seemed to stand still; the pulse-beat of world history appeared to cease. The Anatolian sat lost in thought, losing count of the march of the hours.

He was seldom known to translate his thoughts into words, and, indeed, was hardly able to do so, for no one had taught him this. The thoughts of his peasant nature were profound; he was closely bound up with those things which, he was aware, were round him: his soil and his limited strip of star-strewn sky.

Far from the world he built for himself his own world, a world of belief, of the miraculous and of the supernatural. His life turned him into a philosopher, and he claimed to be conscious of the presence of higher, mysterious powers, which the reason of the inhabitants of big cities refused to recognize. He recognized them, fanatically, devoutly, and with every atom of his being.

His wretched mud hut often concealed thousands of good Turkish gold-pounds, enough to enable him to build a fine country house, enough to permit him to travel—but he had no wish for such things. The money continued to rest where it had already long rested. Once a month he visited the nearest market, sold his cattle, and, if the Beiram Festival was at hand, sold them in herds, bringing home with him more gold-pounds, which he placed in the chest with the others. And there they stayed. He continued to sleep on the bare floor; his life consisted of caring for his soil and of silent thought; occasionally in the evening he smoked his old water-pipe; maize was his principal food.

He was a man of great stature and formidable strength. A long battle with the hard soil had made him so. He was accustomed always to carry arms, for he had to defend himself against wolves. About five centuries ago he came from the dark lap of Turkestan, when the great drought descended upon Asia, driving the nomad Turks westwards.

When the Sultan declared war, he suddenly found himself a soldier, and he displayed in his new profession the same tranquillity that had characterized him as a peasant and philosopher. He was amenable to discipline, loyal and fearless; he demanded little for himself, placed not the slightest value on his own life, and looked up in quiet confidence to the officer whom Allah had destined to be his master and leader.

His uniform was ragged, and the boots given to him by his Supreme War Lord were worn out—but he made no complaints. In the other world Allah was preparing every luxury for those who in this world humbly and loyally served His representatives.

Of such stuff were the soldiers with whom the Divisional Commander, Lieutenant-Colonel Mustafa Kemal, defended his front near Ariburnu against the Anglo-Australian "Anzac" Corps.

It is only to-day that we are able to see these men and their leader in their true light. He was a man who inspired confidence in his subordinates. The Anatolians regarded him with a mixture of awe and admiration, and placed absolute trust in him. There was something about him—they could not explain to themselves what it was—something of magic. . . .

His look pierced one like a bullet. His word of command was like the crack of a whip, and in his movements there was supple strength, a menacing assurance, reminding one of solitary beasts of prey in the jungle.

Undoubtedly there was something electrifying, something spell-binding about the *Kumandan*; and he possessed a forceful personality which captured and held men in its grasp.

He was master over others because he was master of himself. He was a man, looking neither to the right nor to the left, who wasted neither words nor gestures—a man of thought, discipline and will-power.

He lay behind a heap of stones, a sinewy, lean figure, with binoculars to his eyes, watching the beaches where the British soldiers, wet to the skin and utterly wretched, were endeavouring to take cover ; and he watched the burst of the ships' shells, which the enemy continued to despatch in order to consolidate the meagre gains of their first landing attempt.

His stern, clear-cut features, which seemed as though cast in bronze, were immovable, dark, determined and impenetrable. The steel-grey eyes in his sun-tanned warrior face shone with an uncanny, remarkable brilliance. They were eyes in which the supple strength and ruthless self-control and will of the Turanian Grey Wolf were mirrored.

His eyes wandered out to sea, where an amazing spectacle met his gaze : transport after transport, guarded by ships of war. One corps after the other was being set ashore, until the narrow beaches were black with soldiers.

This accursed lack of artillery ! If only a couple of heavy batteries were at hand to take up the challenge of the British naval artillery— not a British marching boot would have been left on Gallipoli soil.

GALLIPOLI

In the present circumstances the enemy had to be left in occupation of a narrow strip of coast. It was not much, but bad enough.

How different things might have been had not Turkey existed in a sort of medieval unconcern of development and progress! The *Kumandan* cursed inwardly. He had seen what a modern army was, five years ago, in Picardy, during the French Autumn Manœuvres. Then he was a junior member of the General Staff, and how his eyes had opened at the sight of the engines and machines, at the organization and smooth co-operation of the various arms.

On his return he had bombarded the higher authorities with requests, suggestions, demands and criticisms: he was determined to create a modern army, an army fit to take its place at the side of its European colleagues.

Regarded as an intolerable nuisance and meddlesome know-all he was posted to Sofia, and at the outbreak of war an attempt actually was made to prevent him from returning to active service with the Army.

Party administration, slackness, corruption and the shameless household policy of the Sultans, the whole being cloaked under the mantle of religious fanaticism—against that progress was impossible.

But now was not the time for brooding and pondering. No matter at what cost, the enemy had to be finally dislodged from the narrow strip of coast now in his possession, and cast into the sea. To wait for the next day, and launch a surprise attack at dawn, was the best policy. He took out his note-book and began to write down orders. "*Activité! Activité! Vitesse, messieurs!*" stood written in bold letters on the first page of the book, which, in addition to observations of his own, contained extracts from the works of Moltke and studies of the Napoleonic campaigns.

Much costly blood would flow. The goal could only be reached through a bayonet charge, for in a hand-to-hand engagement the naval artillery could not participate, was helpless.

At an early hour on 27 April, the 19th Division advanced to the attack. Their commanding-officer was at their head. The enemy were swept from Gallipoli with the bayonet. Mustafa Kemal glanced with pride and emotion at his Anatolian soldiers, who had been victorious over an army many times their own size.

The British had hardly extricated themselves from the Turkish grip, when the naval artillery took a hand in the game. The wounds which it inflicted on the gallant division were rightful. But it had no effect on the result of the engagement. The English landing attempt had been repulsed. . . .

The Vice-Commander-in-Chief, Enver Pasha, lifted his eyebrows. He could see in his mind's eye the thin, stern features of the soldier. He hated and feared the cold, penetrating look of the man who was once his friend and comrade. Even in days gone by, when they had been in league against Abdul Hamid, the fallen despot, Mustafa Kemal had proved himself to be a sharp, troublesome critic and irritating busybody. No one saw through the reserved, solitary individual, who silently retired into the shade when the revolutionary Young Turk Committee seized power and the young captains and subalterns became generals and Ministers overnight.

The Vice-Generalissimo Enver remembered vividly the moment when Mustafa Kemal demanded that the Committee should dissolve, the goal having been reached and the despot fallen. He likened it to a state within the State, and spoke of cliques and party rule. And when he retorted, " On the contrary, the Committee's régime is just beginning," their ways parted.

The thirty-five-year-old Vice-Commander-in-Chief, thanks to the Committee the mightiest man in the Ottoman Empire, had many foes. None was more inconvenient to him than Mustafa Kemal, for he was not a personal enemy or rival, but the representative of another *Weltanschauung*, an ideology that had nothing in common with the Liberal-Democratic views of the Freemason Enver. His well-manicured fingers drummed nervously on the surface of the writing-desk. At the very moment when, despite all precautions, his own failure in the Caucasus was becoming public knowledge—a fearful blunder costing ninety thousand soldiers their lives—precisely at this moment came the news of Mustafa Kemal's victory at the gates of Constantinople !

The telephone bell rang.

One of the invisible men of the mighty Committee announced himself.

" What a dubious success ! To whom are we indebted for the

fact that Mustafa Kemal received a command in Gallipoli, instead of remaining in Sofia to drink tea with beautiful women ? "

" Unfortunately I failed to convince him that that was of greater importance than, in these times, serving at the front."

" To put it more clearly—he left Sofia on his own responsibility and went to the front ? "

" I wasn't here, I was in the Caucasus."

" Where the fortunes of war were substantially less favourable to you . . ."

" I am grateful to you for your repeated reminder of the fickleness of fortune."

" Don't mention it !—The point is this : The Committee entirely agree with the Vice-Commander-in-Chief that, politically, Mustafa Kemal must be rendered innocuous. The Vice-Commander-in-Chief no doubt is clever and capable enough to devise ways and means to rid the Committee, to whom he has sworn loyalty, of a source of acute anxiety. May Allah spread His protecting hand over you and your sons, Pasha ! " . . .

Honours were liberally distributed to the victorious troops on Gallipoli. As representative of the Supreme War Lord, Sultan Mohammed V, the Vice-Commander-in-Chief appeared to convey to the soldiers their sovereign's thanks.

Among the troops who paraded were the 19th Division, the division which bore the blunt of the fighting and which decided the battle. With joyful anticipation the brave Anatolian soldiers looked forward to the arrival of the distinguished visitor. Their ragged uniforms and the big gaps in their ranks were an eloquent, affecting proof that they had well deserved the honour.

Clenching his teeth the commanding officer began to march up and down the trenches. He was already aware that the Vice-Commander-in-Chief was not celebrated for punctuality. He had even allowed, on one occasion, the invalid Sultan to wait three hours for him. The soldiers were patient, but Mustafa Kemal secretly ground his teeth in rage.

Kemal's division waited for some while longer, until the officers could no longer conceal from their men the fact that the Vice-Commander-in-Chief in his inspection of the front had passed over the Ariburnu sector.

Enver was able to permit himself a smile of satisfaction on being informed that Colonel Mustafa Kemal had relinquished his command.

His joy was short-lived. He promptly received a visit from the highly indignant Commander-in-Chief of the Straits, General Liman von Sanders. The German was in no circumstances willing to allow them to hound his best officer from the front. Once more there was a lively exchange of words between the two men. The German officer's criticism of the Vice-Commander-in-Chief was sharp and merciless.

Liman von Sanders spoke with Mustafa Kemal as man to man, soldier to soldier. Neither had need for the employment of high-sounding phrases. And without the need for voicing it, both were in agreement in their judgment of the spokesman of the Committee and in their assessment of the military situation. Mustafa Kemal admired in Liman von Sanders the ideal superior officer, and the German, for his part, made no secret of the fact that he regarded his divisional commander as a soldier born to great things.

Mustafa retained his command at Ariburnu.

In May Turks and British concluded a truce for the purpose of burying their dead, who had fallen in No Man's Land. The stench of the decomposing corpses, above which huge swarms of large blue flies hovered, was unbearable. Among the Turkish soldiers who went forward to the British trenches to bear away their dead comrades was a sergeant, a lean, upright man with very fair hair and remarkable steel-grey eyes. He turned up, soon here, soon there, a spade in his hand, digging the earth and conversing, in very imperfect French, with the British soldiers. In the latter a decent, sporting conception of war had been bred in their bones, and they willingly talked to the pleasant sergeant, who, they guessed, was certainly no Prussian. The active sergeant managed to be everywhere, and, during the work of burying corpses, kept a sharp eye on what was happening in the British trenches. The worthy Tommies, who exchanged cigarettes with him, had little idea that they were hobnobbing with the enemy commanding-officer, Mustafa Kemal.

A couple of days later, instead of exchanging cigarettes they were again exchanging " Blue Beans," and no quarter was given on either side. In the narrow hell of Gallipoli they could not allow themselves the luxury of taking prisoners.

The campaign stagnated into demoralizing position warfare. The Briton failed to advance a single yard, though, at the same time, the Turk was unable to dislodge him from his present gains, for he had no means of reply to the naval guns which commanded the shores. They were still without communications with Germany. If only the German heavy guns would arrive, what a difference they would make to the situation! Thomas Atkins would then be given something to think about. But before that Serbia had to be conquered; until then the Allies could not join hands. When would the German offensive in Serbia open? When would the Central Powers close their grip on the Balkans?

Until that time they must do their best to hold out.

The British were clearly aware of the position, and knew that it was a race with time. But they needed months for the preparations.

In August, 1915, they believed themselves strong enough, having a large numerical superiority, to launch the big attack.

The best army that England had ever set on foot assembled at the Greek islands. Countless transports—floating barracks—churned the waters of the Mediterranean.

"Two minutes from victory!" was the opinion of Sir Ian Hamilton, the Commander-in-Chief of the Anglo-French Expeditionary Corps.

Again the British attempted bluffing tactics up and down the coast, striving to confuse the enemy, and then set ashore a large body of troops at Suvla Bay, north of the Ariburnu sector.

Three Turkish battalions and a few guns were all that remained at the moment for the purposes of defence. Along the whole of Gallipoli hell broke loose. The British naval artillery mercilessly pounded the Peninsula, rending great holes in the earth, casting into the air huge fountains of soil, crushing human beings like ants and taking a fearful toll of valuable, irreplaceable Anatolian life.

Liman von Sanders clenched his teeth. This time things looked extremely critical. Without reinforcements nothing could be done. Over on the Asiatic side a reserve corps had been alarmed, and was assumed to be advancing in forced marches. So far nothing had been seen of it.

At Suvla Bay the British went forward to the charge. On the other side the Turks doubled to meet them. Between the two forces lay the mountain of Sari Bair. That was the objective. It was a race for possession. Soon Briton and Turk were at grips.

There were three Anatolian battalions against an army.

Fighting farther to the north was Mustafa Kemal, unable to stir, powerless to send help, having all his work cut out to hold the enemy in check.

Nothing was seen or heard of the Asiatic Reserve Corps. Its commander's ears must have buzzed with the curses which were rained down on his head. As it happened, with the best will in the world, and by dint of the severest marches, he could not possibly reach the scene of action until the following day. The British, who were always well informed, knew that they had to reach the goal first.

A hellish night, illuminated with flashes and the reflection of fires and made hideous by explosions, cries and the thunder of the guns, passed. Towards morning Mustafa Kemal received a message that the English were storming the commanding Sari Bair. All night he had sought in vain to shake off the enemy, whose hand gripped his throat. Catastrophe seemed inevitable. The Sari Bair in the hands of the enemy? There was no time to lose in speculation. At the last second he formed a quick, bold decision.

Mustafa Kemal withdrew one battalion from the line, placed himself at its head, and hastened to the aid of his hard-pressed comrades on the Sari. The British were about to plant their spades in the summit, when Mustafa's assault burst upon them. There was a murderous fight, which resulted in the Turks regaining possession of the Sari Bair.

They were allowed no time in which to make themselves comfortable, for the British again assaulted the blood-drenched mountain. The men from Scotland and Lancashire and the young fellows from the Australasian Anzac Corps knew precisely what was at stake. The fall of the Sari Bair meant the fall of the Straits, meant at last an escape from the Gallipoli hell, meant the capture of Constantinople and the finish of the war in the East.

The officers, England's best, had no need to tell their men this. They charged with desperate valour, and after fearful bloodshed cast the weak Anatolian detachments from their positions and, finally, halted breathlessly on the summit of the Sari Bair. Below them lay the glittering surface of the Dardanelles Straits, opening in the distance to the wide Sea of Marmora, where, a little farther away, Constantinople lay and beckoned. They could almost see their goal. The soldiers raised a hoarse cheer : victory was theirs !

Rifle-fire brought an abrupt end to their jubilation. Lieutenant-Colonel Kannengiesser, at the head of the 9th Turkish Division, stormed the Sari Bair, and after a sharp engagement drove its occupants back into the valley.

Still nothing was seen or heard of the Asiatic Reserve Corps.

Lieutenant-Colonel Kannengiesser was severely wounded. His men began scratching up the earth to provide temporary cover.

On the following morning the British naval guns took the Sari Bair under fire, and hurled salvo after salvo at the Turkish positions, which could be clearly observed from the sea. There was no refuge from the shells of the naval artillery. But the Anatolians did not yield. Sari Bair gradually became transformed into a huge grave.

Then the British stormed them. The Anatolians leapt out of their shallow trenches and shell-holes and met them with fixed bayonets. In their rear Turkish reinforcements rushing to their aid were mown down by the British artillery.

On Sari Bair the last Anatolian defenders collapsed riddled with shell-splinters.

Abruptly the gunfire ceased. From the summit of the mountain echoed the cheers of the victorious English. The artillery, which had been laying a barage on the other side of the hill, grew silent, and granted right of way to its own infantry, who, intoxicated with the realization of victory, raced down the other side of the mountain to reach the other coast. The battle was decided. What remained of the Anatolian battalions sought refuge amid the rocks.

Suddenly the ships' guns flashed, and a salvo of heavy shells burst upon the Sari Bair, which was crowded with cheering English soldiers. For seconds, which seemed like an eternity, the earth was torn up and flung into the air. Then the thunder rolled away over the water, the dust and smoke settled down, and the mountain again became visible. Of the British soldiers who had been preparing to pursue the Turks there was no sign. But in shell-holes and along the slopes of the hill lay hundreds of mutilated corpses and dying men. Fearful cries rent the air, which still trembled from the shattering force of the salvo that had just been discharged. A wild panic seized the troops.

The Turks saw that for the moment the British had lost all power to think and that they were running aimlessly here and there, the victims of a temporary panic. Immediately the defenders grasped the situation. A salvo from the ships had been fired too late and had burst among its own infantry. The Anatolians realized that this was their last chance. An Allah-sent chance.

With what strength they had left, they sprang to their feet, advanced, and stormed Sari Bair.

Twelve thousand Britons, picked young men, and ten thousand brave Anatolians lay on the field of battle. They would never know that at the eleventh hour the big British attack had failed, and that Sari Bair, and with it Gallipoli, remained secure in the hands of the Turks.

But on Chunuk Bair the enemy still had a firm foothold. Spades feverishly dug the earth, making trenches and parapets.

Mustafa Kemal glanced at his soldiers, who lay on the ground in a state of utter exhaustion, and then looked at the advance area leading to the mountain : it lay under heavy fire from the British naval artillery.

No matter ! The important point was that until Chunuk Bair was reconquered there could be no talk of the invaders having been decisively beaten off. He gave orders for the attack. The men hesitated to plunge through the rain of death. Mustafa Kemal then realized that here commands would not help, and that it was up to him as leader to set an example. He sprang out of the trench, and shouted :

" All right, men, wait, and let me first of all see what is happening forward. When I raise my arm, you can come on ! "

Soon the *Kumandan* was in the midst of that rain of iron, and soon a bullet struck him, flattening itself against his watch. Mustafa Kemal raised his arm.

The soldiers immediately sprang to their feet, and a little later the Crescent banner fluttered above Chunuk Bair.

THE ANGLO-FRENCH FLEET IN THE DARDANELLES, MARCH 18TH, 1915

Triumph
Ocean   Agamemnon   Bouvet
Gaulois   Canopus   Inflexible   Charlemagne   Suffren
Cornwallis   Majestic   Vengeance   Queen Elizabeth   Irresistible

There were three fierce, determined British counter-attacks, and gradually great gaps appeared in the Turkish line, now worn as thin as a veil. Mustafa Kemal's division had been almost completely wiped out, but was still maintaining a desperate, hopeless resistance, when the Asiatic Reserve Corps arrived on the battlefield at the double.

For the Turks the battle was over. The British, as before, retired to the narrow strips of beach, which the naval guns guarded for them. The heights, and with them Gallipoli, stayed in the safe possession of the Turks.

Mustafa Kemal, when he went to report the victory to his commanding officer, Liman von Sanders, produced the shattered watch. The German officer kept it as a souvenir and promoted the young colonel to be officer-commanding in the Anafarta sector of the front.

For weeks position warfare held sway. For six months now the Anatolian soldier had been lying in inadequate, shallow trenches, without a rest, without proper rations and without supplies. There were no supplies, and, moreover, on account of the British naval guns, which commanded the whole Peninsula, none could be brought up. Decent base-lines, thanks to the enemy artillery, simply did not exist. Boots were torn and uniforms in rags, but still the Anatolian soldier had to stick to his post, hug the ground and maintain a strict watch on the enemy lines. There was no night. British searchlights mercilessly pierced the darkness, casting fountains of light over Gallipoli.

This continued for weeks, for months, for a whole half-year. Occasionally the soldiers talked to each other in whispers. Of what did they talk? Of their homes? After what they had experienced they were scarcely able to believe in their existence. Of the Padishah? Yes, they were fighting for him. The C.O.? Yes, he was the idol of every soldier on Gallipoli. Mustafa Kemal.

" Can you see him up forward? " whispered one man.

" Of course I can! He's always in the front-line trench."

" He is holding to his eyes those glasses which bring distant things close. I wonder what he can see over in the English lines? "

" Evening is approaching; they are probably eating, eating a satisfying meal. At home at this time the muezzin from the minaret is summoning the faithful to prayer. The *Kumandan* is watching the *Inglis* while they eat."

"He is just skin and bones, like ourselves."

On the other side a gun barked. With deep concern the soldiers glanced at Mustafa Kemal, who sat calmly on the parapet of the foremost trench, observing the enemy. The shell burst right on the edge of the parapet. They wanted to call out, but their voices failed them. Soon the report of "Shot Two" was heard. Again the shell struck the parapet. But this time it was twenty yards nearer to the spot where Mustafa Kemal was sitting. He gave no signs of moving.

Didn't he understand the danger? Wouldn't he understand? They must call to him, make him realize his peril.

The third shell burst twenty yards nearer than the last. The next shot should strike the exact spot where Mustafa Kemal sat.

The officers began to shout. "Look out! Get under cover!"

The horror-struck soldiers watched the *Kumandan* turn his head. Ah, he had heard, he understood! But to their dismay he remained seated, cupped his hands, and shouted back to them:

"Too late, I can't set you a bad example."

He then searched in his pocket, brought out a cigarette case, selected and lit a cigarette, blew a cloud of smoke through his teeth, and then remained as still as a statue. At that moment the fourth shot rent the air. The flash almost blinded the soldiers, who, when they next looked up, saw their commanding-officer still in his position, calmly puffing at his cigarette.

Actually, it was No. 1 gun that had fired the fourth shot. Apparently the battery had only three guns.

The soldiers were struck dumb by the miracle. . . .

For months the struggle for the Dardanelles continued. Gallipoli became a miniature, indescribable inferno, consuming England's best troops and the *élite* of the Turkish regiments. But London was not willing to yield. The goal was too valuable. Moreover, the prestige of the Empire was at stake.

In the autumn the guns began to thunder on the Danube. In a few weeks Field-Marshal Mackensen had overrun Serbia. Bulgaria had mobilized and joined forces with the Central Powers. Communication was established.

On 3 November Liman von Sanders, to his utter relief and

GALLIPOLI

satisfaction, received the long-awaited telegram from the German Chief-of-Staff:

" What is needed to drive the enemy from Gallipoli ? "

At the end of November the first heavy guns from Germany—morsers, howitzers, *Minenwerfer*—reached their destination.

On 19 December the Turkish soldiers were surprised to find themselves standing before deserted trenches. Under cover of night and mist the huge British expeditionary corps had evacuated the Peninsula. The starving Anatolians pounced on the abandoned supply depots. Tins of pork were handed to the Germans.

CHAPTER II

SALONIKA

A GOOD quarter of a century has passed over the world since the Imperial Ottoman Director of Inland Revenue, Ali Riza, reached in Salonika a decision that was of fatal significance not only to his son, but to the whole country.

In the easy-going 'eighties of the last century the Sultan's Empire, still enjoying the fame of a great past, extended over three continents. The Crescent banner was flown in Danubian regions, Walis collected taxes for the Sultan in North Africa, and in Asia as far as the Indian Ocean the scimitar held sway for the successors of Fahti the Conqueror.

Ali Riza, Imperial Ottoman Customs Officer, who was employed at the Port of Salonika, was one of the few who looked beyond the surface, who realized that the greatness of the Empire was but a façade, behind which the structure of the building was crumbling, and Ali Riza was intelligent enough to recognize the factors leading to this general collapse. He had every day an opportunity of watching his colleagues at their work, to say nothing of the higher officials ! There was hardly one who in the exercise of his office did not firmly close both eyes and fix his attention exclusively on *bakhshish* and bribes. Laws and regulations were simply provided in order that officials might exceed them. And no one seemed to discover anything improper in it. They all had the same dual goal : little work and big rewards. The minor official practised this policy in so far as his confined scope would permit, and the higher official allowed him to proceed undisturbed provided there were decent " pickings " for himself.

Ali Riza, who was not a fanatical Mohammedan, did not accept this state of affairs as something for granted, or as God's will. But, on the other hand, what could he do to alter it in the face of a four-thousand-headed monster of corruption ?

What could he do against the general impotency of a sickly State organism ?

Ali Riza, unlike his comrades, was no waster, to whom all things were indifferent. He followed with keen interest all that happened in the big world. He read in the newspapers how the European peoples were fast growing into powerful, proud nations, how they had great men to lead them, and how a Bismarck was uniting a strong Germany, that mysterious land away in the north, whither the Sultan was sending the pick of his young officers for military instruction and where there were high-schools, which imparted enlightenment and knowledge in generous abundance.

Ali Riza suffered acutely through being condemned to live in a world of ignorance. He told no one of this, but he was keenly aware of it in his heart of hearts. He did not accept the doctrine of Mohammed. He saw how the hodjas, the Islamite priests, deliberately held the people in ignorance, how they encouraged religious fanaticism, and how, on the other hand, they condemned and discouraged Western progress and achievements as the Devil's work of infidel dogs.

And yet Ali Riza knew only too well that recognition of that progress, and its adoption, alone could save the Empire. To him personally it was not a matter of deep concern. He, in any case, would be hardly likely to survive the collapse. But his son, his Mustafa !

After hours of patient thought and long reflection he came to the conclusion that Mustafa had to be provided with a good education. Bold plans and hopes stirred the thoughtful man's imagination. No sacrifice was to be too great. One day Mustafa was to be sent to Germany, to one of the high-schools. He would return as an enlightened, modern man, as a man of character, personality and knowledge—an example and pattern for thousands of Turks.

Everyone had to see or sense that Mustafa was no average child. With such eyes it was evident that he had been born for something great.

Little Mustafa was proud. With his friends he showed a certain reserve. A masterly nature was born in him.

No one had ever seen him weep, nor had anyone ever seen him dirty or untidy. Ali Riza, too, attached importance to appearance. Unlike most of his contemporaries, he did not wear a jersey and baggy trousers, but was seen in a well-pressed European suit of a quiet pattern. He was serious, dignified and careful.

Mustafa kept an eye on his father, copying him in his ways, bearing and manners. He was proud of him and was animated with a desire to do better than the others.

He was seven years old. To-day was the first red-letter day in his young life : he was to be admitted to the Mohammedan school. The door of the little wooden house in the main street which Ali Riza and his family occupied was decorated with green foliage. Inside stood little Mustafa, holding in his hand a golden branch. His mother had dressed him in a white robe, and had placed on his head a gold-embroidered turban. It was the age-old custom.

The mother was happy and excited. She had long looked forward to this day, and she had long struggled for it. The father had wanted to send Mustafa to a secular school. But Zubeida Hanum had opposed him with all the strength she possessed, and her stronger will had carried the day. The time had now come. Mother and son stood side by side. How alike they were ! The same eyes—those hypnotic wolves' eyes—and the same prominent cheek-bones. Mustafa entered whole-heartedly into the ceremony, knowing that it was a day which he would never forget.

A hodja, followed by the pupils of the school, arrived at the house. They halted at the door to say a prayer. Mustafa bowed, touched his forehead and his heart, kissed his mother, then his father, and gave his hand to the hodja. Then the other boys escorted the novice and marched in solemn procession through the city to the school, which lay close to the mosque. All then said another prayer, after which the hodja, taking Mustafa by the hand, led him into the bare schoolroom, opened the Koran, and began to explain to him the significance of the doctrine of Mohammed.

At the Mohammedan school Mustafa made little progress.

After a few days, only his father, smiling happily, led him to the venerable Chemsi, who conducted a private school on European lines. This was the institution which Mustafa was in future to attend.

Quietly and resignedly the mother accepted this change. She had been reared, and devoutly believed, in the tradition of Islam, and desired to know nothing of world progress. Her world was confined to the restricted space enclosed by the four wooden walls of her house, within which she lived her life. She probably realized that Mustafa was dedicating himself more assiduously to a pursuit of worldly knowledge than to a study of his religion, that he was impetuous and that he was ambitious. She was a woman of great strength of character, and she exerted every effort to counterpoise his worldliness. Zubeida surrounded her son with care and attention, and he was never happier than when listening to her teachings and the fables which she used to relate to him. Zubeida came of sturdy peasant stock, was an ardent patriot and intensely loyal to the Sultan and his House.

Family life was strictly conventional. The son on entering the room kissed his father's hand, remained standing, and waited until he was politely bidden to seat himself. Then, with equal politeness, he would reply that he could not dream of taking a seat in his presence. His father then said in a friendly tone, " Then I command you to be seated." The son bowed and said, " I dare not disobey one of your commands."

These conventions and traditions bred self-control and a dignified, measured demeanour, and they prevented temperamental outbursts and imprudent speech. A boy like Mustafa was never encouraged to consider himself as a child. In his parents' house he was always treated as a future grown-up, and each mark of respect which he paid to his parents and instructors was returned in kind.

Thoughts and wishes were, for preference, not expressed directly, but with poetic intricacy, and games were played in deep earnest, almost ceremoniously, at no time noisily or boisterously. A boy aged nine, like Mustafa, gave up games entirely, and conducted himself thenceforth as a man, as a person of knowledge. Younger brothers and sisters were treated with tender care, like very delicate blooms, which bring joy and colour to the household. The elder brother was their guardian and protector—a responsible person. Between brother and sister there was the same conventionality that existed between a gentleman and a lady. The flourishing, decorative, formal greetings when they met consisted of, in the first place, the lady insisting on her right as a woman to play the part of a servant, whereupon the gentleman, the effendi, the bey, requested her to consider herself an equal, and after his request had been many times refused, " ordered " her to abandon the role of servant. Then the lady, smiling pleasantly, took over the command—which is precisely what happens all over the world.

Mustafa idolized his mother, worshipped the little flower, his sister, admired his father and valued his praise. He learnt with facility and studied assiduously at school, where he had an opportunity of distinguishing himself and showing others how it should be done. That was Mustafa's ambition and greatest joy.

The worthy Chemsi had seldom had such a pupil as this bright Turkish lad with the light blue eyes and flaxen hair. He spoilt him and set him above the others, but Mustafa took it all as a matter of course. He seemed to take it for granted that he was superior to the others, and he was inordinately proud to be the son of Ali Riza, the Revenue official, whose bearing and appearance were those of a pasha.

The schooling cost money. Where was it to be found? Zubeida Hanum was thrifty, had mastered the art of managing on little, and was successful in sending out her husband and son neatly and well groomed—Mustafa would have been extremely unhappy if there were the slightest blemish in his suit—but the money would not reach beyond this. Ali Riza, with quick determination, resigned his office and started a timber business, with the object of earning more money. He could, of course, have earnt more as a Government servant had he kept his eyes shut and his hands open. But he would rather have starved than have profited by dishonesty.

From his earliest youth Mustafa had been set an example of the most scrupulous honesty by his father. With the whole strength of his character he develped an implicit sense of honour which, later, was to make him the leader and inspirer of a decadent and disunited nation.

Ali Riza worked like a slave, denied himself every luxury, and maintained a single goal in view: to send Mustafa one day to a European high-school. In the evenings, when he arrived home tired, Mustafa stood and waited, kissed his hand, and then they worked together. Father and son studied. Often it was the son who was tutor.

One day the earnest, industrious man was silent. In the little house there was a depressing stillness, anxious listening, waiting. The doctor came. Before Mustafa had time to realize what it was about, his mother led him to his father's bedside. He was cold and motionless. A little later they carried him out and buried him.

Life meant very little in the land of the Turks. And when a

man was dead, few questions were asked about him. The cemeteries, with green cypresses waving above them, were lonely, places of oblivion, of absolute quiet and ceased existence.

Ali Riza lay under the cypresses. The sun sank, and rose again—as always.

A mother and two children faced poverty.

With lowered heads, their belongings tied in bundles on their backs, they wandered from the city.

Not far from Salonika was a solitary little village, a meagre settlement consisting of a few scattered huts, which, although it did not exactly cry of poverty, certainly did not proclaim prosperity.

Mustafa's new home was in one of these houses, which belonged to his uncle. The latter was a farmer and could find ample employment for so sturdy and intelligent a youth.

Mustafa required no urging, and attacked his new work with typical energy and thoroughness. Soon he was as efficient in the stables with a pitchfork as in the fields with a spade. In due course the lad could visualize no other future for himself than that of farmer, a farmer standing on his own property, a free man owning no master, reaping the fruits of the labour which he sank into his own soil.

When his uncle sent him out to herd sheep and goats he lay in the grass for hours—which seemed like an eternity—gazed at the sky and thought. The Anatolian in him was beginning to show itself, for although Mustafa was born in the Levant, he was of pure Anatolian blood. Family traditions and chronicles were unknown in old Turkey, and no one can say at what period Mustafa's ancestors came to Europe.

Mustafa was nearly always alone. He loved solitude. Not that he was a dreamer. Indulging in pleasant flights of fancy was not to his taste. On the contrary, he was a youth of sober thoughts, with a mind only for the practical and real and with a determination to master the things which came his way.

Two years dragged slowly and uneventfully past. Mustafa had grown strong and self-assured.

One day a shout from his sister startled him out of his reveries.

On entering the house he was surprised to find his mother in a state of happy excitement. Since his father's death she had been burdened with worry. Zubeida Hanum, good woman, had reason for joy. At one time she was against the suggestion of a higher, secular education for her son, but now that she had seen him cleaning stables and herding sheep, leading a hard life and wearing coarse clothes, she was willing to change her mind. For a long while she had wracked her brains to discover a means of restoring him to the city, where he could again attend school. She had prayed, but in this matter was not willing to leave all to the will of Allah. She had not ceased to work for this end, and now, in the presence of his uncle, who wore an unusually solemn expression, made her son aware of an important change. Mustafa kissed the hand of mother and uncle, implored Allah's blessing for them both, and listened in silence while his mother told him how God's hand had given his fate a decisive turn. Mustafa was to return to Salonika. While there he would live with an aunt. His mother would work, denying herself everything, and provide the school fees. She had already obtained a neat suit for him. Without his mother, Mustafa would probably have remained a nameless peasant for the rest of his days. But now he set foot in another world, and began a career which—by no means one without obstacles, but plentifully punctuated with difficulties and reverses—at length brought him to the top rung of the ladder of world history.

As a man he would find things no simpler than he was finding them as a boy. He had to fight his way on, step by step, against his foes and against his friends, until the day came when his name suddenly was famous.

Day by day a sturdy, reserved boy attended the private grammar school in Salonika. His school-fellows seldom saw him smile. He was invariably polite and of unexceptionable deportment, a fellow-pupil of an excellent type, and yet there was none who would have dared to describe him as a friend, for he appeared to exist within an enclosure which no one seemed able to penetrate.

Mustafa was an outstanding pupil, and nothing seemed to cause him difficulties. His keen intelligence, his piercing eyes and his supreme self-assurance distinguished him from the rest of the boys, but at the same time brought him into conflict with the masters. Mustafa found it difficult to subordinate himself, and he had a profound contempt for the legally constituted authority. He was a born rebel. Wherever he happened to be the air was charged. Position and titles failed to impress him. Although he was an outstandingly able pupil, his masters were far from being delighted with him. Mustafa was the son of a poor, widowed mother, who worked hard and suffered want in order to provide her son with a schooling and with clothes that bore favourable comparison with those of the richest of his fellows. To be badly dressed would have been the worst punishment that Mustafa could have suffered. He had a pronounced sense for dignity and appearance. In the streets of Salonika, when he turned to look at officers from the garrison, his wolves' eyes dilated. One day he would wear a similar uniform! And, by Allah! he would cut a very different figure from those shabby, genteel officers, who fell far short of his standards of smartness.

Perhaps because he was poorly off he was constantly on his guard, protecting himself with a shield of impenetrable pride, working by himself, and adhering to a fixed determination to surpass the others in character and knowledge. At the same time he was touchy and easily offended. But he was far from being possessed of an inferiority complex. He was convinced that a man was to be valued for what he was, not for what he had. He knew also that in time of need he had to defend his position, and, when necessary, with his fists.

One of his masters, a man named Hafis, happened to come along at a moment when Mustafa's fists were pounding the skull of a classmate.

Hafis, in any case, was not well disposed to Mustafa, who made no secret of his contempt for Arabic, the master's pet subject. Here was an opportunity for him to make an example of the boy.

Why was Mustafa bullying one of his friends, the master wanted to know?

There was absolute silence in the class.

Then the culprit answered in a hard, abrupt, metallic voice which rang through the room.

He had been insulted. Anyone, in the circumstances, if he was not a coward, was entitled to defend his honour with his fists.

If one boy struck another it would be his turn to be struck, said Hafis. An eye for an eye, a tooth for a tooth. Two grey wolves' eyes stared uncomprehensively at the Arabic master. Mustafa was in the wrong because he had defended his honour? Without further argument Hafis seized him, and a couple of dozen terror-stricken youths watched with malicious joy while the haughty Mustafa was soundly thrashed by one who was stronger than himself.

No one stirred while Mustafa returned to his desk. None dared to grin at the sight of his face, which had the appearance of being carved in stone. They all felt that a strange change had come over the punished boy, that something had collapsed within him.

In Mustafa's silence and calm there was something uncanny. The boys involuntarily moved out of his way when, at the close of the lessons, he proudly stepped out into the street. . . .

It was Mustafa's last attendance at the school. His mother was frantic with despair. She wept, threatened, begged and coaxed, but Mustafa was unrelenting. He had been perfectly within his rights, had been thrashed for it, and publicly trampled in the dust—the disgrace, the humiliation of it! Mustafa would rather have perished than have gone back to that school.

Zubeida Hanum ceased weeping and looked at her son in a hopeless, helpless fashion, for she knew that words would be wasted. There was no taming his wolf nature.

But what was to happen now? Salonika possessed no other grammar school, and there was no money to send him to Constantinople. He was poor, and he had no choice. The logic of that was convincing. Only one thing appeared to remain: return to his uncle's farm, clean stables, guard the sheep, and stay for the rest of his life a poor peasant.

But you want to be somebody, Mustafa! his mother protested.

The appeal to his ambitions was not without its effect.

Without saying a word, he went out. He was twelve years old at the time.

Old Major Kadri, who lived nearby, was not a little astonished when Ali Riza's son came to him and firmly and politely asked him to aid him to enter a military academy. Major Kadri knew Mustafa by sight, and liked the look of him. The boy, alone, of his own accord, had come to him, and now stood confidently and erectly before him.

" He's a born soldier! " was the thought which suddenly struck the old man.

He asked a few questions. The boy replied briefly and to the point. Kadri then knew that the boy would get into the Cadet School—that, somehow or other, he would manage to gain admittance. Very well, he would arrange for him to take the entrance examination.

Examination? It was more in the nature of a conversation. Mustafa fired off his answers like shots from a pistol. And each time he struck the bull.

The examiners looked at each other. If Mustafa held to his promises, then the Cadet School in Salonika would have gained a pupil of whom it could be proud.

Zubeida Hanum again wept when Mustafa came home one day and briefly mentioned that he had been admitted to the Cadet School. She had wanted him to be a scholar. A soldier? In the Ottoman Army? The Sultan was always at war. . . .

Did all the sacrifices mean that, sooner or later, her only boy would lose his life somewhere in the scorching deserts of Arabia? In order to maintain savage Bedouin tribes under the sovereignty of the Caliph?

But Zubeida Hanum somehow knew that she would have to give in and that her son's will was not to be changed. She resigned herself to her fate, and left Mustafa to his. Nevertheless, it was a happy woman who learnt soon afterwards that he was the pride of the academy.

Here the lad suddenly became the model subordinate, and none of his comrades was more amenable to discipline. Not long passed before he was promoted to be a sort of cadet under-officer, and was entrusted with the task of instructing some of the junior classes. Mustafa became a keen mathematician. Mathematics was his ideal subject. The logic and clarity of it appealed to him; he found it an essentially masculine study, providing the mind with vigorous and healthy exercise. For hours at a time Mustafa would be absorbed in the solution of some problem, and the harder the problem the better he liked it. No one ever recalled his putting his pencil down before the equation was solved.

His master was enthusiastic about him. His name, too, was Mustafa.

"There must be some distinction between us," he said one day,

" so in future we'll call you Mustafa Kemal, Mustafa the Excellent."

In old Turkey anyone, if he felt so inclined, could adopt a name that bore no relation to his family name. And so Ali Riza's son was entered on the roll under the name of Mustafa the Excellent, Mustafa Kemal. . . .

In 1897 guns began to roar near Salonika. Turkey was at war. This time Greece was the opponent.

As may be expected, the cadets of the Senior Military Academy in Monastir followed the progress of the campaign with the liveliest interest. Mustafa Kemal, now aged seventeen, a cadet of his Majesty the Sultan, was the keenest of them all. He drew up for his own edification big strategical plans, and was not sparing in his criticism of the old generals.

After the victory national pride swelled the bosoms of the young cadets.

Mustafa shared their pride and enthusiasm, but in a far greater degree. And his patriotism did not stop there. He was anxious to see an overthrow of the old régime and in its place the introduction of European ideas of progress and development : in brief, he desired a complete reformation of the State and of the whole life of the nation.

Mustafa Kemal neither delivered big speeches, nor did he in any way seek the limelight. At the same time, he occupied here a position similar to that which he held at the grammar school : all looked upon him as the strongest and ablest, as the leader whom all followed and obeyed, and as the centre about which they gathered. He had not summoned them to do this, for he was as lonely and as reserved as before. None could boast of his friendship, and he admitted none to the magic circle which surrounded him.

There is little known of him, save that he was immaculately dressed, that he read a great deal and—what is more—gave long thought to that which he had read. To his associates he remained an unsolved puzzle.

Occasionally he was asked to explain what it was that he aimed at, what direction his thoughts took and what he meant to become.

" I mean to be somebody," he answered curtly.

" But what ? "

"I mean to be somebody," he repeated.

"But you can't be Sultan?"

"*Ben olajagin!*" ("I shall be somebody!")

For his evening stroll his trousers had to be freshly pressed each day. The citizens of Monastir turned round to look at him. Here, they saw, was a new type of officer, erect and precise to a "T." There was nothing lazy or slipshod about him. Energy, a smartness of bearing and a subtle strength made him a man who immediately struck attention.

There was a complete absence of Oriental softness and dreamy relaxation in his features, which, on the contrary, eloquently expressed his vitality and eagerness—though the prominent cheekbones clearly pointed to his Tartar origin.

Such in all probability was the appearance of the Turks who, more than five centuries ago, left their homes in the vast steppes of Central Asia, to overrun and conquer the ancient empires of the East, and then gradually to fall victims to temptation and Western softness.

Under the banner of the Grey Wolf warlike nomads—tough, desperate and hardy men—led by powerful, war-loving sultans, conquered the whole of Asia Minor. What were the motives that led them to carry their banners and "Jingling Johnnies" to the very gates of Vienna itself? The need to give rein to a superabundance of energy? A love of battle, a love of conquest?

That past had long been forgotten. It was practically no longer existent in the hearts of the Turks, who were ignorant of, and uninterested in, the origins of their race. Many a conqueror was corrupted by the East. The luxuries and temptations of the Orient were the undoing of Alexander the Great. The Occident was the undoing of the Turkish race.

The Turk, it is true, regarded himself as master in Western Asia and in South-East Europe—by right of conquest. But he retained no inkling of the secret of his blood, and had lost all his former vitality.

Without a scruple the bold conquerors took over a religion and a culture that were entirely foreign to their nature. From the subjected nations they adopted Islam, Mohammed's doctrine, the great paralysing religion, the foe of progress. In recent years every attempt to reform the State and remodel it on European lines was hopelessly frustrated by the obstinate resistance of the reactionary Islamitic priesthood and of the people, whom they had completely under their sway.

And so the Turkish race slowly but surely advanced towards its destruction by the poison which flowed forth from the worst elements of the Mediterranean populations—the Macedonians, Greeks, Jews, Arabs and Armenians—who spread over the country like a pernicious weed. The Turk despised them, but failed to realize that in the course of the centuries he was growing like them, until finally the Tartar features themselves practically disappeared from his face.

The spirit of the Grey Wolf was dead.

Those were the thoughts which occupied the mind of the lonely, brooding Mustafa.

But he felt that the spirit of the Grey Wolf of the old, genuine Turkish race lived in him. He was conscious of a difference of blood, of value.

He began to devote himself to the study of history.

It stimulated his imagination and broadened his vision. Having read something of the history of the nations, he began to see the world in a different light. Mustafa Kemal, too, delved in the past of his own nation, and learnt how mighty sultans led their irresistible hordes from the heart of Central Asia, how they conquered Arabia, Syria, Egypt and Tripoli, how they came to Asia Minor and, finally, crossed the Dardanelles and reached Europe.

Greece fell to them, and then the Balkans. Soon they found themselves at the gates of Vienna. Sultan Suleiman the Magnificent had world conquest in sight. European princes begged for his friendship and help.

His vast empire consisted of huge possessions in three continents. Would his successors be able to maintain it intact? If the Sultan and his armies marched towards the north the Arabs and Egyptians revolted in the south. If he led his armies into the southern deserts, then the flames of revolt burst forth in the north, in the Balkan mountains and in Greece.

For two hundred and eighty-five out of the last four hundred years the Ottoman Empire had been at war. There never was a

ENVER PASHA

TALAAT PASHA

real interval of peace. Who had time to think of internal progress and construction? The whole strength of the Turkish race was being wasted in the eternal wars. Nothing remained for the tasks of peace.

For what were they fighting? It was a question which Mustafa was continually asking himself.

To maintain a motley horde of nations in subjectivity, to remain masters of provinces, inhabited by hostile peoples, who were constantly in rebellion. What an insane expenditure of strength! A brave and capable nation was being sacrificed for futile objects and tasks.

For centuries the deserts of Arabia and Syria had been consuming in regiments the flower of Turkish youth. For a madness. For the notion of Islam, that religious product of the Arabic-Semitic mind, which had nothing in common with that of the Mongolian Turks, but which was corrupting them and degenerating them as a race.

Mustafa Kemal saw clearly and unmistakably the whole extent of the downfall of his nation.

For four hundred years the Turkish people had been punished for the arrogance of their sultans. For four hundred years they had been going steadily downhill. The Turks had been driven into a hopeless defensive position.

They had been obliged to defend their possessions in murderous wars against the European Powers, who seized one province after the other, and still were not satisfied. Now they were taking advantage of the interior rottenness in a much more damaging way.

The Sultan needed money. Where was it to be found? How could the peasant pay taxes, when he was constantly being taken from his plough and placed under arms? And as there was not enough money for the soldier's pay, how were roads, bridges, canals and cities to be built?

The Sultan needed money and still more money. The Western Powers, the British, the French, were only too willing to loan it to him.

In return they did not demand much. Just a few privileges, securities, and concessions for exploitation of the soil. But the net of these privileges grew and grew. To save the money from going to the devil, the right of control was demanded. It meant simply this: the creditor insisted on the right to control the affairs of his debtor.

The Ottoman Empire stood under the business management of foreigners. Not even a railway could be built without the approval of the creditor. The obligations became more and more exacting. Moreover, the foreigners were not under Turkish jurisdiction, and could do on Turkish soil just as they liked.

And there seemed no possibility of escape from this stranglehold. Even assuming that the Sultan had sufficient money to discharge his century-old debts, the Western Powers would not have taken it. They wanted not the money, but the destruction of Turkey.

For some time secret pacts had been signed in respect of a partition of the "Ramshackle" Empire, whose collapse could only be a question of time.

That point would have been reached earlier but for the Iron Chancellor, Bismarck, who at the decisive moment again destroyed the carefully-woven schemes.

Menaced on all sides by foes, the Ottoman Empire counted only one friend: Germany, who sympathized and, as far as she was able, encouraged the efforts which were made in the direction of national solidity.

Russia was the most dangerous enemy. Russia coveted Constantinople and the Dardanelles. Britain was equally eager for their possession, on India's account. Britain reached out for Arabia and Egypt, France for Syria, Italy for Asia Minor.

Sultan Abdul Hamid, who began his reign in the 'seventies with far-reaching plans of reform, was like the man in the fable who fell into a pit. Above him, at the mouth of the pit, waited the wild beasts, while below him were the open jaws of a dragon.

None was hated more heartily than Abdul Hamid.

He quickly buried his ardent, independent ideas. Reforming the Empire, matching it with Europe, meant sending it to its doom. Islam, too, would permit no changes. In addition, external enemies allowed him no peace for domestic construction.

The unsociable despot saw but one way to hold together temporarily what remained of the squandered estate of his fathers:

a studied policy of cunning, striking at the one weak point of the European Powers—their mutual jealousy of each other. In that way it might be possible to hold out for another decade or so. And then—all lay in Allah's hands. ...

The internal enemy followed close upon the heels of the enemy from without. Europe had become Democratic, and the word "freedom" was in everyone's mouth. It was, therefore, not surprising that the Turkish youth also embraced the idea.

It was European, and therefore it must be good. All nations expected blessings from Democracy. Perhaps, too, Democracy was the magic medicine that would cure the sickness which was crippling the Ottoman Empire. People began to clamour for freedom, a constitution, a parliament.

Abdul Hamid smiled scornfully and cynically. In the face of grim political reality he had long since buried such plans. His police agents began to scour the whole Empire, scenting treason and rebellion everywhere. Many a dream of freedom expired behind the walls of the Red Prison, and many a mouth that had called for a constitution and a parliament closed for ever in the dark waves of the Bosporus.

Every now and then rumours of another palace revolution reached the public. Some general had once again attempted to assassinate the tyrant and place one of his brothers upon the throne. It was then known that a night or two later a long stretched-out form wrapped in a white cloth, and carried on the shoulders of herculean life-guardsmen, would set out on its last journey to the Bosporus and be cast into the waves. Torches shed a dim and uncanny light on the scene. The revolt had been stamped out, having been discovered at the last second by one of the police spies, or having been betrayed by one of the conspirators. The Bosporus swallowed the mortal remains of the would-be assassin.

Constantinople gave a slight shudder and bowed deeper before the despot, whose shadow darkened the city. . . .

Ali Riza's son passed all his examinations with flying colours, and now the career of officer stood open to him. He went to Constantinople.

Constantinople, the holy city and resort of wealth, splendour, luxury and light-hearted enjoyment! Here the whole world met, and here nothing was too costly for the big men of the Empire and the foreigners. The most voluptuous capital of the pre-War world opened its doors to the young, recently-gazetted staff-officer.

How Zubeida Hanum had dreaded and trembled at this translation from the Cadet School in quiet little Monastir to the Staff College in the capital! How was she to find the money to enable him to live in accordance with his rank? If a man desired to be somebody in the Ottoman Empire he had to cause notice, get himself talked about, exhibit himself at all the places where people of importance met, attend balls, visit the clubs, and frequent the international hotels....

In this way the piastres and gold pounds disappeared like raindrops on the parched desert sand.

Mustafa was not born to stand on one side. To Ali Riza's son a certain atmosphere of elegance and culture was an indispensable necessity.

Fate once more took a significant hand in his affairs. A wealthy citizen of Rhodes had proposed marriage to the widowed Zubeida Hanum. It was not easy for her to consent to a second marriage, but she had Mustafa's future to consider, and could not afford to dash aside the hand which Providence had stretched out to her. She accepted.

The news cut Mustafa to the quick. A stranger to be his father? This marriage seemed to him a betrayal of Ali Riza.

Mustafa, usually so sparing in his comments on personal matters, openly voiced his disapproval. He was as fond of his mother as she was of him, but now an estrangement had come between them—this second father, Morali Ragib, son of the well-known Lord Abbas of Morea.

A long time passed before he understood the sacrifice which his mother had made and before he was capable of accepting it. In reality, what Zubeida had done was anything but a betrayal of Ali Riza. Prepare Mustafa's way to a great future was the deceased man's testament. A wish to fulfil this testament led Zubeida to take the step. All for Mustafa, all for one!

But the son's love for his mother was deep and genuine, and after this first disagreement had been settled relations between them were even better. At the same time he would have nothing to do with his stepfather, preferring to ignore his existence.

Behind her tears Zubeida was happy. Away in the capital Mustafa must succeed, all eyes must turn to him. She imagined how, with his wiry, erect frame and soldierly features, forceful personality and easy self-assurance, he must stand out.

Already in her mind Zubeida saw him as a general, a governor, a minister.

And so a terrible blow struck her when one day fearful news arrived, crushing everything, hopes, wishes and prospects. . . .

Mustafa Kemal had now been in Constantinople two years. He was one of the few picked men who were destined for the General Staff Class. That meant that on conclusion of his studies he would pass out with the rank of captain.

As in Monastir, Mustafa kept himself a little apart from his comrades. They were not quite sure what to make of him. He felt that he was being sharply watched, and that he was being sercetly discussed. One day someone placed in his hand a book containing some poetry written by an exile. Mustafa now knew what he had long suspected: among the picked men of the Staff College there was a spirit of revolution. They read banned books, which attacked Islamitic fatalism, attacked despotism and attacked the foreign influence; and they read the poetry of an exile, Namik, who summoned his fellow-countrymen to take action and rebel.

Mustafa could not understand why the reading of such patriotic literature was prohibited, nor why the word *Vatan* (Fatherland) might not be uttered aloud.

Intense indignation filled the born rebel.

The Inspector-General of the Staff College, Ismail Pasha, patrolled the corridors and rooms of the institution: he seemed to have ears and agents everywhere. His aim was to curry favour with the Padishah and to serve Abdul Hamid and the Mohammedan Church.

The Commandant of the College began to notice how things were hastily concealed when he approached and how conversations were suddenly broken off, the young staff-officers endeavouring to assume as harmless an expression as possible. However, he pretended not to notice these things, and passed on his way. In his heart he sympathized with the discontented young men.

The word *Vatan* (Fatherland) was forbidden. That was enough to cause Mustafa to use it as the name of a secret society. Briefly, he had marshalled all the discontented, revolutionary elements and organized them on a strict revolutionary basis. Definite and clear aims were set before them; there was no place for ambiguous or immature plans. In addition, he exercised his friends in the art of making a speech. In the intervals between lectures he would stand, watch in hand, and then suggest a certain subject. That subject had to be dealt with fully and briskly, within the few brief minutes that were at the speaker's disposal. For a time he edited, and published with the aid of a duplicating machine, the *Vatan Magazine*, which was issued in manuscript.

His associates themselves could not say what it was that drew them to him or what made him their leader, for, to tell the truth, they knew nothing at all about him. He never by any chance mentioned personal matters. And there was none who would have dared to confront him with questions of that nature. With a look or slight movement of the facial muscles, he could have held the most importunate of them at bay.

During this time he was living like a lord. . . .

Several young officers from the General Staff had assembled in a small café close to the Galata Bridge. They were those who, a short time before, had passed their final examinations and were now waiting a short while until they were gazetted as captains in the Regular Army.

They met often in this particular café, but so unostentatiously that not even Ismail Pasha's eagle eye was likely to discover anything unusual in it.

On this evening one of the fraternity, Fethi Bey, was to bring with him a friend of similar views whom he wished to introduce to the circle. Slowly and deliberately, Mustafa Kemal smoked a cigarette, and waited patiently for the arrival of the two men. Fethi was an old school friend, reliable, slightly older than Kemal, and had already been cashiered from the Army on account of revolutionary activities. He was maintained by the *Vatan* society.

Nearly all the members were present. Fethi arrived, bringing with him the new recruit. He made a good impression on the assembly, who soon began to tell him of the objects of the society. That seemed hardly necessary, for the new man was already surprisingly well informed. He started to ask questions and displayed a keen interest in the aims, organization and members of the society.

After some time, he rose, smiled courteously, and introduced himself.

Conversation abruptly stopped, and faces turned pale. Mustafa pressed his lips together.

The " recruit " was an aide-de-camp to Ismail Pasha, the existing régime's truest servant. With acid politeness he invited the gentlemen to accompany him on a short stroll, during which the gendarmes, who were waiting outside, would be honoured to escort them, and happy to be permitted to pilot such a select body to solitary confinement in the Red Prison.

Many weeks passed behind prison walls. Rats and other vermin —it was ghastly! Nothing happened to relieve the monotonous existence of the prisoners, who waited in anxious uncertainty of their fate.

A despairing mother journeyed to Constantinople. Her face concealed by a veil, she wandered from one office to another, refused to be turned away, and clung to the officials, who merely shrugged their shoulders. Not the least was known regarding the fate of the conspirators. Everything rested upon the decision of the Padishah.

The unhappy woman's voice threatened to desert her. . . .

Was Mustafa still alive?

A horrible dread lay behind the question.

Shoulders were shrugged.

Did he live? Had he, like so many others, been consumed by the waves of the Bosporus? Did he languish behind prison walls?

No one could say. Perhaps he had been quietly and secretly stabbed with a dagger. Or he might have died slowly and wretchedly from poison.

Utter obscurity surrounded his and his associates' fate.

The weeks passed. Zubeida Hanum's sight was growing dim. The terrible shock and an unending flood of tears had practically robbed her eyes of their power to see. She was approaching blindness. But the despairing woman paid no heed to it. What mattered her sight now that all was lost, now that Mustafa had come to this end—and at the very moment when he was due to receive his commission as a captain in the Army?

An audience at the Yildiz Kiosk. Ismail Pasha stood humbly before his lord and master, Abdul Hamid Khan, and begged imploringly for the heads of the conspirators.

The revolution had dared to enter the Staff College, and under the very eyes of the Padishah and his most loyal servants spread its poison. Exemplary punishment was needed as an example and deterrent to others.

The Sultan stared out of the window and said nothing. There seemed some doubt that he was listening to what the pasha was saying. . . .

Abdul Hamid was in an extremely thoughtful mood on this day. In his serious, misanthropic eyes there was a faint glimmer of benevolence and understanding. Who were the conspirators, he wanted to know?

Their conduct at the Staff College?

There was no denying it—the Commandant had reported well of them, but then he himself was one of those freedom-coveting sons of dogs, and was long overdue for the gallows.

The despot thought for a while longer. Obviously, the best, the ablest members of the College were inclined to oppose the fatal policy that was ruining the Empire. Allah's ways were inscrutable. If fate decided that the Padishah was to fall, he would fall.

Abdul Hamid shook his head. Why should he desire the death of these young men, who had rebelled against something which he himself secretly loathed. He had had the same ideas, but had been forced to capitulate before grim reality. One day these young men would have to do the same. He would help them to mature as quickly as possible. No one was to learn—under pain of incurring the Padishah's wrath—of the places to which they would be banished, separately, each to a remote province on the frontiers of the Empire, where loneliness and the absence of civilized comforts would be conducive to profound thought and contemplation.

SALONIKA

At the Golden Horn, as always, the gay sails of the ships filled in the breeze. Ships ploughed the water and gradually disappeared from the view of the onlookers on shore.

Few paid attention to the vessel which slowly and steadily proceeded on its course to the Sea of Marmora. And few had any interest in the heavily-veiled woman who stood watching the ship slowly pass the Imperial Seraglio and recede from view. She then almost collapsed.

The ship was bearing her only son, her Mustafa, into the unknown. She had not been able to exchange a single word of farewell with him. In absolute secrecy, the conspirators were embarked and sent forth on their voyage into exile.

The woman stood motionlessly at the Golden Horn, still gazing at the corner of the Seraglio, behind which the ship had disappeared. She can have had little idea that one day, on that very spot, they would erect a statue of her son, looking out over the Bosporus and appearing as though stepping towards the East. . . .

Captain Mustafa Kemal, transferred for disciplinary reasons to the scorched deserts of Syria, an exile, soon received his baptism of fire in a skirmish with Arabs, who were constantly in revolt.

Mustafa saw how fanatically the Arabs hated the Turks, how they craved for an independent Arab national State, how they sympathized with all Turkey's enemies and how they set hopes on England.

And in Constantinople and Salonika young revolutionaries were dreaming of a fraternity of all Mohammedans under the Crescent and of the resurrection of the great Turkish Empire.

What do the Mohammedans, the Arabs and the Syrians mean to us?—Mustafa Kemal continually asked himself.

It was evident that something drastic, a radical change, must happen for the Turkish race to be saved.

The revolution also had its nests in the garrisons of Damascus, Jerusalem and Jaffa, though the central seat remained in Salonika in distant Macedonia. There all the best brains were sent, and there, unsuspected, met all those army men who planned an overthrow of the Government. At the cost of a little wangling, Mustafa Kemal also succeeded in getting transferred to Salonika.

Affairs as they existed in Salonika were an acute disappointment to him. The revolutionary Young Turks lacked any pretence of unity and were divided into groups and sections, cliques and parties, among whom there were bitter squabbles. They gathered at the premises of the European Masonic Lodge, which had already gained a predominating influence over the whole Movement.

In the centre of Salonika a big, well-cared-for house struck the eye. There was a very quiet air about it. Occasionally only, in the evenings, officers in uniform and men in civilian dress were seen passing in and out of the house. At those times lights in the top storey could be seen until late in the night. But nobody discovered anything strange in this, for it seemed perfectly reasonable that if Mustafa Kemal, a major on the General Staff and Inspector of the Turkish Railways, desired to entertain his male friends in his mother's house, he was entitled to do so.

Nor did Zubeida Hanum at first find anything unusual about it. Only that the quietness of these entertainments seemed to her a little strange. Mustafa Kemal was accustomed to take care that the door was well guarded. The only member of the household who was permitted to have access to the room was the parlourmaid.

And this maid confessed to the mother that she found these meetings uncanny. Zubeida Hanum, mistress of the house, shook her head. She knew, without being told, that Mustafa was an extraordinary child. Child?—naturally, to her, the man was still a child, who at times was in need of guidance from his mother. He had been allowed great freedom to develop his character and personality in his own way, but from time to time the mother's strong will, which the son had inherited, asserted itself, and there was a considerable row.

All tension between mother and son had vanished. Some time ago Allah had summoned the stepfather to him, and Zubeida was left with a substantial fortune. All was for Mustafa!

A few days later, the same gentlemen again gathered in the major's apartments. The maid served tea, cigarettes, cognac and wine. When she came downstairs, she reported that large sums of money were heaped on the table and that a strange conversation was in progress.

Zubeida guessed what was taking place. Quietly, she climbed the stairs, stood in the corridor, and listened, however without being able to learn anything. The conversation was being conducted in lowered voices. Zubeida was a strict adherent to her faith and a woman of very conservative views. Permit conspiracies to take place in her house ? . . .

Mustafa had noticed nothing. For the past few days one thought had been filling his mind: they were on the eve of revolution. If only everything functioned without a hitch! An enormous amount of industry was still needed to marshal the conflicting elements of the party and direct them towards the common goal. And Abdul Hamid's spies were on the alert.

It was long past midnight when the men left the house. Mustafa quickly gathered up his papers, locked them in a drawer, extinguished his cigarette and retired to his bedroom.

A noise suddenly startled him. The door opened, and his mother quietly entered.

She stood by his bed, her face lined with care and anxiety. To affect innocence would be idle. Mustafa at once realized that his mother knew everything, and he looked at her expectantly.

"My child," said Zubeida, scarcely able to restrain her agitation, "there is one thing that I must know. It is true that you mean to revolt against the Padishah ? "

"Yes! But the man who, you say, is endowed with the strength of seven saints is in reality weak. We want to rid the country of him. Your world is a different one from mine. You may not be able to understand me, but you will never wish to place obstacles in my way."

Several minutes passed before the mother could master the shock which the acknowledgment of the truth, Mustafa's confession, had caused her. But she was too strong and too proud to complain. Moreover, mother and son were not in the habit of discussing their feelings. They listened to what lay behind the bare words. And that was enough.

And yet, at this moment, the mother, who had lost her son once already, and who could not stand another such blow, felt that she had to give more expression to her feelings.

"You will fail!" she protested. "And—you are my only son—I don't want to lose you. The very thought of it is more than I can bear."

" I can't turn back "—Mustafa gave his answer clearly and emphatically—" things are already taking their course. You wouldn't like me to break my word ? "

" No ! "

The deeply-religious woman and her son faced each other—two blunt and determined characters. The woman was fighting a hard battle with herself; in the room it was quite still. Then Zubeida's strong voice rang out, calmly and firmly, without the slightest trace of hesitation.

" I understand nothing about these matters, which you know better. I have not had the education that you have had, but always bear this in mind : what has been begun must be carried through to the bitter end. You must succeed ! Do everything that is humanly possible to achieve victory."

In July, 1908, revolution broke out in Salonika.

The blessings of Western Democracy, of Liberalism, were to come to the aid of a land which still existed in a state of medievalism.

With miraculous suddenness, there rose a man who later played such an important part in the fate of the old Empire : Enver, a youthful, radiant hero of the same age as Mustafa, a passionate opponent of the old Turkish idea, an Imperialist of boundless imagination.

Who were his disciples and followers ?

No one could say precisely what the Committee of " Unity and Progress " really was. Its members remained invisible, their traces being lost in the dark, in Masonic Lodges, in the clubs and international circles. It had all the appearance of a secret society, but was surrounded by a weird atmosphere that was half European enlightenment and half Asiatic mystery.

The *coup d'état* of 24 July, 1908, placed power in the hands of the Committee. Its power was supported by the bayonets of the Salonika garrison. In Constantinople the Reaction rose in counter-revolution.

Mustafa Kemal was appointed chief of staff of a division in the Young Turk army which advanced against the capital.

Mustafa, as one of the army which defeated the counter-revolution, had a hand in deposing Abdul Hamid.

Insignificant subalterns and company-commanders became field-officers and generals overnight. Mustafa Kemal disdained to take part in the general scramble for posts and promotion.

Events took their course. Members of the Committee were full of extravagant plans and illusions; they talked much, made rash promises and created a state of wild confusion, under which conditions, instead of getting better, grew steadily worse. Everyone strove for popularity with the crowd, and parties were formed which fought among themselves.

Mustafa Kemal turned away in disgust.

That was not the purpose of the revolution. Worlds separated him from these men. He maintained close relations only with Jemal, later Proconsul of Syria, whose star was just in the ascendant.

The two men, emerging from one of the clubs or a session of the Committee, would walk for hours in the streets, debating and exchanging opinions. Jemal was a staunch adherent of the Committee and swore by its leaders, the big men.

" Don't be tempted, as most people are to-day, by a desire to be popular with every idiot you meet," Mustafa admonished him. " Mass applause has neither range nor importance. Greatness does not consist of echoing the words of others and of throwing sand in people's eyes, but of doing that which is of real necessity to the country and in marching straight to one's goal. All sorts of people will come along to you with their own ideas, and will try to divert you from your path. But stick to it! People will place all kinds of obstacles in your way—in the conviction that you are not great, rather a weakling, without friends or supporters. But in the end you will triumph over all difficulties; and then when you have attained greatness, and people tell you so, you can simply laugh in their faces."

Jemal paid no attention, and soon the friends lost sight of each other. One rose to success, while the other, from conviction and of his own accord, remained in obscurity, in haughty isolation.

On behalf of the Committee, Mustafa visited the African colony of Tripoli, for the purpose of popularizing the revolution there. His observations were similar to those which he had made in Arabia and strengthened his conviction that the Young Turks were on the wrong road, a road leading the country into even worse difficulties.

Personal differences grew more pronounced. The mission to Tripoli had returned. Mustafa rapidly became a menace and intolerable nuisance to the men of the Committee. And so they sent him to attend the French Autumn Manœuvres, and got rid of him for the time being. But on his return, he opposed the Committee even more vigorously, and his endless suggestions and obstinate insistence on practical reforms drove the authorities to distraction. Where would they be if he followed up his words with actions ? Or if he gave up words entirely and confined himself to deeds ?

To make things worse, the Committee's spies reported that the General-Staff Major, Mustafa Kemal, had gathered round him in Salonika a circle of men, not all of whom were officers in his regiment. There was reason for assuming that the eternal rebel, with his sharp criticisms of Government policy, had stirred up the officers of the garrison in opposition to the authority of the Young Turks.

The secret Council of Seven demanded disciplinary punishment.

They dared not proceed too viciously against the renegade, but he had to be shown, once and for all time, that the Committee could not be opposed with impunity.

Mustafa Kemal was relieved of his command and given an office job in the capital.

Subsequent events showed how justified were his criticisms of, and his lack of confidence in, the new men.

Bosnia and Herzegowina were lost, annexed by Austria. That was the first step towards the great world catastrophe. And tempers had hardly cooled down when the Italians invaded Tripoli. This time Mustafa was in complete agreement with Enver and the Committee. Although a war in far-off Africa was hopeless, military honour had to be defended. In company with Enver, Mustafa went to Tripoli to mobilize the Berber clans to fight against Italy. After an adventurous journey, disguised as an Arab, Major Mustafa Kemal reached Tripoli through Egypt. The British kept a sharp look-out, but he got through.

Mustafa and Enver attacked the Italians with energy. They whipped the tribes into a fanatical war passion, organized the

SALONIKA

savage Bedouins, and conducted a hopeless, but heroic struggle against the superior forces of the Italians.

Enver made full use of the limelight, lived in a magnificent tent, and sent optimistic, false despatches to Constantinople, with the object of encouraging the Government to continue the war, which was making his name famous throughout the world.

Mustafa's honesty and sense of reality were outraged. There were angry scenes between the two men. The mathematician and realist opposed the dreamer and visionary. Enver began wholeheartedly to fear and hate his friend. But the day would come when he would have his revenge for the reproaches to which he had been obliged to listen in the camp at Derna.

Suddenly, before their quarrel could develop into an open breach, catastrophal news from home completely altered the situation. While Turks and Bedouins were being sacrificed by Enver, and for Enver, the Balkan States had mobilized and declared war.

The Young Turk Government, the Army, all failed miserably and lamentably. With the utmost dispatch, and at any price, peace had to be concluded with Italy. The dead who filled the valleys and ravines of Derna had sacrificed their lives in vain. . . .

In a roundabout journey, which took him through Egypt, Italy, Austria and Rumania, Mustafa Kemal made his way home. During the journey he read in the papers of the frightful defeats of the Turkish Army, and could hardly believe his eyes. But there it stood, in black and white: Turkey was facing complete annihilation. The proud, mighty Ottoman Empire was collapsing under the blows of the Balkan kings, a society who were the laughing-stock of Europe.

The full extent of the catastrophe was not apparent to him until he arrived in Constantinople. The Committee had been thrown out of office. The great men of yesterday were dangling from the gallows. Starvation and cholera added to the disaster.

Fresh anxieties came to Mustafa. Salonika was in the hands of the enemy. What had become of his mother and sister? Rendered half insane by the disgrace of his country, he threaded his way through the lines of the defeated army and the endless columns of refugees, and sought his lost relatives. He was torn by doubt and despair—were they still living? The refugees whom he met related appalling stories of the scenes of brutality and frightfulness in Salonika, where the Greeks were cold-bloodedly massacring women and children.

At the gates of Constantinople there was indescribable confusion. Cholera victims, maimed and starving people clamoured for assistance; the troops had degenerated into a disorderly rabble; the authorities had lost all control; there was a steady stream of distracted refugees towards the capital. From Macedonia the enemy were advancing in rapid marches. None had any desire to fall into the hands of those troops.

A few years before, Zubeida Hanum had trembled for the life of her son and had combed Constantinople to find him or learn of his whereabouts; now it was the son who feverishly searched Macedonia for traces of his mother.

The suspense continued for days. But something told him not to surrender hope. He continued the search.

When at last he found them, speech almost deserted him. His mother was nearly blind.

After an exhausting and terrible journey, he succeeded in bringing them from the Macedonian hell, and he placed them in safety. Scarcely had this been accomplished, when unconfirmed news came that large bodies of troops had assembled on Gallipoli. Reinforcements were also reported to be on their way from Anatolia. In the chaos that existed, reliable information was simply unobtainable. Mustafa reported for active service.

The enemy advanced against the capital. Inside the capital people spent their time hanging the Young Turks.

Nothing was done to rescue the country. Everything was confused and obscure. On Gallipoli, too, there was the most indescribable chaos. People waited and waited, until they were driven almost to insanity.

Constantinople was not captured. On reaching the Chatalja Lines, the Serbs and Greeks turned tail. No one could say with certainty why. The Bulgarians, left to themselves, made no progress. By a miracle the worst seemed to have been averted.

But in the capital feelings which had been bottled up were suddenly uncorked. Enver, taking advantage of the situation,

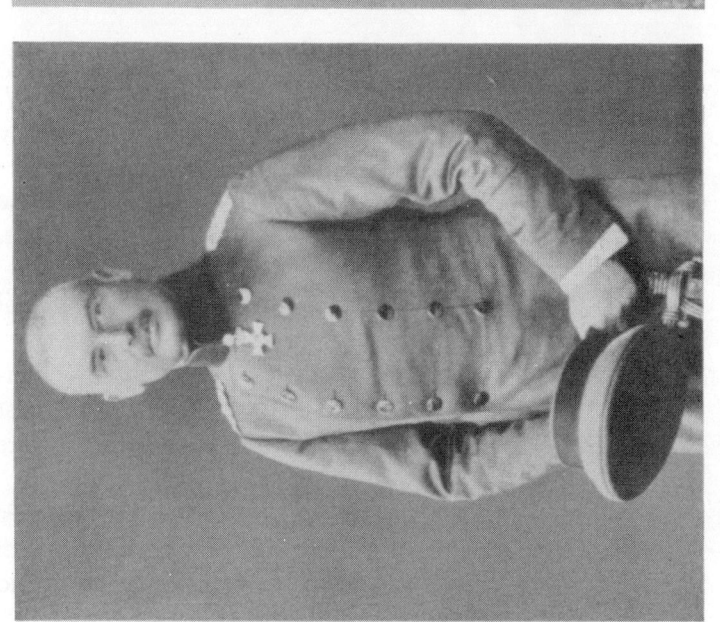

GENERAL LIMAN VON SANDERS
(1855–1929)

A WAR-TIME PORTRAIT OF KEMAL ATATURK

stormed the Sublime Porte, where the Peace Conference was in session. Nazim, the War Minister, was killed by a bullet. Mahmud Shevket, the leading man of the Committee, became Head of the State.

A State of Siege was proclaimed in Constantinople. Now it was the turn of the Young Turks to hang the Old Turks.

Enver decided to continue the war. Mustafa was with the army in Gallipoli. Orders were received to advance. They went forward, made contact with the enemy, and came to blows. In Constantinople nobody seemed to care a straw for the handful of troops who were fighting unaided on the Peninsula. Mustafa Kemal received yet another proof of Enver's incompetence. The fighting ended in the withdrawal of the Turkish troops, whose condemnation of the mismanagement of affairs will not bear repetition.

A little later, Mahmud Shevket was assassinated by the Reaction. A bullet struck him as he was entering the Mosque.

Mustafa's friend, Jemal, became Military Governor of Constantinople, and instituted a horrible tribunal of vengeance. Not even the Sultan's stepson was able to save his neck from the hangman's noose.

Meanwhile, the Balkan kings had started to squabble among themselves. With quick determination, the Committee ordered out the Turkish Army. Mustafa Kemal and Enver, both appointed to the General Staff, drove their troops northwards against Adrianople. Shortly before reaching the fortress, after the resistance of the Bulgarians had broken down, Enver placed himself at the head of the advance-guard cavalry to be first to ride into the reconquered fortress, and thus be able to proclaim to the world that he was the conqueror of Adrianople. He was now the big man. Sultan Mohammed V, when he heard that the thirty-three-year-old Enver had been appointed by the Committee to be Minister of War, was horrified. But Abdul Hamid's successor was nothing more than a figure-head, whose reluctant duty it was to append his signature to the documents which the almighty Committee placed before him.

The newly appointed Minister of War lost no time in making his power felt. All officers whom he considered as a nuisance or danger to him were dismissed from the Army.

Among those who might be considered as belonging to the above category was, in the first position of all, Mustafa Kemal. But he could not be dealt with in such summary fashion. He had supporters, and Enver could not advance against him with the same courage that had distinguished him in his dealings with the others. Mustafa Kemal must be disposed of in a different way.

Mustafa Kemal was promoted to the rank of lieutenant-colonel and sent as Military Attaché to Sofia. The Turkish Minister in that city was none other than Mustafa's old friend Fethi. The latter received secret instructions to keep the new attaché as much as possible away from his work and to see that he was well equipped with introductions to the leading members of society. It was thought that it would be better if he spent his time dancing and flirting with beautiful women than spend it in meddling in political and military matters.

Mustafa rapidly became a familiar figure in the clubs, where men gambled and debated, and in the drawing-rooms, where interesting women were the attraction. At the same time, at regular intervals, lengthy exposes and recommendations found their way on to the War Minister's writing-desk—demands for reforms; vigorous criticisms of Government measures; complaints about the lazy and incompetent individuals who were fattening themselves at the nation's expense. Opposition to the policy of Enver and Company became increasingly violent, notwithstanding the attractions of the ladies of Sofia and the claims which they made on the attaché's time.

The most irritating feature of these annoying criticisms was the fact that, in the end, people were forced to admit that he was right.

Mustafa Kemal, in his gilded exile, followed developments at home. The Talaat-Enver Government had invited the German, General Liman von Sanders, to reorganize the Army on German lines. Soon Mustafa Kemal was to discover that collaboration between the German Military Mission and the Turkish War Ministry bristled with difficulties. No two men could have formed a greater contrast than Liman von Sanders and Enver Pasha. Moreover, Turkish economic affairs were under the control of Turkey's creditors, whose agents and spies were everywhere and who were untiring in their invention of tricks to frustrate the work of construction and progress. Financial matters were entirely in the hands of the Levantines, Jews, Greeks and Armenians, who were the truest allies of all foes of the Ottoman Empire. There was no money for reforms. " *Para yok!* " (no money!) was the expression which caused all plans and projects to wither.

Nevertheless, Liman von Sanders managed it.

Not more than about a year after the collapse, he paraded the Ist Army Corps on the Taxim Square. No one had ever seen Turkish troops like them. All those present, Turks, Russians, Frenchmen, Britons, Italians and the rest, were unanimous in their opinion: Faultless! Incredible!

On the barrack-square in Belgrade were practising those marksmen who, shortly afterwards in Serajevo, assassinated the heir to the Throne of Austria-Hungary.

Mustafa Kemal was in close proximity to the Balkan witches' kettle. In Sofia the secret machinations of Belgrade and St. Petersburg were known. At the end of July the flames rose, and by the commencement of August Europe was on fire.

The Turkish Military Attaché in Sofia began to fidget at his post. He was well aware that in the course of time the Ottoman Empire would be swept into the cataclysm. At the beginning of August a secret treaty of alliance between the German Empire and Turkey was signed. In mid-August Turkey was to all intents in a State of War with the Western Powers and Russia. Finally, in November, the official declaration of war was despatched.

Mustafa Kemal sent in an application to proceed to the front. Enver wired back that he was to stay at his post.

In war-time there is only one post that matters to a soldier, and that is at the front. Mustafa Kemal again appealed to the Minister of War and Vice-Commander-in-Chief to alter his decision. The order to remain in Sofia was repeated. Enver left for the Caucasus and sent ninety thousand men to their death, without achieving the slightest success.

When he returned, a sober and depressed man, Mustafa Kemal was in command of a unit of the Dardanelles Army. . . .

Mustafa, now that Gallipoli had ceased to be a scene of war made the capital his venue.

He was seen at all the Ministries and at all the principal military offices. The great men behind the writing-desks groaned when a secretary placed before them a card bearing the name " Colonel Mustafa Kemal." That could only mean an interview in which grouses, charges, criticisms, demands and recommendations would play the chief part.

In addition, it was well known that the Committee were keeping a strict eye on him. It was dangerous, therefore, to converse with him in any other than a cool, conventional tone. The suspicions of the powers-that-be might easily be attracted to oneself.

The Foreign Minister, Achmed Nessimi, attempted to crush the obstinate and unwanted visitor by telling an attendant that Mustafa Kemal was to be kept waiting.

"His Excellency sends apologies to the colonel, but his Excellency is overwhelmed with work. Would the colonel mind waiting?"

Mustafa waited, and saw one visitor after the other admitted without question to the Holy of Holies and after some time leave.

Mustafa sent in a reminder.

The Minister cursed.

" Tell him to wait ! " he shouted at the attendant.

The latter hardly had the courage to pass on the message.

Mustafa knew exactly what was on foot, struck up a conversation with one of the minor officials in the ante-room, and waited patiently while the Minister took his time over another audience.

The time grew late, and his Excellency began to get tired. Oh, yes, Mustafa Kemal was still outside—talking to one of the officials.

The Minister resigned himself to the inevitable. He wanted to shut up the office and go home.

The attendant solemnly opened the door and told the colonel that his Excellency would receive him.

" Tell him to wait," said Mustafa with unconcern, and quietly finished his conversation with the minor official, while the great man sat open-mouthed in his room, taking a lesson in the art of waiting.

The victory at Gallipoli, that brilliant test of the soldierly qualities of the Ottoman Army, roused the Turks from their despair and lethargy. They began to regain confidence in their own strength. But Enver and the whole Committee of Union and

Progress completely lost their heads. With absurd over-estimation of their strength, they began to strike out at hopelessly unattainable goals, dreaming not only of preserving the Empire in its present form, but of uniting all Mohammedans under Turkish sovereignty.

A Holy War was proclaimed.

The call went forth into space, and produced no echo.

Enver planned the conquest of Egypt. It was to be achieved with a mere fifteen thousand men. Actually, the expeditionary corps performed miracles, and after great hardship endured in the desert succeeded in reaching the Suez Canal. Germans and Turks provided an example of unequalled heroism. Naturally, they were forced to retreat before the crushing superiority of the British, who quickly recovered from their shock and carried the pursuit into the desert.

But the British advanced gradually, establishing good, well-organized base-lines (which Enver had omitted to do), until one fine day they reached the other side of the desert and stood on the southern boundary of Palestine.

Liman von Sanders issued a warning. The numerical weakness of the Turks would prove catastrophic. In the long run, with such slender means, it was impossible to defend all the frontiers of the Empire. But the Vice-Commander-in-Chief had foolhardy, offensive plans. He wanted to march through Persia and Afghanistan to India. The breach between Enver and the Head of the Military Mission was now public knowledge. The best officers of the Ottoman Army firmly supported Liman's views, and Mustafa Kemal also belonged to those who considered the Vice-Generalissimo a mortal danger to the country.

Enver feared conspiracies. In order to make them more difficult, he was constantly transferring officers and formations. Several times a month a unit changed its commanding officer. As soon as a regiment had settled down in its position, it was given orders to proceed to some distant part of the front. The result was that most of the Army spent the time on the move, leaving the fronts deserted.

The officers did not know their men, and the soldiers became demoralized. They were semi-starved and lacked all proper attention.

Enver was well aware of the sorry state of things, and knew that conspiracies were being carried on in secret. But still the game of General Post was continued, to make it as hard as possible for the conspirators to bring their plans to a head.

The famous Dardanelles Army, with its splendid officers and seasoned men, had been scattered to the four winds.

Mustafa Kemal was sent as a general to the Caucasus, where nothing was happening and where no laurels were to be gained. His chief of staff, a young colonel, worked himself nearly to death: Ismet. Mustafa made a note of the man.

The Vice-Commander-in-Chief could not prevent the formation of plotting cliques. In Constantinople, under the very eyes of the Government, Major Yakub Jemil was working for the downfall of the present régime, and went among the officers with the slogan: Get rid of the men who imagine they are great, but who in reality are small.

A sharp eye was maintained on the conspirator, though at present the authorities were not quite clear what he intended. But general incompetence was so obvious, and the Vice-Commander-in-Chief's blunders so apparent, that Yakub Jemil received a ready hearing.

More and more officers rallied round him. The revolution grew apace. All that was lacking was a leading personality whom one could nominate as successor to the hated Enver.

Yakub Jemil then pronounced the name of the man who was needed: none other than Mustafa Kemal, the greatest soldier in the Ottoman Army and Enver's most unrelenting opponent.

There was now a rush to join the conspirators. Cold perspiration stood upon the brows of the Committee. It was high time for intervention! Mustafa Kemal *ad portas!*

The police apparatus still functioned admirably. One morning, without noise or fuss, Yakub and his fellow-conspirators were liquidated. Only one escaped, pursued like a hunted stag through the rocky deserts of Anatolia to the Caucasus.

General Mustafa Kemal was not a little astounded when they brought to him a trembling, half-starved specimen of humanity, which introduced itself as Dr. Hilmi and implored the general's protection.

SALONIKA

Shortly afterwards a telegram arrived from the Government. It contained the order to arrest immediately the traitor Dr. Hilmi and send him back to Constantinople.

Enver ground his teeth when Mustafa Kemal's reply was placed in his hands.

Mustafa Kemal declined to deliver up the fugitive who had put himself beneath his protection.

In Constantinople there was a conference. The opinion of the majority of the Cabinet was in favour of allowing matters to rest where they were. An open disagreement with the Victor of Anafarta was too dangerous.

Enver was forced to yield. Angrily, he determined to make of the victor a vanquished. Somehow a defeat had to be hung round Mustafa's neck; people had to be discouraged from looking upon him as the " Invincible." He would send him to some lost post and allow him enough rope to hang himself. Some opportunity would present itself.

In the distant Caucasus General Mustafa Kemal examined the conspirator, who confessed everything, including the name of the man whom they had marked out to be successor to the Vice-Commander-in-Chief.

Mustafa's features did not move.

Ismet ventured to ask whether he would have accepted, in the event of the plot succeeding.

The general shrugged his shoulders.

Could he have brought himself to accept a post under such circumstances? And supposing he had—his first duty on arriving in Constantinople would have been to hang this Yakub Jemil and his associates from the highest tree.

CHAPTER III

SYRIA

IN the streets of the Holy City of Mecca there was a sound of rifle-fire. People shouted, and horses, handsome Arabian thoroughbreds, upset by the crowds and the din, reared and shied. Arabs with flashing eyes, riding up and down in the square outside the Government House, were discharging their silver-inlaid rifles in the air.

Dazzling white burnouses ballooned out behind them as they rode. Everything was white, all other colours having been destroyed by the fury of the sun.

An angry, howling mob thronged outside the residence of the Turkish Governor; dark-brown faces, whose features were distorted with rage, kept watch on the entrance gate.

Suddenly horsemen scattered the crowd with whips and backed their frightened horses against the walls of the houses. Make way! The Grand Sheriff was approaching at the head of a solemn, imposing procession.

Surrounded by a horde of shouting, pock-marked warriors—sinister, dangerous-looking fellows—came Hussein, King of Mecca, a man with an evil, forbidding, despotic countenance.

He had just renounced the Sultan and had proclaimed himself ruler of the Holy Cities.

" *Allah il Allah!* " yelled the Arabs.

Daggers flew from their scabbards as the gate of the palace now opened and the Turkish Governor made his appearance. The Grand Sheriff's cavalry escort cold-bloodedly charged the yelling, infuriated mob, forcing them back. Periodically shots were fired, and keen-edged Damascus blades flashed through the air.

Soon the crowd broke through the ranks of the horsemen and, like a giant wave, flung themselves on a squad of captured Turkish soldiers. In the *mêlée* flashes of knives and an occasional shot could be seen and heard. Eventually the quivering mass of human bodies was separated by the Sheriff's cavalrymen. Mangled soldiers made their appearance and were led away. They uttered not a sound: the hellish heat, if nothing else, had dulled their senses. Rifle-butts pounded their backs.

The Governor with set features negligently handed the keys to the Grand Sheriff.

Mecca, taken completely by surprise, had been stormed and taken by insurgent Arabs.

The revolt had spread through the deserts with lightning speed.

The war had suddenly a totally different aspect. A new situation had been created, and completely fresh problems had to be faced.

As yet few people realized that here, in the burning heat of the deserts, the grave of the Ottoman Empire was being dug.

Coming from Cairo in an English warship, a young man disembarked at Jedda on the southern shores of the Red Sea, where no Turkish troops were stationed. Wrapped in a white burnouse, his features half-concealed by the flowing head-cloth, he rode into the heat of the deserts mounted on a camel.

He rode from tribe to tribe. Often, owing to the heat, his skin burst, he bled, and the glare of the sun practically robbed him of his sight. Sandstorms overwhelmed him as he rode, and thirst nearly drove him insane—but he carried on, summoning the Arabs to fight for an independent Arabia.

Wherever he appeared, he whipped the tribes into a frenzy. The country resounded with the fanatical yells of the Bedouins, who staged time after time displays of horsemanship in honour of the man who had mastered all their dialects and who lived, thought and felt as though he himself were a son of the desert.

But this man, when he sat in Sheriff Feisal's tent, cast off his head-cloth and spoke English. The Arabs could hardly believe that he was an Englishman; and although they knew that he was, pretended to ignore the fact. To them he was Urens, the great magician Urens.

To the British General Staff in Cairo he was Colonel Lawrence, who, more or less on his own responsibility, had gone to Arabia to spread revolt in the desert, for he knew that from there the Ottoman Empire could be checkmated.

By the commencement of 1917 there was in existence an Arab national army under the command of Feisal, son of the Grand Sheriff of Mecca.

In close proximity to Mecca lay the second Holy City, Medina. There a Turkish division was in station and still holding out against the Arab revolt.

Medina was the terminus of the Hedjaz Railway which, running for several thousand miles parallel to the Red Sea coast, extended as far as Damascus.

Enver, for the sake of preserving political prestige, had got it into his head that Arabia and the railway must be held. The Chief of the German Military Mission, as well as Mustafa Kemal and many other officers, knew that this was madness. To defend this great area, in Turkey's present weak state, was glaringly absurd.

The Englishman was counting on Enver's arrogant self-confidence. The former had troops in plenty and could establish as many fronts as he fancied. And his policy was to force the Turks to defend as many points as possible, and so divide and weaken their forces.

No one as yet saw any connection between the Arab revolt, Colonel Lawrence's work, and the formation of a British front on Palestine's frontier.

Bravely and tenaciously, the Turkish soldiers fought in the desert with the tricky Arabs, who from 1917 onwards were equipped with English war material and supported with Egyptian troops, English sappers, armoured-cars and aeroplanes.

In distant Mesopotamia Bagdad fell. Enver's position seemed untenable. There was a general clamour for his resignation, and shouts for Mustafa Kemal grew loud. Enver journeyed in hot haste to the German Headquarters to beg for assistance.

In vain Marshal Liman von Sanders, the only German with a real knowledge of local circumstances, warned against sending an expedition to recapture Bagdad. Nevertheless, it was determined upon. The German Asia Corps arrived. A mixed army group, known as the " Blitz " Army (Lightning Army), was formed under Falkenhayn's command. Turkish and German soldiers marched shoulder to shoulder to eject the British from Bagdad.

Mustafa Kemal was recalled from the Caucasus and given the command of a section of the " Blitz " Army that was in station near Aleppo.

The whole undertaking was accompanied by disagreements and rows. The Chief of the German Military Mission was treated in a manner which aroused the intense indignation of all those who had come to hold him in the highest esteem. The German Headquarters, which was completely misinformed, and which placed absolute reliance in Enver, regarded the opposition that was displayed to the Vice-Commander-in-Chief as an outrage.

Mustafa Kemal, who had managed to establish so excellent an understanding with Liman von Sanders, was quickly at cross purposes with Falkenhayn. Falkenhayn was totally ignorant of the position of Turkish military affairs, and with Enver in his path found it quite impossible to arrive at an independent assessment of the situation. The Vice-Commander-in-Chief with his intrigues eventually succeeded in winning over the German commander to his side, and in gaining his confidence and recognition.

Someone must have the courage to create a public demonstration against this state of affairs. But the officers just moaned and groaned, and things stayed as they were.

Mustafa Kemal finally risked being court martialled when he unexpectedly resigned his command at Aleppo and refused to take part in an adventure which he knew was hopeless, participation in which would have been against his conscience..

They did not place him before a court martial, but sent him once more to the Caucasus. He was urged by other officers to make a more vigorous demonstration, but this he declined to do.

The people of Constantinople, fearing that the affair might produce unpleasant repercussions in the capital, now decided officially to place him on the sick list and grant him indefinite leave.

The rebel was left in Aleppo without financial means. It is true that he was the owner of a valuable string of horses, but who was in a position to buy them from him? Who in Syria had any money? Mustafa Kemal, with his pockets empty, sat helplessly in Aleppo and brooded over his situation.

Then there came to his assistance an old friend, Jemal, who gave him five thousand pounds for the ten horses. Mustafa could now return to Constantinople.

There he was accorded a "warm" reception. Zubeida Hanum, in particular, was anything but satisfied with the son who rebelled against everything, made everyone his enemy, and wrecked his own career.

She utilized the opportunity to take him severely to task, as she had done in the days when he was a child. To-day she repeated the process. And if he had been a general and defender of the Dardanelles ten times over, he would still have had to contend with his mother, who now insisted that he should display some loyalty and concentrate his energy on progressing in the world.

First he had rebelled against the Sultan, and now he was rebelling against the Committee. That was a little too much for Zubeida Hanum.

Mustafa Kemal was always happiest when he was entirely alone. Oceans separated him from the views held by his mother, and when his family and relatives began to pester him with advice, and sought to exert their influence on him, he knew that something had to be done about it. His path lay clearly marked out for him; and there was no one who could persuade him to desert it. He did not wish to contradict his mother for fear of hurting her feelings, and so he came to the conclusion that it would be better if he ceased living at home. Mustafa took a room in an hotel, stayed there quite alone, indulged in melancholy meditations, and waited to see what would happen.

It was as he and Liman von Sanders had predicted: the expedition to recapture Bagdad ended in a glaring failure. The desert climate and the complete neglect of proper communications and supplies had defeated the undertaking. Again valuable lives, which could never be replaced, had been vainly sacrificed. Again the Turks and their Allies sustained a severe loss in prestige.

In the autumn, 1917, the British assumed the offensive in Palestine. Near Ghaza there was a long drawn-out, grim and bloody battle which ended in the defeat of the English. But the situation behind the Turkish front was developing dangerously. Palestine and Syria had joined in the Arab revolt.

Colonel Lawrence now began to lead a number of raids behind the Turkish lines that were the height of boldness. Again and again he appeared at various points of the impenetrable desert, destroying the rearward communications of the Palestine Army and sowing the seeds of revolt among the local population.

The bearers of responsibility viewed the future with increasing anxiety.

Spring, 1918.

In Constantinople Mustafa Kemal was instructed to join the

suite of the Heir to the Throne, who was about to pay an official visit to the German Imperial Headquarters.

He received the intimation with satisfaction, sensing that here was an excellent opportunity for getting to know the future Sultan.

Crown Prince Mohammed Vahideddin was a thorn in the Committee's eye. They knew that he was a fanatical Reactionary, but at the same time did not dare to take action against him.

The first meeting between the two men produced keen disappointment on both sides, but when they found themselves in the train, and Constantinople had been left behind, Mustafa experienced a surprise. The Crown Prince suddenly cast aside his mask, and the sleepy, degenerate cretin transformed himself into a man of energy and vitality. They had not long been speaking together before Mustafa Kemal realized that he had opposite him one of the most cunning and resourceful men he had ever met. The Prince appeared to recognize that Mustafa Kemal was the coming man and treated him with consideration and kindness.

Did the two men realize, as they sat opposite each other in the train passing the time in pleasant conversation, that one day they would become the bitterest of enemies? Did Prince Vahideddin guess that this same Mustafa Kemal would later drive him from his country as a traitor?

Mustafa Kemal no longer had faith in victory and was firmly convinced that Germany was in no position to provide adequate help, but rather that it was her duty to apply all her strength in an effort to solve her own problems.

They arrived at Spa, the German Headquarters, and made the acquaintance of the big men—Ludendorff and Field-Marshal von Hindenburg. The Kaiser was unable to bring himself to like the impenetrable Turkish general, who made no secret of his want of faith in victory, who spent his time in asking awkward questions, who wanted to know everything and who seemed to have infected the Crown Prince with his own inquisitiveness.

Mustafa Kemal was not there to find fault, but he could not evade the unpleasant feeling that all was not well. The Ottoman Empire was utterly ruined, at the end of its tether and no longer able to maintain any appreciable resistance to a determined attack on any one front. All the sources of material aid and man-power had been expended, indeed frittered away, in Enver's extravagant political adventures.

Only a hundred per cent German victory on the Western Front could now alter matters and save Turkey from complete collapse. Enver had blind faith in that victory. Not so Mustafa Kemal. He began to approach Ludendorff with inconvenient questions—which were left unanswered. Mustafa felt the need of turning to someone who would understand his emergency, someone whom he liked and who appeared to like him—Hindenburg.

His despair gave him courage. On one occasion, after dinner, when Hindenburg drew him aside for a long, confidential talk, the Victor of Anafarta determined to speak his mind. Mustafa Kemal then launched out with a question which, he knew, would cause the field-marshal considerable embarrassment:

"*Herr Marschall*, you are about to open a big offensive, and it seems to me that you are placing far too much confidence in its success. Would you mind telling me, just between ourselves, precisely what objective you hope to accomplish by it?"

The field-marshal looked at him, in a way which told the young general that he understood what was on his mind and in a manner which appeared to indicate that he himself was tormented with the same doubts. But to Mustafa's surprise, he ignored his question, and turning to a smoking-table nearby said:

"Will your Excellency have a cigar, or do you prefer a cigarette?"

Mustafa Kemal helped himself to a cigarette.

Realizing that he would not gain the information he sought, the Turk then remained silent.

Mental strain was beginning to affect him physically. Mustafa Kemal was stricken with a disorder of the kidneys, had to go into a hospital in Vienna for treatment and afterwards to Carlsbad.

That was in July, 1918.

About this time Sultan Mohammed V died, and Vahideddin became Emperor of the Turks. Immediately, the new ruler curtailed Enver's authority. Mustafa hastened back to Constantinople and was received in audience by the new Sultan, upon whom he urged a complete change of policy. But the Sultan had not the courage to consent to anything so drastic. Even if this Mustafa

SYRIA

was an adversary of the Committee, he was altogether too downright in his views and too daringly enterprising. Such men did not appeal to the oily, diplomat nature of the new Sultan, who preferred secret, tortuous paths to all other ways.

Mustafa Kemal thereupon began to make an insufferable nuisance of himself at the various Ministries, until there was an unanimous decision that he was to be ousted from Constantinople without delay. Enver then saw a way, a grand opportunity, of ridding him of his label of " Invincible." On the Palestine front the situation had radically changed. There England's most highly-reputed soldier, General Allenby, had assumed command, and for the past few months had been accumulating great quantities of war material for the big onslaught. An abundance of men were at his disposal, and most of the units were above war strength. Well-nourished, splendidly-equipped men waited for the signal to storm the Turkish lines.

A Turkish front? It merely existed on paper. It consisted in reality of a few divisions, tragically under strength, which were slowly perishing from disease and hunger; whose soldiers, who had been months without stores and munitions, had become completely demoralized. Why?

The Vice-Commander-in-Chief had other cares.

He was busy in the Caucasus planning the conquest of Turkestan, Persia and India, utterly blind to the fact that in the south of Palestine the British were quietly and comfortably preparing the decisive blow, which they could deliver at any time they fancied.

Even in December, the previous year, when Jerusalem fell, the Vice-Commander-in-Chief had not been alarmed.

The Governor of Syria and Palestine was Mustafa's old friend Jemal, who lived in Damascus in a marble palace, held court like a monarch, lived on the fat of the land, and complained bitterly whenever it was necessary for him to journey to the " front." In fact, journeys to the front had become exceedingly dangerous since Colonel Lawrence had been paying his unwelcome visits to the Turkish base-lines. One day, when the train abruptly halted at a small station in the middle of the desert, when bullets began to fly and soldiers leapt out of the train to drive off Lawrence and his

Bedouins, Jemal began to gain a little more insight into the state of local affairs.

That nothing could be done with this army of sick men, most of whom were suffering from chronic tuberculosis, Jemal knew. And wisely, he quickly cancelled his visit, travelled by the shortest route to Damascus, and continued to hold court.

Somewhere an efficient commanding officer had to be found, especially as it had been learned from spies that the British were intending to strike on 18 March.

There were two men who made it hard for the Vice-Commander-in-Chief to sleep at night and whom he would like to get rid of—Liman von Sanders and Mustafa Kemal. The latter was still in Vienna.

And so the command was handed over to Liman von Sanders. He refused to accept it. Enver then telegraphed to the Kaiser, who sent back orders that Sanders was to take command. The general obeyed and set out to take over, burdened with the responsibility for one of the most appalling catastrophes in the history of war—a catastrophe that was inevitable long in advance—while those who were really responsible just snapped their fingers.

Soldiers deserted by the hundred. Equipment and supplies were simply unobtainable.

Despite that Liman von Sanders held at bay the English assaults, launched by a tenfold numerical superiority consisting of the best troops at the enemy's disposal, and actually delivered a counter-attack forcing the British to withdraw to Jerusalem.

Allenby then called on more cavalry, more guns, aeroplanes and armoured-cars, and on 19 September attacked again.

Liman von Sanders was forced to remain inactive and await the enemy's coming. The Vice-Commander-in-Chief had broken his word and had sent neither troops, nor food supplies, nor munitions, nor medical outfits for the war in the desert. The men in Syria were completely cut off from the world and left to defend themselves as best they could against the British and Arab insurgents.

The circumstances were horrifying. On account of the hostility of the local population to the Turks the transmission of orders was practically impossible. Runners and messengers disappeared without trace, having been ambushed and liquidated by the Arabs.

ZUBEIDE HANUM, MOTHER OF KEMAL ATATURK

KEMAL ATATURK

Telephone-lines, bridges and railways as soon as they were repaired were again destroyed. That was the work of Lawrence, whose Arab revolt had the effect of a stab in the back of the Turkish front.

A new commander was needed for the VIIth Army. Mustafa Kemal had just returned to Constantinople and had already been taxing the ministers' nerves.

Enver decreed that he should be given command of the VIIth Army in North Syria, and arranged that he received his orders to take up the command from the Sultan in person.

" Bravo, my friend, you managed that very well," was Mustafa's bitter comment to Enver, whom he found smiling blandly in his Majesty's ante-room.

When he arrived in Syria and saw the VIIth " Army," he suffered the first and only nervous breakdown of his life.

Lying in bed, he carried on the command of the undisciplined rabble that had once consisted of brave soldiers. To make things worse the supports which Enver had despatched from the snow-covered mountains of the Caucasus were half-grown lads of fifteen, the only recruits that remained for service, boys, who had not the least inkling of what it meant to be a soldier.

On the eve of the big Allenby offensive Mustafa rose from his bed. The Vice-Commander-in-Chief quickly withdrew the German *Scharfschützen* (Rifle) Company, Liman's last dependable troops. The German Marshal stayed in Nazareth, and marvelled that he was still sane.

On the 19 September, 1918, the Valley of the Jordan was a scene of terror and gruesome slaughter. The crushing weight of the British attack descended in full force upon the remnants of the Turkish armies. Where had the troops gone? Whole divisions had vanished without a trace, and no one could possibly imagine where they were.

Liman von Sanders was no longer in communication with the various sectors of the front. The telephones were silent; runners fell to Arab knives; no orders were received and no reports arrived.

The chaos was appalling.

From innumerable ambushes Bedouin horsemen rode forth, cutting down fugitives or selling captives into slavery.

Only one route of retreat lay open, and that was a narrow defile through the Esdralon Valley. In indescribable confusion, with no pretence at any kind of order, the Turkish divisions stampeded between the steep, rocky walls of the valley, driven by a single thought—to get out of that hell and strike for Damascus !

But Allenby was not willing to allow the Turkish Palestine Army to escape, and attacked the sorely-wounded enemy from the air. With roaring engines the air squadrons suddenly came upon them, and a rain of bombs descended upon the human masses, who soon lay struggling in the blood and dust of the narrow valley. There was no escape : wedged between the steep walls of the Jordan Valley a whole army lay at the mercy of the British air fleet. The terrible slaughter lasted four hours. When one squadron had expended its cargo of bombs another took its place, while the first returned to its base for a fresh supply.

Gradually it grew quieter—in the air and on the ground. The airmen vanished, and in their stead came the vultures, who circled over the pass and then swooped down.

Allenby's airmen had completed their work.

Belated revenge for Gallipoli !

With one giant sweep of the scythe the Syrian Army had been mown away. The few scattered bands that remained fled wildly towards the north relentlessly pursued by swarms of bloodthirsty Bedouins.

The Holy Land was turned into a scene of terror and unbelievable horrors.

Colonel Lawrence hastened from point to point, ahead of the extremely slow-moving British army, directing his Arab hordes, who left a fearful story of devastation in their trail.

Once only did he halt and ponder—when he came upon the remnant of the German Asia Corps. They made the war-seasoned Briton and foe seem small, and aroused his respect.

" They were two thousand miles from their homes," he wrote some time later, " without hope in a strange, foreign land, in a situation desperate enough to break the strongest nerves. Nevertheless, their units remained firm and disciplined and steered their course through the surging sea of Turks and Arabs like armoured ships, silently and with heads held high. If they were attacked, they halted, took up a position, and returned well-directed fire.

There was no rush, no shouting, no hesitation. They were splendid."

On Syria's northern frontier, where Anatolia, the real Turkey, began, Mustafa Kemal brought the scattered bands to a halt, and near Aleppo the troops were re-formed. The general's energy succeeded in creating from the wreckage of the Syrian Army a solid formation consisting of freshly-formed units for the defence of the city.

But Aleppo was in revolt. Mustafa Kemal again had to act.

The front had to be taken back still farther. Mustafa Kemal issued fresh orders from the mountains on the Anatolian frontier.

" The enemy will not pass this line," he declared in an Order of the Day.

Then from Constantinople came the command to lay down arms. Bulgaria had capitulated and thrown herself at the mercy of the Western Allies. The French were advancing from Macedonia against Constantinople. They had already crossed the Maritza near Adrianople, and were within a few days' march of their goal.

But that did not suit the Briton's book. The French in Constantinople? As masters of the Dardanelles?

Orders were hurriedly issued for the British fleet assembled near the Greek islands to raise steam.

Once again Enver decided to place everything on one card and assembled the remnant of the army to oppose the French.

He was too late; his hour had struck. The shout for capitulation, armistice and peace resounded through Constantinople. Quite unexpectedly Sultan Vahideddin emerged from his reserve and seized the reins of government to himself. Since the fall of Abdul Hamid the Sultan had exercised no control in his country's affairs, was simply a figure-head, but now things were to be altered.

His first step was to arrest all the Young Turks on whom he could lay hands. Enver fled to Germany. The former Vice-Commander-in-Chief's brilliant red car, tearing at breakneck speed through the streets of Constantinople, followed by his life-guard of picked giants, with their inevitable revolvers and carbines, vanished from the capital.

Sultan Mohammed VI, Vahideddin, established a dictatorship and ruled with a rod of iron.

He sat one day in his study holding in his hand a telegram from General Mustafa Kemal Pasha, which caused him to think hard. The despot puckered his forehead. Mustafa Kemal had proposed the formation of a new Government, with himself in the role of War Minister.

Vahideddin agreed that there was no man more entitled or better equipped for the job, but at the same time he deemed it rather unwise, now that they were begging the British for peace and pardon, to present to them a man whom they hated like poison, and whose name was an unhappy reminder of the severe reverses on Gallipoli.

No, Mustafa Kemal must not be Minister of War. But instead of sending him a blank refusal Vahideddin exercised his customary diplomatic cunning and held him at an arm's length. He was very much obliged for his Excellency's suggestions and would be delighted to discuss them with him later. At present he intended making Marshal Izzet Grand Vizier. General Mustafa Kemal, on the other hand, was not to be sent away unrewarded, he was to take over from Marshal Liman von Sanders the command of the entire Syrian Army.

The British Mediterranean Fleet meanwhile steamed to meet General Townshend, who had been taken prisoner at Kut el Amara and who was now on his way to conduct negotiations for an immediate armistice on behalf of the Ottoman Sultan.

Vahideddin, in accordance with good Turkish tradition, maintained a strictly correct attitude where his German allies were concerned, but Germany could no longer help, and returned to Turkey her liberty to take independent action.

Admiral Calthorpe sighed with relief when the officer with the flag of truce came aboard his flagship. Most certainly, he would grant an immediate armistice, if only for the purpose of keeping the French out of Constantinople. The conditions under which the armistice was to be granted were hastily drawn up in the Admiral's flagship, which lay by the entrance of the Dardanelles.

Surrender of the fleet, immediate demobilization of the army and occupation of Constantinople as security for fulfilment of the undertakings were the main conditions of the truce.

In far-off Adana, in the south of Anatolia, a guard of honour had paraded on the station platform, and the soldiers presented arms for the last time to Marshal Liman von Sanders, who made a short speech of farewell and handed over his command to General Mustafa Kemal Pasha. The two officers then shook hands.

"There is just one thing that I have to console me in my misfortune—that I am leaving you behind as my successor," said Liman von Sanders.

Mustafa Kemal was unable to find words in reply.

The train then slowly drew out of the station.

Alone and abandoned, the new commanding officer stood and surveyed his soldiers.

What was the next step?

PART TWO
THE REBEL

CHAPTER IV

CONSTANTINOPLE

THE narrow strip of glistening water at the Golden Horn, separating the Turkish City of Stambul from Galata and Pera, echoed the sounds of the French *clairons*. The famous old Galata Bridge groaned under the weight of the marching battalions.

France's troops were entering Constantinople. It is true, not as conquerors—the British had cleverly taken care of that—but at all events as victors.

There they were, Poilus of the notorious Salonika Army, which marched into neutral Greek Macedonia and held there a veritable reign of terror—wild, insolent fellows, maintained at high pitch by their officers. The light blue of their uniforms vied with the blue of the sky. They had shaken the war-filth of Macedonia from themselves and now appeared, in immaculate new uniforms, as triumphant heroes in the disillusioned wonder city on the Bosporus.

The old Galata Bridge was used to bearing noisy crowds on its back. A throng of people, of all nations and all hues, had passed over it day and night since time immemorial. It was Constantinople's main artery, the place where the bustle and picturesque life of the old city reached its peak.

Here the small merchants and beggars gathered. Proud Turks and foreigners in search of novelty mingled with the motley company of Levantines, Jews, Greeks and Armenians. Deeply-veiled women threaded their way, keeping their eyes averted, through the crowd, among which the bright-red Turkish fez was the most conspicuous head-gear. Fortune-tellers and vendors of charms and knick-knacks pestered the passers-by. Sinister-looking Dervishes in flowing robes strode unconcernedly along. Everyone moved aside when an officer of the Ertogrul Life Guards rode up on a fine, perfectly turned-out horse. These men, with their bronzed features and (often) blue eyes and with their blue tunics and dove-grey breeches made an impressive show.

Or sometimes a four-horse carriage containing a powerful pasha drove along, its occupant not deigning to cast a single glance at the colourful scene which surrounded him. . . .

That was the old Galata Bridge. During the War its scene was a different one. Business-like motor cars, carrying officers and officials, then tore across it. The foreign element dived out of their way; the Turks were busy fighting on the various fronts.

But now the old life was beginning to show itself again, in an even more intensive, altogether more demonstrative form.

But one saw only the foreign element of the population. These swarmed round the newly-arrived victors like moths round a candle, but in their enthusiasm they did not forget to speculate on the personal gains which they hoped to derive from the soldiers, who after four years of war had made up their minds to enjoy life.

The columns headed in the direction of Galata and Pera.

Suddenly the troops were met with flags. The streets were decorated with triumphal arches and garlands; windows and balconies were draped with bunting; it was impossible to see the sky for the ceiling of Allied flags that was spread over the streets.

Business premises were closed. Pera, on the " Far Side," was according an extravagant welcome to the victors, representatives of the great France, who at last had brought liberation from the Turkish masters, the masters of yesterday, who had robbed and cheated them for centuries and who had left to the people of Pera that which was their life purpose—their businesses—earning for themselves in return the name of oppressors.

Pera cheered itself hoarse. The streets were hardly big enough to hold all the people.

" *Vive la France! Vive la liberté!* "

At every street corner the French were greeted with new signs of reverence and enthusiasm. General Franchet d'Esperay was completely overcome by the magnitude of the welcome that was accorded to him.

Not even in his wildest dreams had he imagined such scenes possible.

The troops marched, rode and drove further, until they had traversed the whole of Pera. Shouts of welcome and ringing cheers and an avalanche of flowers accompanied them on their way.

On the other side of the Galata Bridge all was quiet. Stambul, the Turkish City, resembled a great white tomb. There was not a person in the streets, and all the shutters in the houses were drawn. No sounds disturbed the stillness. Even the perpetually running fountains in the forecourts of the mosques had dried up. Stambul was without water.

Vanished were the active craftsmen usually to be seen working outside the houses, squatting in the Arab or Oriental fashion on the ground, the roof of a porch serving them as shade from the sun. Gone were the carpenters, smiths, pottery-makers and carpet-weavers, the cobblers, tailors and others, who for centuries had made the streets their workshops and who worked silently and honourably before all eyes.

They were not to be seen. You would have found them, inactive, motionless and in despair, crouching behind the walls of their houses.

Even the big bazaar was silent, the world's most fantastic stores, a city in itself, with thirty-five streets and approaching three thousand shops, where in the ordinary way throngs of people inspected goods, haggled over their price and finally bought; where thousands sipped their coffee and smoked innumerable cigarettes, whose fumes covered the whole scene in a bluish, aromatic haze.

All that was at an end. Everything was dead, silent, shut.

The massive, unornamented Hagia Sofia loomed ominously above the maze of houses which stretched as far as the harbour.

Turkish sentries—starved, battered creatures in ragged khaki—stood guard at its gates.

The sounds of cheering in Pera were borne to them across the water.

Night cast a black mantle upon Stambul. Pera was ablaze with light. On the windows of the palaces could be seen the shadows of the officers dancing. The latest tunes from Paris could be heard.

Rich Levantines had thrown open their drawing-rooms and had staged balls in the honour of their liberators.

In the harbour all was still. The heavy forms of English battleships lay in the gently-moving waves of the Bosporus. Floating side by side, their guns were pointed as a silent threat against the Magic City. . . .

On the Galata Bridge stood two Turkish officers, tall, wiry men with the figures of horsemen, who looked over the sides of the bridge at the water below.

"Have you heard anything yet about negotiations? About peace?" asked one of them.

"The victor has plenty of time, my friend. First of all Germany has to be strangled. Then it will be our turn," was the reply.

"What became of the German Asia Corps? Where is Liman von Sanders?"

"They demand the surrender of the Germans..."

"That would be the last straw..."

"They can do what they like with us, but hands off our guests and brothers in arms! We have been defeated, but we're not cads. I am told that Marshal Liman von Sanders is at Kadikoi. German units are said to be forming there."

The younger of the two men looked towards the west; his eyes were misty.

"Gallipoli," he whispered. "Would that we had remained out there with the others. How we suffered in those shallow, narrow trenches at Anafarta and Ariburnu when the ships' guns were trained on us! The earth was drenched in blood, but we held out. Was it all in vain? Have all the sacrifices we made, the victories and the bloodshed been forgotten?"

"It's fate, my friend. It is Allah's will. There is only one thing we can do, and that is to preserve manly dignity despite all misfortunes."

"What will happen?..."

"*Inshallah!* God alone knows."

"What has become of the men who brought about this unfortunate state of affairs—the men we thought were great?"

"They've flown. Enver and Talaat have escaped to Germany. Here, to satisfy the British, they have been tried and sentenced to death."

"There was something wrong in the aims of those men."

"Something? Is that how you describe it?"

"Where is Mustafa Kemal?"

"Mustafa Kemal? If you travel out to Shishli you will find a small country house. There you will be received by an unemployed general, a private man, an unwanted individual like ourselves—Mustafa Kemal. He is another one of those whom we prefer to hide, for he was unfortunate enough to defeat the English. No, my friend, Constantinople is no place for soldiers. What's the best thing to do?"

"They need soldiers in South Russia. Wrangel is planning to attack the Bolsheviks."

"Sell our lives as mercenaries?"

"Bad enough. But there's no more room for us here. The whole country is occupied by the enemy...."

"Quiet, my friend, it is his Majesty's pleasure that we call the English our friends..."

"Very well—occupied by friends. Anyhow, we Turks are unwanted, we've become strangers without rights on our own soil."

Not far from the two officers stood a couple of ragged hollow-cheeked, under-sized Turkish boys. They gazed inquisitively at the khaki uniforms and the medals decorating them.

The older officer felt in his pocket and threw a few coins to them. The boys made a wild rush at the money, and having picked it up immediately recovered the dignity and solemnity which are characteristic of Turkish children.

"Poor little devils! What will become of these children, I wonder? They will form part of a homeless nation, without rights, without hope—humiliated, fettered, dishonoured...."

"Spare me that! There must be a way out."

"There is nothing we can do. The Ottoman Empire is finished, destroyed. Soon the last of the Ottoman race will perish from starvation in the rocky deserts of Anatolia, whither we shall soon be driven. It's fate, my friend. It is the will of Allah. Face it bravely!"

"Let's move on, some English soldiers are coming this way. We'll turn to the right and go in the direction of the Bourse. To have to stand to attention before the men whom, a few months ago, we were fighting near Jerusalem would be impossible."

Sitting on an ottoman in one of the luxurious apartments of the Seraglio Palace was a lean man. A tall fez made his face appear even longer than it was, and a black "Stambul" frock-coat emphasized his gloomy appearance.

Sultan Mehemed Vahideddin, apparently uninterested, was listening with his eyes closed to the words of his brother-in-law, Ferid Pasha, who was standing at a respectable distance from him.

Damad Ferid Pasha understood his Imperial master, and was not misled by the mask of indifference behind which, he knew, the Sultan's brain was working feverishly.

"In conclusion," said Ferid Pasha, "I should like to point out to your Majesty that all the Asia Minor ports, on the Black Sea as well as on the Mediterranean, have been seized and blockaded by the Allies. In addition, the stations on the Anatolian Railway have been occupied by troops. His Highness the Grand Vizier, Izzet Pasha, sees in this an infringement of the conditions of the Armistice."

The Sultan raised his flickering eyelids and shot a venomous glance in the direction of the speaker.

"Izzet Pasha will resign. He no longer possesses our confidence. I hope soon to greet my exalted brother-in-law as Grand Vizier."

Damad Ferid Pasha held his breath and bowed low.

"There remains the question of the surrender of the German troops, your Majesty. . . ."

The Sultan suddenly grew alert.

"No power in the world can force us to infringe the sacred laws of hospitality."

"But the High Commissioners insist on it, your Majesty."

"Not another word about it!"

The pasha humbly lowered his head.

Vahideddin relapsed into silence, looked at the golden ornaments which stood about the room and at the damask on the walls, which in the dim light looked like dark red fire.

"The world is breaking up, and thrones are tottering," he whispered. "Arabia, Syria are lost beyond hope of recovery—more than half of our Empire. The coffers are empty, debts and obligations are accumulating, we face an empty future. There is only one thing that can save the throne of Osman—the goodwill of the English."

Damad Ferid Pasha perceptibly livened up.

"England, exalted Majesty, England is big-hearted. If we show good intentions England will accord us just treatment. In London they know that we are not to blame for the recent misfortunes. If the English see that we intend to deal relentlessly with all enemies of law and order, they will show understanding for our problems, and then I foresee no danger to the throne of Osman."

The Sultan nodded.

"No will shall exist beside our own. If necessary Constantinople shall be a forest of gallows—so much the better if it is. Our English friends will at least recognize that we are serious. It would be a good thing if all our servants joined the Society of Friends of England. We are in the hands of the victors. Anyone who provokes them is a traitor and a rebel, a foe of the Sultan-Caliph."

"Preserve the throne, preserve the throne!" murmured the Sultan, nervously fingering his prayer-chain. . . .

The brightly-lit rooms of the *Herrenklub* in Pera were in a haze of blue cigarette smoke. There was a buzz of conversation, and from one of the rooms came the sounds of a gramophone. In the card-rooms, on the other hand, there was absolute silence. Their occupants seemed to have forgotten the world and were studying their cards with an intentness that seemed to indicate that their lives must depend on the result of the game.

In another room a number of men had gathered round a military officer of high rank. They were trying to persuade him to see their point of view. One must support unconditionally the Sultan's policy, someone argued, qualifying his opinion with a detailed explanation. He further urged that drastic measures be taken against the powerful men of yesterday—that is, against those who had not sought refuge abroad, and, of course, those who had already been hanged—as a warning and an example to the whole world.

Another vigorously opposed this view. It was scandalous, he said, to condemn men who had done their best, merely to curry favour with these questionable victors.

Several men gave a warning "Shhh!" It was dangerous to give vent to such expressions. All looked at the man in the centre of the group, who listened in silence, nodding to those who spoke to him and quietly puffing at a cigarette.

Slowly and gradually the discussion flagged and features relaxed. The men ordered cognac, stared aimlessly at the lights of the big candelabra or smoke from their cigarettes, and relapsed into silence. Although no one expressed it, all had the same thought—*Inshallah!* as God will.

The taciturn man strode up and down the room, his eyes fixed on the tips of his patent boots. Closely following him was an officer, equally erect, whose similarity to him in bearing and features was extraordinary. One had to look closer to discover a certain irresoluteness in his visage which distinguished him from the man whom he followed with the uncanny certainty of a shadow. His face, that of the bold, typical soldier of fortune, wore a fixed, contemptuous, sarcastic smile.

He, too, was silent, and when he occasionally did open his mouth to speak it was to utter some remark of a caustic, biting nature. Those who heard him laughed at the unfailing acuteness of his acid wit, but at the same time had a feeling as though someone had cut them with a whip.

Nobody liked him. This did not worry him in the least; on the contrary, he seemed to derive enjoyment from making people his enemies by wounding them in their most vital spots.

Although this was so, no one attempted to quarrel with him. He was an audacious fellow—a wild, ruthless, sword-rattling soldier. Externally he was an elegant, cultured man, but below the surface he was a hundred-per-cent Tartar.

He was as strong as a horse, had muscles of iron, and was as lithe as a panther.

Since the Armistice Mustafa Kemal had been seen constantly in the company of this feared man, who might have been his brother.

It was a strange friendship, even stranger than the fact that Mustafa Kemal, a man who kept to himself and went his own way, had made a friend.

And what a friend!

What was known of this man, who had suddenly attached himself to the Victor of Anafarta, whom he followed like a dog?

Who was Colonel Arif?

He was supposed to have been at the Military Cadet School at the same time as Mustafa Kemal, afterwards going to Germany where, like Enver and other picked men, he underwent a course of training in the Prussian Guard.

During the War he was employed on the Ottoman General Staff, and like many other men whom the Committee of Union and Progress did not implicitly trust, was held on a short rein. People

A PEASANT WOMAN OF ANATOLIA

who came into contact with Colonel Arif were generally pretty quick in concluding that it was just as well that he was held short. He was a fearless dare-devil, as light-fingered with his revolver as he was ready with his tongue.

He was one of a numerable company of grousers, the rebel element of the Ottoman Army, whose eyes since Gallipoli had been fixed on Mustafa Kemal. At this time the two men, whom anyone would have taken for brothers, and who seemed to understand each other so well, were never seen apart. They spent hours together in Mustafa's villa at Shishli, on the outskirts of Pera, smoking cigarettes, occasionally talking about the War, passing sneering remarks about the leading men of the Empire, drinking at intervals a glass of cognac, and voicing disrespectful views on Mohammed and Islam—whatever it was, they were of the same opinion. Mustafa Kemal could listen for hours while Arif gave vent to his mischievous wit, which respected nobody and stopped at nothing.

They rode together, fenced, went to the balls, and were to be seen wherever there was anything happening; in brief, they lived like lords.

Among those who now frequently sought Mustafa's society was a Colonel Refat, a smart, alert cavalry officer. An erratic individual, whose head was always full of the wildest ideas, he was also a man with a keen sense of humour, abundant vivacity, and was an exceptionally good conversationalist, whose presence was an asset in any drawing-room. He too was aimlessly killing time in Constantinople, like all the other officers whom the Armistice had thrown out of employment and who, despite an appearance of not worrying or caring, had the same thought—to do something, no matter what it was, to put an end to the paralysing inactivity.

In addition, there was another young colonel, Colonel Ismet of the Ministry of War, who had been with Mustafa Kemal in the Caucasus and Syria. He was a quiet, unassuming man wearing a fixed smile, who was rather hard of hearing and who deliberately kept himself in the background. His thoughts and his views on current affairs he communicated to nobody. When Mustafa Kemal was about, he generally managed to place himself in close proximity to him, where he would stay, smiling, reserved and silent.

Of a very different type was the fourth of the fraternity which collected near Mustafa—a giant, pompous man with coal-black eyes gazing steadily and truly into the world, who feared neither hell nor the Devil. This was Fevzi Pasha, one of the best soldiers in the Ottoman Army, at present Chief of the General Staff.

Stars twinkled above the minarets and towers of Constantinople when the men dispersed late at night. Mustafa strode in silence through still and deserted streets, a cloak thrown carelessly over his shoulders. Behind him, a little to one side, his shadow, Arif, faithfully followed.

"You are keeping something to yourself," said Arif softly. "Your present life is a deception, a deliberately-worn mask of indifference. We are all aware of it, and are wracking our brains to discover what is behind it all. The Sultan's friends say that you belong to them; his enemies say you are theirs; those who want law and order are waiting for you to lead them; and the others who can't wait any longer before undertaking a *coup d'état* also swear by Mustafa Kemal. And I say that they are all fools, for the truth is that you belong to none of them, and nobody knows what your intentions are. But one thing is clear : you will not be content to leave affairs in their present state. You least of all."

"How's your old favourite the bear? And what's Ayesha doing nowadays?" asked Mustafa.

Arif ignored the question, and continued in a quiet voice, all traces of his normal cynicism having been shaken off.

"How much longer is this sort of thing to go on? We must have a go at somebody—if not at the Government, then at the foreigners. There are plenty of fellows about who would only be too pleased, if necessary, to slit the throats of the whole Army of Occupation, hang some of their exalted friends at theYildiz Kiosk, and keep to good old customs by sinking their devoted servants in the Bosporus. Let's do something; at least let us feel that we are soldiers once more ! One day we must seize power. Is it to be said of us later that we missed our chance?"

They had reached Mustafa's villa. The general peered for some while at the sky, and then whistled softly.

"Come inside," he then said, and unlocked the door.

They entered the house. On the other side of the road a shadow moved. In one of the windows of the villa a light appeared.

Mustafa Kemal walked slowly up and down the room. Arif watched every movement.

"Founding a great empire embracing many nations," said Mustafa after some time, "may be a very enticing goal, but a State cannot be strong when it consists of a number of disunited peoples with varying interests. To be able to carry on successfully a national policy, you must first have a united nation behind you. Our forefathers carried their conquests to the gates of Vienna. Suleiman came very near conquering the world." He laughed contemptuously. "Conquest of the world! You seldom have an offensive without a counter-offensive. Europe's counter-offensive has arrived. To-day we are experiencing its last phase . . ."

He then turned to Arif.

"A *coup d'état*, a *putsch* at this moment would be a madness and a crime. We have had enough of that sort of thing. But"—he lowered his voice as though speaking to himself—"something different must happen, something very different. Let the old order of things collapse in order that a new State may arise, a State formed with the aid of the most modern means provided by human knowledge. . . ."

Arif took in every word.

"In order to do that we must have complete freedom," said Mustafa, "and that, I grant you, means that we shall have to fight."

Arif's eyes sparkled at this announcement.

"We shall have to fight as, perhaps, no generation has had to fight before. We shall stand alone against the entire world, and no one will help us. And for the very reason that we shall be thrown on to our own resources, our cause will be victorious."

"I'm afraid I don't quite understand, I can only guess . . ."

Mustafa Kemal sat down at his writing-desk, took a block of paper and a pencil, drew sketch-maps and wrote down figures and letters, and in a low voice began to speak of his plans, supplying his companion with a far-reaching survey of future history. It was nearly dawn when Arif rose from his chair, and said in all seriousness:

"I have no one in the world, I believe in nothing and love nothing. But—if you can do with a dog that will never stray from your side—take me."

CHAPTER V

ERZERUM

DEEP in the dark lap of East Anatolia, covered in a mantle of snow, lay the old, crumbled fortress of Erzerum, the scene of fierce fighting between Turks and Russians during the Great War. The lofty peaks of the Caucasus looked down upon a maze of low houses, walls and turrets. Filth and dust filled the ruined casemates, and the forts under their white coating of snow looked buried and deserted.

A man, glancing suspiciously about him, advanced cautiously towards an old, weather-beaten fort situated some distance from the town. He wore a heavy fur coat tightly buttoned at the throat, and on his head there was a tall astrakhan cap; a carbine was slung across his back; his riding-boots sank deep into the snow.

Presently he reached the old fort, halted, looked carefully in all directions, and then knocked a certain number of times at the door. After he had waited several seconds, the door opened slightly.

There was a brief, whispered conversation, the man disappeared into the building, and the door closed behind him.

The eye had first to accustom itself to the darkness of the interior of the small casemate; and a thick cloud of cigarette smoke did not make visibility any easier.

Greetings were exchanged in silence; thumbs were pressed to lips and heart in accordance with the old Turkish custom.

Steaming-hot tea was served. Mountains of cigarettes lay on the table.

About a dozen men were sitting or standing in the room. Carbines were piled in the corners. Near by, in a wretched shed, were tethered a number of frozen horses, who shifted restlessly. The icy breath of the Caucasus had settled over the countryside.

In a quiet voice the eldest of the men present began to speak.

"I now open, in the name of Allah and his exalted representative, Sultan Mehmed Vahideddin Khan, the session of the Association for the Defence of the Rights of the Eastern Provinces. Before we begin our discussion, we will join in silent prayer for our Sovereign, whose liberty of action has been taken from him by the foreigners."

For several minutes there was silence.

ERZERUM

The old man then spoke again. His hard, coarse peasant features were just visible in the dim light of the room. He called out the names.

A man was missing; as his name was called there was silence.

He had probably been shot, and now lay outside in the snow.

The route to the old fort was long and dangerous. Patrols from the Armenian Legion and Greek bandits kept a constant lookout for representatives of the Turkish peasants, who assembled in the old building to organize protection for their land.

The old man made his report, quietly, despondently.

There no longer existed any doubt that the Eastern Provinces of Anatolia, the real Turkey, were to be separated from the Motherland. They had been promised to the Armenians. As a reward for treacherous conduct in the War the Eastern Provinces were to form an Armenian State. The Turk of the future was to be an Armenian subject. The Armenian legionaries, equipped by the ex-enemy with arms and munitions, were already acting as though they were the masters. The peasants were having bitter proof of that every day. One act of violence followed the other. Turkish property was no longer secure. And farther north, in the Black Sea direction, hordes of Greeks had settled themselves in the hope of establishing there a Pontic State of their own.

An infantry captain jumped up to protest. What were the Government in Constantinople going to do about it?

The old man shrugged his shoulders.

The Padishah was in the power of the English.

The Padishah was not aware of what was happening to his most loyal subjects in the East! objected the captain bitterly.

" The Padishah is surrounded with traitors ! "

There was a murmur of indignation, and the captain relapsed into silence.

A country doctor then spoke.

" We have weapons, and no enemy commissioner has yet appeared to take them from us. We must look to our own defence, and do the best we can. We must fight to preserve our country. Singly we can do nothing, but united everything is possible. The Padishah can't help us, so the Association for Defence of the Rights of the Eastern Provinces must assume responsibility for protecting the people from these Armenian and Greek jackals."

The captain then told of the fighting that had been taking place at Ersinghian.

The old man then distributed weapons for the different peasant sections. The deputies were to arrange for their transport to the villages and begin at once to enrol their inhabitants in defence contingents.

Under cover of the darkness the men left and parted company, each proceeding in the direction of his native village.

A violent snowstorm met them as they emerged from the building, and the marks of the horses' hooves were obliterated almost as soon as they were lifted from the ground. Gradually the shadows of the horsemen vanished into the winter night—a night made perilous by the presence of lurking, spying Armenians.

・　　・　　・　　・　　・　　・

Coming from the Galata Bridge, a motor car sped in the direction of the Sublime Porte.

The vehicle came to a halt at the big main entrance of the palace of the Imperial Ottoman Government. The officer of the Turkish guard sprang to attention and saluted the Allied High Commissioners, who ignored him and entered the building. A little later they found themselves in the study of the Grand Vizier, Damad Ferid.

Extremely disagreeable news had been received from the Eastern Provinces, and the Allied Commissioners found it hard to reconcile with the declaration of submission that had been made by the Imperial Ottoman Government. Armed peasantry; associations for Defence of the Rights of the Eastern Provinces; violent conflicts with Armenians and Greeks, who were under Allied protection. . . .

The Grand Vizier, dressed in the English fashion, expressed the deepest regret and, smiling courteously, offered his guests some excellent tea and cigarettes manufactured from some of the finest tobacco obtainable.

Having, as it seemed to him, partially dispelled their ill-humour, he proceeded to put it to them that the Ottoman Government had left no stones unturned to give evidence of their goodwill. Allah knew—Damad Ferid, the devout Mohammedan, raised his voice—that the Imperial Ottoman Government was fully conscious that is represented a Power defeated in the World War, and craved the indulgence and help of the generous victors.

The French High Commissioner for a few seconds wore a faint suggestion of a flattered smile, but immediately afterwards recovered his dignified, official expression. The expression on the face of his British colleague remained unchanged.

The Grand Vizier extinguished his cigarette and started to recite in detail the many things that had been done to give satisfaction to the victors. They had executed all who had been found guilty of persecuting Armenians, and agitators sent out by the Committee had been hanged high above the heads of those to whom their fate should serve as a warning. Was it necessary for the Imperial Ottoman Government, who had passed the death sentence on Enver and Talaat—unfortunately in the absence of those gentlemen—to give further assurance that it condemned every form of excess where foreign minorities, Armenians especially, were concerned, and that it turned in disgust from such barbarism?

The English High Commissioner was not so much interested in what became of the Armenians as in the fact that Turkish peasants in the Eastern Provinces were armed, and that Turkish troops still stationed there, together with fanatics and trouble-makers, were stirring up strife.

The British member of the Commission sought to make it clear that if the Imperial Ottoman Government wished to be accorded generous treatment at the forthcoming Peace negotiations, it should do its utmost to avoid anything which might aggravate the present situation and lead to unfriendly relations.

The others agreed.

What was it that the High Commissioners of Britain, France and Italy demanded of their humble Turkish friends?

The proud Grand Vizier secretly bit his lips as he said this—being defeated was bitter.

The Englishman then requested the Grand Vizier to appoint a Turkish officer of high rank to proceed to the Eastern Provinces, to be responsible there for the strict execution of the conditions of the Armistice, and, in particular, to collect all existing war material and complete as quickly as possible the disbandment of the remaining Turkish military units.

Damad Ferid Pasha consented and implored Allah's blessing upon the heads of the Allied High Commissioners, who soon afterwards left by car.

Damad Ferid began to wonder where he could find a reliable officer, who possessed enough authority in the Army to be able to assert himself in the face of possible opposition from crazy fanatics and nationalists. . . .

Then he remembered that his Majesty at the last Selamlik, the big monthly reception which the Ottoman Sultan held after the ceremony of public prayer, had spent a long time in conversation with Mustafa Kemal. Moreover, his Majesty had afterwards declared that Mustafa Kemal enjoyed more respect than anyone else in the Army. . . .

He would, therefore, send Mustafa Kemal to East Anatolia with instructions to disarm the Eastern Provinces. The Minister of War was at once informed and directed to get in touch with the general.

· · · · · ·

"Take your time, your Excellency, and carefully study the instructions which the Allied General Staff have provided for you."

The War Minister stepped to the window.

Mustafa Kemal, wearing the full uniform of an Imperial Ottoman general, glanced quickly at the documents which had been placed in his hand.

"Thank you, Pasha. I think I can let you have particulars of the amendments in three hours," he said.

"Amendments, your Excellency? The Allies won't be bargained with."

"Neither will I!"

Mustafa Kemal's bronzed face again bent over the papers, as in a strong soldier's hand he crossed out here and made additions there. The Minister of War grew hot as he watched him. The general's steel-grey eyes, which he was secretly studying, betrayed nothing, were inscrutable.

No one had yet succeeded in solving the puzzle of this man, a book with seven seals—he was uncanny.

Mustafa Kemal had correctly estimated: in three hours he had finished.

The Minister of War's expression grew even more worried as he scanned the documents and started to look for the extremely arbitrary alterations which he assumed had been made to them. However, on examining the alterations, he discovered that they related only to small points. What could that mean? There must be something behind it, otherwise Mustafa Kemal would not have been so insistent.

Resigning himself to the will of Allah, the Minister of War forwarded the documents to Damad Ferid Pasha, who without troubling to look at them appended his signature. Back they went to the Ministry of War.

The Minister's hand shook imperceptibly as he furnished them with his seal. Why, he could not say...

. . . .

The 15 May, 1919, was anything but a friendly day. A cutting wind blew from the Black Sea, and grey-black clouds chased across the sky. The waves of the Bosporus were dark and rough.

Colonel Arif was ready to start his journey. Ayesha, his elderly housekeeper, was busying about, giving advice, issuing orders and swearing. Several soldiers came and took his luggage to the quay.

The colonel went into the garden. From a small iron cage came a growl. Colonel Arif turned the key and the door sprang open. A huge brown bear trotted out and licked his hand.

Arif patted him and spoke kindly to him. He was not to be miserable, although he was going to be left alone for a considerable time. "Will you miss your master very much, old fellow? Do you remember how he captured you many years ago?" he said, pulling the animal's ears.

"You were very very small then. But you haven't had such a bad time all these years, have you, old boy? By Allah, there is no one I know whom I would have treated as well as you, my old faithful bear."

There was nothing cynical or contemptuous in the glance which

Arif bestowed upon his pet, the only creature in this world for whom he displayed anything like love or affection, whom he was now bidding farewell.

"Come on, old fellow, let's wrestle once more!"

Obediently the bear stood up on his hind legs, placed his paws on his master's shoulders, and began to wrestle with him. At the end of a few minutes he growled and slipped to the ground.

"Cheat!" said the victor laughing and patting him on the back.

Old Ayesha joined them. Arif could not remember his mother, and Ayesha had fostered him, reared and spoiled him. There was a warmth in his voice as he spoke to her.

"The devil only knows when I shall come back, old Ayesha."

"It rests with Allah, you infidel dog," the old woman snapped back at him, and straightened his belt, as though he were a boy just leaving for school.

And Arif listened like a good boy to her parting advice and admonishments. He then kissed Ayesha, made her swear to give the bear his daily ration of milk and honey, and in return promised not to get into mischief and not to get mixed up in conspiracies and violence.

At Shishli, Mustafa Kemal was saying good-bye to his mother.

"Child, my child," she wept, "I have seen you leave so often for wars and revolutions—and there is no end to it. As soon as you are back, you have to leave again..."

"Quiet, Mother, don't weep. This time I have a big task to perform. This time, perhaps, we shall not see each other again for a long time, and I shall not return until I can say: It is done. If I cannot say that, then never! But don't weep, Zubeida, we're not living for our own sakes, but for something else..."

"For God, my child."

"As you will! But you are the mother of a soldier and must suppress your tears. And why should you weep? I am going to Anatolia on a mission for his Majesty, as Inspector-General of the Army. You need not be afraid."

"But I am worried, my child, that you may be hiding something from me. On a mission for the Sultan, you say, Allah's shadow on earth? Be loyal to him, my son!"

"That, my dear Mother, depends on him."

"I'm afraid of not seeing you again."

"Be brave! Remember that you are a soldier's mother. Don't worry! Mustafa's faith is different from yours. It points out his road to him and makes him unflinching. But my time is up, good-bye!"

But Zubeida Hanum, although strong in her faith in Allah, refused to be comforted. Mustafa had said that he was journeying on a mission of peace, for the Padishah, but she instinctively felt that something was wrong, and her mind was uneasy.

A small steamer, the *Ineboli*, a wretched little vessel securely roped to the quayside, bobbed up and down in the choppy waves of the Bosporus.

At the gangway waited Arif, Refat and three other officers, the staff of Inspector-General Mustafa Kemal. No words were passed between them. Thick clouds of black smoke emerged from the funnel of the little steamer, which was ready to put to sea. Officers' servants were busy stowing away luggage.

Heels clicked as Mustafa Kemal arrived and keenly scrutinized the faces of his five colleagues.

"Let's go aboard, gentlemen!"

The picturesque outline of the wonder city of Constantinople gradually sank in the waves of the Bosporus. Last of all, the great dome of the Hagia Sofia dipped beyond the horizon.

The *Ineboli* set an easterly course and made for the Black Sea. Castles and ancient strongholds dotted about the green hill-sides on both sides of the water sent silent greetings to the travellers. Presently the channel widened, the land became two thin strips, and the sea opened.

Mustafa Kemal briefly observed that he possessed a secret code for communicating with the Ministry of War. Ismet and Fevzi were also in possession of it. Messages, uncensored, could be sent and received.

CHAPTER VI

ANATOLIA

LAPPED by the warm waves of the Mediterranean, the white and bright city of Smyrna stood out against its more colourful background of mountains, which extended farther than the eye could reach.

A strong, narcotic aroma from the fig and olive groves made the air heavy and stupefying.

In the harbour there was more noise than usual. Cranes, moving boxes and bales, creaked and groaned. Most of the other parts of the town seemed strangely quiet and deserted. But in the Greek quarters flags were flying.

It was known that enemy troops were to occupy Smyrna, though no one could state a reason why; and in those days, when tyranny seemed to reign supreme, no one cared to waste time in such idle speculation. Lying in the harbour was a fleet of British war vessels, which had dropped anchor at dawn, and whose guns were now directed against the city.

A car sped through the streets carrying British officers towards the port. They had been to fetch the Turkish Governor. The admiral, waiting on his flagship, had a communication to make to him.

With lowered head and lips pressed close together, the Governor listened while the Admiral of the British Mediterranean Fleet informed him that Smyrna and the Province of Aidan were to be occupied by Greek troops. It was the decision of the Allied Supreme Council in Paris and was unalterable.

The admiral saw how for a few seconds the Turk lost self-command and how tears filled his eyes.

The Governor implored, begged. . . .

Anyone but the Greeks! Let the English, the French and the Italians put as many troops in Smyrna as they liked, but save them from the Greeks! Had no one any feeling for the appallingness of such a humiliation? The Greeks, those despised parasites, as masters of Smyrna and Aidan?—Who accepted responsibility for the measure?

The admiral shrugged his shoulders. It was no good wasting words; orders were orders.

Then at least send in addition a few detachments of British sailors!——

A little later the streets of Smyrna presented a very lively spectacle. Turkish troops were hurriedly withdrawn into the big barracks opposite the Governor's official residence, the Greek, Levantine and Armenian sections of the populace flocked through the streets leading to the harbour, and windows and doors in the Turkish city were barred and bolted.

Standing in front of the crowd at the quayside was the Greek Metropolitan. He raised the Cross as the Greek soldiers disembarked and lowered their rifles, which he blessed.

A crusade! Down with the Mohammedans! Beat the dogs to death, destroy them! Smyrna and Aidan for the Greeks!

The troops formed up and marched in the direction of the Turkish barracks. The soldiers remained inside the building and anxiously waited for developments. At present they had no knowledge of what was taking place or of the attitude they should adopt. . . .

They had a fore-feeling of coming evil.

"Long live Venizelos! Long live Venizelos!" shouted the crowd which had gathered outside.

Suddenly a shot rang out.

French observers afterwards reported that it was fired by a Greek agent.

The crowd screamed and started to stampede. Greek troops then rushed forward, and with their machine-guns opened rapid fire at the barracks.

The troops herded in the barrack-rooms and corridors began to show signs of panic, and it was only with the greatest difficulty that the Turkish officers were able to maintain discipline. To defend themselves was forbidden.

The commandant ordered the white flag to be hoisted and himself walked boldly to the gate to offer the official surrender of the barracks to the Occupation authorities.

He collapsed riddled with bullets. The Greeks sprang over his body and began to slaughter the unarmed Turks. Long columns of prisoners were then escorted to the harbour. *En route* the Greek mob assaulted them. Most of the prisoners were bayonetted before they reached their destination. The way to the harbour was strewn with dead and wounded. Then began the sack of the Turkish city.

Exterminate them! The Turkish population must be reduced to a minority for the world to see that Smyrna was a Greek city ...

Four days later.

Black-grey, foam-crested waves lashed the pier at Samsun, a port at the eastern end of the Black Sea. On shore silent groups of people stood looking out to sea. Presently the *Ineboli*, rolling heavily, and creaking in all her joints, struggled towards the pier. She had had a very rough voyage. She had been obliged to hug the coast and make the best progress she could against a high sea.

Silently, the inhabitants of Samsun bowed in greeting, as Mustafa Kemal and his staff of five stepped ashore.

So that was the hero of Gallipoli. They studied him intently, observed his tall, strong, erect figure, and were favourably impressed. In his look there was something fascinating, something compelling. Below his tall astrakhan fez a strip of fair, smoothly-brushed hair was visible. Close behind him was his shadow, the gloomy Arif. A short distance away stood the vivacious, friendly Refat, his thin lips smiling strangely.

The people respectfully formed a lane, and the young general passed on. For seconds his eyes softened at this sight of Anatolian people, then he walked quickly towards the Governor's house.

" What is the pasha doing here? "

" They say he has been given a command."

" What command? Over whom? "

" I know better," said another of the crowd, " he has come to take the last of our weapons away ..."

Quietly and dejectedly, the people dispersed and went to their homes. The storm continued to pound the shore, now deserted.

Silent rage seized Mustafa Kemal when, at the Governor's house, he was told the news of the scenes of terror in Smyrna.

He went at once to the telegraph office, where, to the astonishment of the clerks, he began to make himself comfortable, as though for a long stay. The spies and agents of the British Occupation authorities, however, seemed to find nothing suspicious in his action.

For the next few days the general hardly stirred from the telegraph office. It was long since the lines had been so busy. His orders went out to all parts of Anatolia, and from all parts of Anatolia came the replies, telegrams signed with the names of important, well-known generals.

There were six army corps stationed in Anatolia, though an army corps in this case signified a general with staff and about a couple of thousand men.

The telegrams which were exchanged were long and weighty with contents. Mustafa Kemal personally sat by the apparatus, and the results of his labour, which knew no distinction between day and night, appeared to give him satisfaction. Arif never left his side. At night they spent much of the time in long, secret talks.

Communication had been established with the headquarters of the various armies, whose commanding officers had assured him of their support.

The first important step had been taken.

Now began a new exchange of telegrams, but this time the orders went to the civil governors. Mustafa Kemal had exceeded his instructions and was now in touch with the civil authorities.

Things all at once began to stir in Anatolia.

. . . . . .

Sultan Vahideddin turned livid with rage on reading for the second time the report of a loyal Anatolian governor. So that was the explanation of the disturbances which for some weeks past had been reported in Anatolia.

The Grand Vizier was being bombarded with protests from the British authorities regarding national demonstrations that had been, and were being, held in Anatolian towns and with complaints about a number of national societies and organisations whose careful and systematic planning indicated that they were being controlled by a particular, central authority.

It was all the more disquieting at a time when the victors were showing a remarkably benevolent mood. Lying at anchor in the port of Constantinople was a French cruiser, which was to take the Grand Vizier to France, where he would have an opportunity of personally handing the Turkish Notes to the Supreme Council in Paris, before they settled down to a discussion of the Peace conditions.

But the report in front of his Majesty disclosed other, even more disagreeable facts.

So this was the work of Mustafa Kemal! This was how he carried out his instructions!

Sultan Vahideddin balled his fist—crush him!

He read one of the telegrams that had been received by the governors of Anatolian provinces:

"The country is in peril. The Central Government is unequal to its task. Only through the determination and energy of the nation can the independence of our country be saved. It has been resolved to hold a General Congress at Sivas. Each district is to send three deputies. The intention must be kept secret."

Sultan Vahideddin, schooled by his elder brother, Abdul Hamid, at once saw the peril, of which most other people would never have dreamed. With the vision of a clairvoyant he saw what was behind this conspiracy and guessed the goal at which this general was aiming.

There was no time for hesitation; the matter had to be dealt with at once, and nipped in the bud.

He immediately telephoned to the Grand Vizier's palace and gave instructions that Mustafa Kemal was to be telegraphed forthwith.

So far so good—but where was he? He had left Samsun a long while ago, and he was no longer to be reached at Amassia. They tried Sivas, the venue of the Congress, but he had not yet arrived.

Vahideddin grew furiously impatient; in his rage he was hardly able to contain himself.

Eventually the Grand Vizier announced himself on the 'phone. Mustafa Kemal had been found in Erzerum and he, the Grand Vizier, had ordered him to proceed at once to the telegraph office.

"Come home on leave," said Constantinople over the line to far-off Erzerum.

"No," said the answer.

Vahideddin bit his lip and tried gentler means of persuasion.

"Go where you like, but cease all activity."

"No."

"The Padishah wishes it."

"No."

ANGORA
The Yeni Buyuk Kourchounlov Djami Mosque.

"The Padishah commands!"

"I request to be allowed to resign my commission in the Army."

"Then you will be relieved of all duties in connection with your command."

Vahideddin turned pale, and trembling in every limb barked out his orders to the Grand Vizier.

It was to be at once made known throughout the country that Mustafa Kemal Pasha had been dismissed from the Service. Any communication with him would be considered as high treason.

The despot sat on the edge of his ottoman and began to think.

If a congress was to be held at Sivas then it seemed fairly certain that all the rebels would assemble there. What a grand chance to capture the lot and bring them back to Constantinople to face a court martial!

Damad Ferid then thought of the Governor of Malatia, Ali Galib, a loyal servant of the Sultan. He would be instructed to mobilize, in the deepest secrecy, the Malatia Gendarmerie and Kurdistan cavalry, surround Sivas, and take the Congress prisoners. As much money as was necessary would be placed at his disposal—but exceptional caution was essential! The English District Officer at Malatia would take charge of the organization of the undertaking.

Somewhat easier in mind, Sultan Vahideddin sank back in the cushions and imagined the satisfaction he would obtain from seeing his enemies dangling from the scaffold.

And yet he was unable to rest. Night had long since fallen over Constantinople, and stars shone above the minarets of the mosques and the roofs of the marble palaces.

A lonely despot standing by the tall, narrow window of his Seraglio had no eyes for the magic of the fairylike night scene, or for the dancing lights of the ships passing the Golden Horn.

He saw only the man whose features appeared as though sculptured in Anatolian rock, features which he had suddenly grown to hate, but which at one time he had found so friendly—during the train journey to the German Headquarters.

Those features now haunted him.

Suddenly an idea occurred to him.

The English must help. They were no less interested than

himself in the removal of the rebels, and there was still time. Two good, full-strength divisions would be adequate to make a clean sweep of Anatolia and stop talk of sovereignty of the people and independence for years to come.

The English were clever and would not hesitate. He decided immediately to get in touch with the British High Commissioner.

．　　　．　　　．　　　．　　　．　　　．

On the outskirts of the tumbledown Caucasian fortress of Erzerum stood an old vacant building, for which no one appeared to have any use. In other days it might have been a school or assembly hall.

At the entrance door two Circassians in gay, picturesque uniforms stood guard. They wore curved swords stuck in their waist-bands, and on their heads tall fur caps. Their long, baggy trousers turned down over the edges of short red riding-boots, and their *Kasak* cloaks reached down to the knees. Carbines loaded with ball cartridge, with their safety-catches released, were slung across their shoulders.

Inside the building a meeting of representatives from the Eastern Provinces was in progress, while at the same time deputies from all parts of Anatolia, on horses, in cars or on camels, were on their long journey to Sivas, where the big Congress for the whole country was to take place.

Erzerum was the curtain-raiser for the main act at Sivas.

Mustafa Kemal was standing before a number of army commanders and a mixed company of officers, civil servants, priests, school-teachers, doctors, chiefs of Kurdistan tribes, Circassian warriors and Dervishes, and was preaching national revolution.

The deputies listened attentively. Occasionally there were expressions of approval or objection. In a special position of honour sat a fine old general, a kind but stern veteran who commanded universal respect. He was Marshal Kiazim Karabekir Pasha, Commander-in-Chief of the East Provinces, their host. In the dimly-lit background stood a number of men, civilians and officials, with their arms folded. A superior smile was on their lips, and from time to time they exchanged stolen glances with each other.

Mustafa Kemal was preaching.

He was no longer in uniform. He had been travelling from village to village, calling upon the people to follow him, and wore a plain suit of English tweed.

"Anatolia is in a state of national revolution," he said. " Our goal is complete freedom and independence from the Motherland. No power in the world can stifle a nation which is resolutely determined to preserve its honour and existence. The foreign provinces—we'll hand them back to their original owners. Their fate will then be in their own hands. But we will not surrender a single inch of Anatolian soil. The Turkish nation constitutes an indivisible whole. We acknowledge battle as the greatest principle in life, and are resolved to make ourselves strong. A nation which voluntarily surrenders its power deserves to be treated as a slave. But the Turk has noble blood in his veins, and he is proud of it. A nation formed of such men can go down fighting, but can never stand the dishonour of slavery. We shall fight, and the worst that can happen to us is defeat. It is better to die with honour than to live in dishonour. We have unshaken faith in the strength which the Turkish race derives from a great past, a strength which is now reviving and which will assert itself. Two things are open to us—freedom or death !" Marshal Karabekir nodded.

The two Circassians on guard at the door listened to the hard, metallic voice of the soldier. The eyes of the elder flashed.

" The Grey Wolf has risen again. The signal for the assault, my friend ! The Grey Wolf has been born again in Mustafa Kemal."

" He is a messenger of Allah, sent in the hour of need, a new prophet."

" Quiet, my friend, I can hear them quarrelling. Shall we shoot them down, the cowardly jackals who are afraid to follow the Grey Wolf ? "

Mustafa Kemal's voice rose above the din.

" The Turkish nation is an indivisible whole. A united East will oppose the foreign occupation and interference. If the Imperial Government fails, then a revolutionary Government will take over the reins."

" That is revolt against the sacred person of the Sultan-Caliph," someone leaning against the wall at the back of the building immediately objected.

Mustafa Kemal, like a skilled fencer, parried the attack.

"The aim of the Movement is to free the Sultan-Caliph from the clutches of the foreign enemy."

There were murmurs of approval.

Marshal Karabekir's forehead was deeply lined; he was thinking hard. There were many things about this Movement that were still not clear to him. The debate continued.

"Who is to assume the leadership?"

A number of voices exclaimed, "Mustafa Kemal!"

"Not one person—form a committee pledged to adhere to a clearly-defined, fixed policy."

Again one of the men in the background shouted something. Arif jumped up from his seat and assumed a menacing attitude.

"What a row!" said one of the Circassian sentries. "It's impossible to understand anything at the moment."

"Quiet, my friend, I can hear the Grey Wolf's voice."

Mustafa Kemal was speaking again.

"Gentlemen, history proves without a shadow of doubt that if great undertakings are to succeed the presence of a capable, resolute, energetic leader is an absolute necessity. A committee will never find the way to success."

At the lower end of the building there was sarcastic laughter.

"You are your own advocate."

"Gentlemen, I leave it to you to elect the most deserving man. I am nothing more than a loyal servant of the people."

There were loud cries of "None other than Mustafa Kemal shall lead us!"

"You are not even a son of the Eastern Provinces," said a voice from the back.

"Order!"

"We'll take a vote—in secret!"

The Circassian tugged impatiently at his moustache.

Inside the building the votes were collected, and there was absolute stillness while the oldest man of the assembly counted them, slowly and thoroughly. . . .

"His Excellency Mustafa Kemal Pasha has been elected President of the Representative Committee."

Applause. Then sudden silence.

A messenger entered, saluted, and handed a telegram to Marshal Kiazim Karabekir.

The general slowly unfolded the paper, read it, then raised his head and looked at Mustafa Kemal. The room remained silent. Behind the old marshal's forehead the thoughts were busy.

"May I speak with you alone for a few moments?" he said at last in a quiet voice.

The two men left the room and stood together in the entrance lobby.

"Pasha," began Karabekir with a worried expression, "his Majesty orders me to arrest you and dissolve the Congress. I have given my word to support you, but at the same time—I am bound to obey the Sultan."

Handed over to the English, deported to a concentration camp in Malta, court martial, gallows—were the thoughts which flashed through Mustafa Kemal's brain.

"It rests with your Excellency," he said quietly, "whether we Turks are to be slaves or free men."

A fight was going on within Kiazim Karabekir, who was unable to make up his mind how to act in the circumstances.

"Give me time to consider my position, Pasha," he begged.

The meeting was adjourned.

In a small room sat Mustafa Kemal and Arif brooding over the new crisis, while next door Kiazim Karabekir could be heard tramping up and down, fighting out with himself which of his two oaths he was going to keep.

"I have done my best to remove his doubts," said Mustafa quietly. "I have tried to make it clear to him that loyalty to Constantinople is treason to the nation."

Arif drew at his cigarette, exhaled the smoke through his nostrils, and laughed contemptuously.

"The great Karabekir! A stubborn old fool!"

Mustafa Kemal shrugged his shoulders.

"The future lies in his hands."

The two men grew silent. In the next room the steps continued, while the honest, conservative old general strove to come to a decision.

Unlike the untrusting Arif, Mustafa Kemal had consideration and understanding for the cruel situation in which the old marshal now found himself.

The footsteps next door died down. Karabekir had ceased his marching. The two men held their breath. Had he succeeded in making up his mind?

Arif amused himself by making cynical remarks about the rats and bugs in the Red Prison in Constantinople, rope and gallows.

Mustafa Kemal rose, stood in front of Arif, seized him by the shoulders, and fixed him with his grey wolves' eyes.

" If he decides against us—you understand me—as a Turkish officer I am not going to allow myself to be dragged off to some filthy dungeon. If there is no other way out, I shall go straight to the enemy commander-in-chief's tent and sell my life as dearly as possible."

" I'm with you," said Arif quietly but firmly, " to the last bullet. And we'll take a good many along with us when we die."

Mustafa solemnly nodded.

" To the last bullet."

They shook hands.

The door flew open, and framed in the entrance was the broad, massive figure of the old marshal, nervously swinging a riding-whip. He came a step nearer, and Mustafa and Arif exchanged glances. The window was open. Standing outside was Mustafa's car. And both men carried two fully-loaded revolvers with them wherever they went.

" Pasha," began Karabekir in a hesitating voice, " you say that the Padishah is a prisoner in the hands of the foreign enemy, that in that case power has reverted to the people and that the orders from Constantinople are not the orders of the Sultan, but of the English. I have thought it over, and you may be right. Furthermore, you are my friend, and I give you my word."

With slow, deliberate movements, he tore up the Sultan's order.

" You can rely on me, Pasha."

Refat, Bekir, Sami and Rauf forced their way into the room, closely followed by the other officers and deputies. Their spurred riding-boots crunched the scraps of paper which lay strewn on the floor—the Sultan's order.

Arif laughed.

" Karabekir has saved you all."

He patted his revolver.

Mustafa Kemal called him to order.

" Gentlemen, let us set to work and elect an Executive Committee to take charge of the affairs of State, the Central Government being no longer capable of discharging its duties."

. . . .

The British desired to strengthen the force in occupation of Samsun, the only outlet to the sea, which had to be kept open at all costs. A strong force in occupation of Samsun would be in a position to upset completely the calculations of the Sivas Congress.

It was a tricky situation.

Refat was given orders to thwart the English plan at no matter what cost. For this task he was given a hundred Nationalist soldiers. These were to argue matters with the English, which seemed hardly wise in view of the report that the latter were bringing up two full-strength battalions.

Refat whistled a cavalry march, slipped into his saddle, and set off at a trot. Behind him were his hundred men.

An English ship had come to anchor in the port of Samsun. The officer commanding the British troops, a colonel, and his staff had already arrived, and were studying the local terrain. *En route* Refat did some thinking, and suddenly remembered an incident which he had seen at some theatre. There was a scene in which a number of troops marched on to the stage, and it had made a deep impression on him.

He quickly explained to his officers the plan of action, and the latter in their turn quickly passed on the information to their men.

Refat announced his presence to the English commander. The latter talked very big, and then mentioned his two battalions. Refat smiled to himself and pointed through the window. Looking up, the Englishman saw a number of Turkish troops—smart men and in step—marching over some cross-roads. Several minutes passed, but the marching still continued, and the Englishman began to feel hot. That was a pretty strong contingent that intended entering Samsun; he asked Refat to explain. The latter smiled imperceptibly and asked the Englishman if he were still prepared to risk his men against so many Anatolians.

The Briton admitted that it was rather a lot to ask, thought for a few moments, then asked more questions and, finally, started to negotiate. Meanwhile, there were no signs of the marching outside coming to an end—they were still at it.

Eventually, the English officer decided that it was a bit too much of a good thing. Why, it was an army! No thank you! Let the Devil occupy Samsun, if he wanted! He took his leave, went straight on board, and steamed away. What he had not seen was this: Refat had ordered his men, on reaching a certain point, to double round a block of houses, and fall in again at the rear of the column. Just as they do it at the theatre.

CHAPTER VII

PARIS

THE Allied Peace Conference had assembled in the Champs Elysées. The Treaty of Versailles had been signed, peace had been dictated to Germany, and now they could slowly turn their attention to the South-East and consider the Oriental question.

Actually, the secret pacts for the partition of Turkey, signed before the War and supplemented and amended at various times during the War, had the largest say in the dictation of peace; but there were at the same time certain squabbles and jealousies among the victors which made the matter more difficult.

As a grand gesture, they had invited to Paris the Grand Vizier, whom they proposed to hear.

A squat figure, with muscles and nerves all tense, and with his nostrils moving slightly, the Tiger, Clemenceau, sat in an arm-chair at the head of the big conference table. A long moustache drooped down over lips that were twisted from the many acid words, like barbed arrows, which had shot forth from them. Next to him could be seen the massive Welsh skull of Lloyd George. The third delegate, the Italian, was the reserved, gentlemanly Count Sforza.

Surrounding the three big men were a crowd of satellites, secretaries of state and departmental experts.

There was an oppressive atmosphere in the room, which reminded one of a court of justice.

The door opened, and into the centre of the " U "-shaped table stepped the brother-in-law of the Ottoman Sultan, Grand Vizier Damad Ferid Pasha, in appearance—save for the Turkish fez—a typical English gentleman. With a dignified bearing and stern, steady features, he advanced into the room, followed by his suite, under a cross-fire of glances from the big, feared men who were assembled to share out the world and decide the fate of nations.

Greetings were cool and formal; the Tiger gave a slight snort; and Lloyd George's head transformed itself into an untakeable fort.

The Grand Vizier was too much a man of the world and too

skilful a diplomat to show surprise at the extreme coolness of his reception. But for the first time an uneasy feeling of depression overpowered him on realizing that he was there not to be treated on equal terms, but as a helpless defendant in the dock.

Damad Ferid began to state his case, but his words, he could not help noticing, fell on empty ears. The judges of the world were not listening to him. In the Tiger's eyes there was a look of scorn, a gleam of hatred. . . .

The Grand Vizier cited Wilson's fourteen points in support of the sacred principle of self-determination for the nations. The Ottoman Government acknowledged that principle. They were willing to accord self-administration to the Arab provinces and desired to remodel themselves in harmony with the rest of the civilized world and contribute their share towards the tasks of civilization. The entry of Turkey into the War—the Imperial Ottoman Government freely admitted it—was a crime. But the guilt lay with the men who held power at the time, Enver, Talaat and the Members of the Committee of Union and Progress, who without reasonable justification plunged the country into war. . . .

A chair was suddenly pushed back, and the Tiger jumped up to attack this last sentence. Here was a chance for him to use his claws.

They had heard, from the mouth of the Grand Vizier of the Ottoman Empire, that Turkish statesmen bore the guilt for the crime of war. That confession substantially simplified the trial and clarified the position. Outside that the Grand Vizier seemed to have already forgotten that his country was completely in the hands of the Allies and that it was the place of the conquered to remain silent.

The Tiger warmed to his subject.

Did they remember the Levantine proverb—Where the Turk treads no grass will grow? Had they forgotten that the Ottoman race had always been barbarians by nature and that the world had never known anything from them save brutalities and atrocities? Was it not, therefore, perfectly natural that the military clique should get together with a similar clique in Berlin to destroy human civilization and freedom? Who would attempt to estimate the number of war crimes with which the Turks had aroused the disgust of the whole world?

" Be silent, your Highness ! Relieve Paris of your presence ! You will honour us by returning to your country as quickly as possible, where you may yet have the opportunity of dedicating yourself to the tasks of civilization ! "

CHAPTER VIII

SIVAS

FROM the inhospitable mountains of Kurdistan galloped swarms of horsemen into the valleys, wild, villainous-looking fellows with long, drooping moustaches and gaily-coloured, flowing robes.

They were striking for Malatia, the capital of the province.

On arrival they pitched their camps outside the gates and staged wild exhibitions of riding, discharging their carbines and pistols in the air and aiming at slender tree-stems with knives which buried themselves up to the hilt in the soft wood.

In the Governor's house the Governor himself, Ali Galib, was entertaining the tribal chiefs with home-distilled spirits, tea and cigarettes, not forgetting to place in the saucers of their tea-glasses a number of shiny coins. The chiefs were in a specially gay and abandoned mood, particularly as the Governor had promised that if the ambush were successful, his Majesty's loyal Kurdish subjects would be left uninterfered with to plunder the town of Sivas.

For the Kurds it was a festive and joyous occasion.

There was only one man in their midst whom they regarded with undisguised animosity, and whom they would have dearly loved to transform into a target for their daggers—that infidel dog of an English major who turned up every now and then to whisper something to the Governor. But they had heard that he was simply rolling in wealth and that while he remained there were prospects of more coin-filled saucers. And that protected him.

The Chief of the Gendarmerie scratched his head at the sight of the wild tribesmen and wondered how he was going to tame and lead them. If they failed to obey his orders in action, the police would mercilessly mow them down, he decided. The Imperial Ottoman gendarmes of Malatia were no milk-sops.

Already that rebel hound, Mustafa Kemal, had reached Sivas; but they were holding back until all the deputies had had time to arrive. There were many, it is true, who would never see Sivas, men who were waylaid and captured in the mountain valleys of Anatolia. Mustafa Kemal himself only escaped capture by the skin of his teeth. The Imperial Ottoman gendarmes were just

SIVAS

a few minutes too late, and swore as they caught sight of the fleeing figure of the man whom they thought they had and on whose head such a high price had been set.

More and more swarms of horsemen surged in the direction of Malatia. The mountain valleys of Kurdistan rang with the echo of the horses' hooves. A great plunder expedition attracted them, and, moreover, an expedition that was pleasing to Allah. Who killed the rebels gained paradise.

. . . . .

The Congress had assembled and was in session at Sivas. For days past the debates had been in progress; at times the excitement had risen to fever-pitch; at other times the interest had flagged and the proceedings had been dull.

"Let us guard against striving at extravagant, unattainable goals," advised some of the deputies.

"On the contrary—everything or nothing!" was the opinion held by another section.

"Let's make absolutely sure of our position."

"And we'd better not allow one man to have all the power. We had enough of that from Enver and the Committee."

And so the arguments continued until, at last, Mustafa Kemal sprang to his feet.

"Gentlemen, we are not here to form a political party or to launch a *coup d'état*. The whole nation is in the process of regeneration, and our aim is to create a new, Nationalist State of the most modern type. We are neither a party nor a committee; we are the delegates of the whole nation. Our sacred mission is to fight to relieve the distress which is being suffered by the whole of the people. We do not rely on the support of a few army corps, we have authority to fight on behalf of the whole Turkish nation, whose faith in its own invincible strength is fast reviving. We will go forth as preachers. I warn you that there is no place here for half-hearted people. The tasks which lie ahead of us cannot be achieved in secret, nor can we, by majority votes and parliamentary talk, force our enemies to acknowledge our claims and rights. We must carry our message to the villages and markets, get in touch with the people, study their needs, and rouse them.

I have been declared an outlaw, and there is not the least doubt that an unpleasant fate is in store for me, if I am caught. And all who work openly with me would share that fate. Who intends to support me must resolve never to forsake the holy cause of the nation, come what may."

" We want you, you as Leader of the Movement," the assembly shouted.

" Provided," exclaimed an old general, " that you do not turn against the Sultan-Caliph."

Arif smiled ironically and satanically. The Grey Wolf, unseen by the deputies, clenched his fist and inflated his nostrils. After a few seconds he relaxed, and said quietly :

" I propose that the Congress should send a message of loyalty to his Majesty."

" Let us take the oath ! "

The soldiers were the first to rise.

The Grey Wolf gazed steadily into their eyes.

" To-day I am an ordinary civilian. I have been dismissed from the Army. But if we are to be successful, my orders in future must be carried out with the same implicit obedience as though I were Commander-in-Chief."

" The Army is behind you, Pasha, if you are fighting to liberate the Sultan from his enemies."

The generals shook hands with him, and then a vote of the assembly was taken. Mustafa Kemal was elected President of the Congress, although a few votes were cast against him. . . .

Coming from the direction of Malatia, a horseman galloped towards the north, towards Sivas. The wind whipped the foam from the horse's mouth, until the animal's flanks were covered in white.

The rider's legs closed still tighter round the sides of his speedy horse as it tore on its way to carry a warning to Sivas.

Soon the horse was pounding the bare, deserted high plateau, casting up stones as it galloped on. The rider, in the khaki uniform of a Turkish officer, bent low over the withers. Suddenly bullets flew over his head, the body of the rider shot erect, and the horse continued riderless in its wild career across the plain.

" *Allah il Allah !* " shouted the Kurds, going in pursuit of the

SIVAS

valuable horse, and in a few minutes both hunters and quarry had vanished from sight. A head sagged and fell back as the mortally-wounded horseman breathed his last. The thin, coarse grass of the high plateau bent in the dust-laden breeze.

Towards evening the Kurdish horsemen returned to Malatia bringing with them the captured horse. Their leader went to inform the Governor that the bullets had proved faster than the fugitive.

Meanwhile, outside, the men were flying at each other's throats for the booty—the horse and its saddle and bridle. . . .

Ali Galib interviewed the Gendarmerie Chief and said he thought it was about time they started for Sivas.

" Very well ! " said the officer. " The expedition can leave in a few days."

" May Allah's hand guard all true servants of the Padishah ! "

.   .   .   .   .   .

Mustafa Kemal for the past few days had hardly left the telegraph office. Messages had proceeded in all directions. Arif had been charged with many secret missions. Mustafa clung to him like a brother, and there was hardly a secret in which he did not share. Arif's active brain and his grim and unfailingly accurate judgment made him an ideal adviser. He was now a divisional commander, but the Grey Wolf kept him at his side. The man believed in nothing, and nothing was holy to him, but at the same time he gave his whole heart to the National Revolution, and that drew Mustafa Kemal to him.

Meanwhile Mustafa Kemal found much of his time occupied by Congress debates, which seemed to drag on interminably.

" Why do you make things harder than they need be," said Arif, trying to tempt him during a confidential talk one evening, when they were resting after a strenuous day's work. " To hell with the Congress and representation of the people ! You have the Army behind you, and we are ready to acknowledge you as dictator. Give us our marching orders, and we will soon see if there is anyone who dares to oppose you in Anatolia."

Mustafa looked at him severely.

" As I have said before, we are not *Putschists*. We are preachers. And if we ceased preaching before the last compatriot and patriot had been won to the cause we should be guilty of self-betrayal. Not bayonets, but something quite different is going to decide this issue—faith, will, conviction. That's not a *Putsch*, but a regeneration of the nation. The blind must be made to see. We will march through the country not as soldiers of fortune, but as prophets, agitators, and we will not rest until we have gained the support of the last citizen for the nation's sacred cause."

"It rests with you," said Arif humbly, at the same time smiling scornfully. Mustafa Kemal, the matchless soldier and warrior, degrading himself to the status of a national orator?

Arif had no intentions of copying his friend in that respect, though he would stick to him through thick and thin. And, he told himself, there would come the day when shots would be fired.

Until then he would have to restrain himself and listen patiently to the idle chatter in the Congress.

In that particular assembly the talking and the arguments seemed never ending.

"What is to be done?"

"We can't do anything without foreign help."

"A State without sources of revenue, with a population ruined in three bloody wars and with a national debt amounting to untold millions, cannot exist in the twentieth century."

"We must have foreign aid."

"Do you want to place the country under the protection of England, who has sent nation after nation to slavery?"

"Then what else can we do?"

"We must obtain America's help."

"Bravo!"

"What is the use of thinking of fighting while the whole country is occupied by foreign troops?"

The Grey Wolf sat in his President's chair, ready to spring at any moment. Standing behind him was Arif, boiling with impatience. Mustafa remained silent and let the deputies talk themselves to a stop. His eyes bored their way into each speaker. All the while his brain was working feverishly.

Finally, he stood up and began to speak quietly and calmly.

"Let us postpone the discussion of these points until a later date, and let us now come to an agreement on the National Pact,

JULY 14TH, 1920. GENERAL GOURAUD (*right*), COMMANDER-IN-CHIEF OF THE FRENCH ARMY IN SYRIA, MARCHES INTO BEYRUTH

which aims to secure, above all, the inviolability and independence of the Turkish nation. . . ."

"The National Pact goes too far. We must be realists!"

"I have already warned lukewarm people to keep out of the National Movement. All or nothing!"

A strange light appeared in the Grey Wolf's eyes, although he spoke the words quietly and without passion.

He stood with legs apart, resting his balled fists on the speaker's desk. His prominent cheek-bones stood out below eyes which seized each deputy and held him, like prey held in the claws of a prairie wolf—there was no escape from them. Arif's blue eyes flashed, and his cold, metallic voice cut in on the momentary silence like a knife: "May the Pasha live a thousand years! Long live Mustafa Kemal!"

All at once recognition and enthusiasm seemed to seize the assembly. The breath of the Grey Wolf had settled among them; the nation's battle signal had been hoisted once more.

"Freedom or death! All or nothing!" they shouted.

The National Pact was unanimously adopted.

Once more Arif shouted: "Long live Mustafa Kemal!"

"Long live the nation!" said Mustafa.

. . . .

Ali Galib was enjoying his tea and listening to the Chief of the Gendarmerie, who was complaining bitterly of the unbridled conduct of the Kurdish horsemen, those unmentionable sons of hell.

"We need them," said the Governor, making himself comfortable in the cushions. "But we'll attend to them as soon as we have that rebel dog Mustafa Kemal and his band in irons. By Allah! what was that? Can you hear the shooting in the street? What the devil can it be . . . ?"

"Save yourself, your Excellency! The soldiers . . ."

The Governor turned pale and jumped to his feet. At that moment a burst of rifle-fire struck the wall, throwing out splinters and dust.

"What soldiers, you dog, or I'll have you whipped . . ."

"Infantry, your Excellency, on mules. Mustafa Kemal sent

them. They have been marching night and day and are now occupying the town . . ."

"You ass, you sleeping jackal!"

The Governor seized the police officer by the shoulders, and shook him vigorously. Suddenly he stopped.

"Good God! if they catch me . . .! Let me get away, let me escape!"

"The southern part of the town is still open. We can make for Urfa. The French are there . . ."

Major X . . . as soon as the shooting began, made a quick dash for his quarters. In hot haste, he threw his things into a bag, and was about to lock it when the door burst open. A Turkish officer rushed into the room. . . .

"Excuse me, Major." He took the bag.

The British officer was about to make an effort to retrieve his property when he caught sight of two Turkish soldiers with fixed bayonets, who advanced towards him.

The Turkish officer opened the bag, felt inside, and presently brought to light a sheaf of documents. "Damnation!" cursed Major X . . . whose hands itched to snatch them away; but standing near him were the two sentries, tall Anatolians, strong, sinewy fellows. He had met their sort in Gallipoli.

The Turk smiled courteously.

"We owe you the deepest gratitude, Major. This correspondence is of inestimable value to us. From it it appears that the Imperial Ottoman Government has been organizing an expedition against the National Movement with the help of foreigners."

He placed the documents in his pocket.

"I am afraid, Major, you must allow us to arrange for your return to Constantinople, where you will no doubt find better scope for your work. And you mustn't be angry because we were quicker."

Major X . . . at the thought of the scolding which awaited him on his return, felt like fighting the world.

. . . . . .

Constantinople was already at rest beneath the dim light of the stars and the Grand Vizier was just about to doze off when he was rudely aroused. In his study a little later he found waiting the head clerk of the telegraph office, who with many signs of respect handed to him a bundle of telegrams.

The blood rose to the Grand Vizier's temples and swelled the veins in his head until it seemed as though his obstinate Albanian skull must burst.

The telegrams were from Anatolia. The Congress at Sivas and all the army corps commanders had wired to his Majesty Sultan Mehmed Vahideddin demanding the resignation of the treacherous Damad Ferid Cabinet. The telegraph office had declined to forward the telegrams to the Sultan at the Yildiz Kiosk.

The Grand Vizier briefly thanked the head clerk.

This was the sequel to Malatia. Mustafa Kemal had spread news of the sortie throughout Anatolia, and the effect was amazing. In Anatolia now they could coolly call the Grand Vizier a traitor, and the corps commanders demand his resignation.

" Wire to the gentlemen in Anatolia saying that all communications to his Majesty must be made through the usual channels, that is, they must first reach the Grand Vizier."

" Very good, your Highness."

The telegraph official departed.

Despite the lateness of the hour, the Grand Vizier, in consideration of the urgency of the matter, dared to disturb the slumbers of his Imperial brother-in-law.

A palace official telephoned back his Sovereign's decision.

His Majesty refused to receive telegrams and demands from rebels.

Over the Grand Vizier's features spread a triumphant smile.

The wires had no rest that night. In Anatolia the corps commanders at Erzerum, Sivas, Angora, Diarbekr, Malatia and Konia sat glued to the receiving apparatus. Orders came through from his Excellency Mustafa Kemal.

The Grey Wolf sat beside the machine in Sivas and directed the campaign. His lips were pressed tightly together, and in his bright, steel-grey eyes there was a gleam of irrepressible energy and determination.

The reply came from Constantinople: the Sultan declined to receive the telegrams.

Clear the line to the Yildiz Kiosk! The lines to Erzerum, Angora, Diarbekr, Malatia and Konia bore the text of the next telegram, which Mustafa Kemal dictated.

Shortly afterwards a bombardment of telegrams from these places struck the Imperial telegraph office.

"Clear the line to the Yildiz Kiosk!" It was signed by the corps commanders at Angora, Konia, Erzerum, Diarbekr and Malatia.

Damad Ferid ground his teeth and wired back: "No!"

There was an interval while Mustafa Kemal, in Anatolia, wired the new message to the generals. Then began another telegraphic attack on Constantinople.

"If at the end of one hour the line to the Yildiz Kiosk is not cleared, communications between Anatolia and the Central Government will be severed." It was signed by the military commandants of Angora, Sivas, Konia, Erzerum, Diarbekr and Malatia. . . .

The Grand Vizier shook with rage, and again notified the Palace. The answer came by 'phone.

"His Majesty would not dream of allowing rebels to confront him with an ultimatum. His Highness the Grand Vizier may act accordingly."

Damad Ferid Pasha tossed his head and dictated the answer to a telegraph official.

"No!" it said.

Immediately the message was transmitted to Anatolia, a great country only partially opened up, on whose coasts there were narrow strips of land of extraordinary fertility and beauty, but whose interior consisted of desolate, rocky deserts and plains meagrely dotted with villages and towns.

The Grand Vizier sat motionless at his writing-desk. The ends of his costly dressing-gown lay in thick folds on the carpet. He drummed nervously on the surface of the desk. This obstinate Albanian was suddenly seized with an uncomfortable feeling of loneliness and depression. He drew the wrap closer about his neck—he felt cold.

There was deathly stillness; nothing moved; no sounds disturbed the silence. He stepped to the window and looked in the direction of the east, in the direction of Anatolia, which lay silently on the other side of the Bosporus.

Presently he could no longer stand the stillness, and began to worry the people at the telegraph office. They were still sitting at their machines, but these suddenly had grown silent.

Anatolia's voice had ceased.

" Attempt to get in touch with Anatolia at all costs ! " ordered the Grand Vizier.

The head clerk tried to ginger up his staff, but their efforts were in vain. No sounds came from the other side.

" Signal every station in Anatolia ! "

There were no answers, not even from the stations occupied by Allied troops.

In Anatolia, punctual to the minute, Kemalist soldiers and volunteers, when the hour's ultimatum had expired, occupied all the telegraph offices and cut the wires connecting with the occupied places. In addition, guards were set over the points at which the lines had been cut.

At many of the stations it was noticed that some of the officials were arrested and marched off, for there were many who showed opposition.

The Grey Wolf had struck the first critical blow. Anatolia was in his power and the Imperial Government was eliminated.

. . . . . .

Sultan Vahideddin thought over the position.

How was he to solve this fresh problem ? Might Allah scorch these English in the flames of his wrath ! They stubbornly insisted on the demobilization of the Army and refused to permit troops to cross to Anatolia to put an end to the rebellion. Indeed, they probably rejoiced at the domestic confusion created in the defeated Ottoman Empire, knowing that it would become weaker and more defenceless the longer such a state of affairs continued. Let them destroy one another !—it will save us a lot of trouble.

The Padishah knew his British friends, and he himself was a diplomat and intriguer of the Abdul Hamid school.

Anatolia in the hands of the Grey Wolf. Constantinople was a capital without a country, the Sultan a sovereign without subjects —but the Allies turned a deaf ear to him. . . .

Vahideddin dug his finger-nails in the cushions as he came to the decision to yield. There was no other way open to him. He could no longer overpower the Grey Wolf with force. But with cunning. . . .

. . . . .

"Damad Ferid Pasha's Cabinet has resigned. The Sultan extends the hand of reconciliation. Enough of hate and self-destruction! The Nationalists are invited to approach the Sovereign with their wishes. The Padishah is willing to summon a Government possessing his confidence and that of the men in Anatolia. The Padishah is even willing to consent to the election of a parliament."

In Sivas thankful and relieved people clustered round Mustafa Kemal, paid homage to him, and congratulated him. They were no longer standing in opposition to Allah's representative on earth, and a load was removed from their minds. There were few of them who had not suffered some misgivings when they had been called to form a front against one of Osman's descendants. That honest old soldier, Kiazim Karabekir, breathed freely once more; doubts no longer tormented him.

Now everything would run smoothly. There would be concessions on both sides, both parties would make cuts in their extravagant programmes, and they would come to a mutual agreement and frame a sane policy.

The one thing that now worried them was the gloomy look which Mustafa suddenly wore, and they could not understand why he should abruptly turn his back on the people who came forward to congratulate him. Soon he would be Grand Vizier, the most powerful man in the Empire, and in a position to conclude a reasonably tolerable peace.

They would not be able to deal quite so drastically with the representative of Nationalist Turkey as they had done with Damad Ferid.

For the first time in a long while the generals were seen to smile —and that despite the serious position in which the country still found itself.

Mustafa Kemal alone knew that the Young Movement was just entering upon a most critical time. He noticed the relief of the generals, civil governors and deputies and observed how they still worshipped the Padishah.

But if it is true that the Grey Wolf was strong and courageous, it is true also that he was clever, cunning and—when it was necessary—tricky.

He intended measuring himself against the elaborate trickiness of his Imperial rival, for in his own cleverness lay his strength. Above the tortuous route along which he was to travel hung the torch of a great, sacred ideal.

When telegraphic communications were re-established, the first message which Mustafa Kemal sent was an address of gratitude to Sultan Vahideddin.

Vahideddin was sorely tempted to tear up the paper, which he held in a trembling hand.

" In the name of the nation," said the rebel, presuming a right which belonged alone to the Sultan-Caliph. The wolf's claws were concealed beneath a cloak of devotion.

Vahideddin knew that they would one day break forth, and so he deemed it advisable first to rob them of their destructive power.

He would do his best to speed up the parliamentary elections. Both Anatolia and Turkey in Europe were to send deputies.

Vahideddin smiled maliciously.—But this National Assembly would be convoked in Constantinople and hold its session under the eyes of the Sultan—within reach of the guns of the British Fleet.

The Grey Wolf would think twice before walking into this trap. Good, then let him stay in Anatolia and grow stale. They would be able to deal satisfactorily with the deputies. And if gentle means were of no avail—then let the English take a hand !

The first thing to do, therefore, was unostentatiously to remove the National Movement from Mustafa Kemal's hands. When the National Assembly was called, this revolutionary government at Sivas would have to dissolve, as it would then be superfluous and illegal. The Grey Wolf would be left in the desert alone, to-morrow a nameless civilian, the day after—forgotten. . . .

CHAPTER IX

ANGORA

ON the Anatolian high plateau the December wind blew with such force that one expected at any moment to see the irregular batches of houses, which formed the town of Angora, uprooted and swept away. Peasant huts, low-built and small, appeared to be ducking down to dodge the storm. Alone the old castle, a wild and awe-inspiring edifice perched high on the rocks, seemed unaffected. But the slender, gracious minarets of the mosques appeared strained almost to breaking-point.

As far as the eye could reach was a series of reddish brown cliffs. Cutting into them were ravines of dizzy depth.

The town, as though driven there by the wind, had nestled in the shelter of the great cliffs, whose summits were sharply silhouetted against the sky.

The roads were carrying unusually heavy traffic. Picturesque crowds were streaming from the town and proceeding in the direction of Chankaya, which lay about half an hour's walk east of Angora and which was on the main road to Sivas. Tall, sinewy peasants, with sunburnt faces and, in many cases, with clear, blue eyes, came from the surrounding districts. They carried rifles slung across their backs. Their fezes had been turned a dull red by the sun. They had brought their drums and shawms with them. They spoke very little, but went silently on their way to Chankaya. Hope and expectation were written on their faces.

A human avenue had been lining the road from Sivas to Chankaya since dawn, and as the day grew the crowds increased. Huddled on the rocks, apart from the men, were numbers of heavily-veiled women. Boys had climbed the neighbouring hill-sides and shouted from time to time when they imagined that they could see something in the east, but stopped abruptly as soon as they grew aware of their error.

Soon a monotonous sing-song was heard, and presently from a nearby monastery came a solemn procession of pious Dervishes, who took up a position in a raised stand at the roadside. Fluttering above their heads was the green flag of the Prophet.

Hours passed. The crowds waited patiently and conversed in whispers.

"He is our saviour."

"A new prophet."

"Allah sent him in the hour of bitterest need."

"He disposes over mysterious powers; nothing is impossible to him."

"He has come to save us."

"Was there ever another pasha who made our cares his own? Do you ever remember another pasha visiting us in our markets, villages and even our huts?"

"May Allah bestow a thousand blessings upon him."

In the distance could be seen a small cloud of dust. The boys, still climbing about the rocks with the agility of Angora goats, started to shout, and this time did not cease.

"He's coming! He's coming!"

The drums began to beat and a fanfare of trumpets rang out. The crowds held their breath and watched the cloud of dust grow bigger. In its midst was Allah's messenger, the great pasha who was summoning the people to revolt and fight. They wondered what this great man, the Grey Wolf, would look like.

The rolling of the drums increased, women on the hill-side began a weird, shrill chanting, and the trumpeters sounded another high-pitched fanfare. With a squeak of the brakes the old car, which aroused awed astonishment, came to a stop. He had arrived.

In the old car was the Grey Wolf, the great pasha, the Chosen One of Allah, Mustafa Kemal. A man in a simple tweed suit worn under a heavy travelling ulster. On his head a big, dark Astrachan *Kalpak*. It was he.

He had no carbine, no revolver, no dagger, nothing in the way of a weapon. Instead he held in his hand an ordinary, unromantic walking-stick.

But his eyes, his lips, his forehead—they were his weapons!

"Long live the pasha!" yelled the crowd.

The high wind caught up the cheers, bore them away, and scattered them over the vast high plateau, letting them fall, like seeds of corn, on the hard earth.

Mustafa Kemal was on his way to Angora to establish the headquarters of the National Revolution in that town.

He made his own, personal quarter in a small, simple room in the telegraph office. There he sat day and night leading and controlling the enormous organization which in the course of a few months had been summoned into life throughout the length and breadth of a great territory, hard of access, lacking both railways and good roads.

For weeks past he had been travelling the country, speaking to the people, rousing them, compelling them. Then the Anatolians voted.

Only National deputies, the Grey Wolf's followers, were elected. Damad Ferid was unwise enough to set up an opposition party, and the Friends of England sustained a crushing defeat. The people wanted Mustafa Kemal.

The deputies then went to Constantinople. They talked, debated, took tea in the Pera drawing-rooms, and were handed round. Constantinople revealed itself with the whole of its charm, temptations and magic, against which even the officers of the Army of Occupation were not proof. The soft, voluptuous air of the capital caressed their temples and made them satisfied, indulgent, pleasure-pursuing and yielding.

The Grey Wolf stayed in primitive, poverty-stricken Angora, watching with deep distrust the course of events. Had he foreseen what would happen ? Had he foreseen that the rebels would rapidly become transformed into devoted subjects of his Majesty, or that they would unsuspectedly walk into the trap which a treacherous monarch, with the help of the English, had prepared for them ? Arif was at his side, casting bitter remarks about the " heroes " of Constantinople, growing ironical and scornful and pressing for action.

Vahideddin's intrigue proved hard enough to parry, and it was only with great difficulty that the dissolution of the Representative Committee was prevented. It still existed, thanks to skilful tactics on the part of the Grey Wolf, who promised dissolution only if the new Government gave proof through deeds that it was equal to its task.

On the other side of the Bosporus the National Pact, the revolutionary party's most sacred possession, was treated with contempt. It was regarded as a sort of political toy, and no one took it seriously.

Mustafa Kemal, much to his own regret, was forced to see that deeds alone could now save the National revolution from collapse. Deeds of a bold and startling nature were what was needed, he explained to Arif, who received the new plan with undisguised enthusiasm.

Armed volunteers tramped the streets of Angora, and bold Circassians in their brilliant uniforms rode into the town. In the absence of other accommodation, they camped in the public squares, ready for battle, their eyes on their leader. Officers and men of the old army impatiently awaited their orders. They had had enough of the parliamentary farce in Constantinople.

For some time past British agents had been reporting remarkable activities in the Anatolian barracks, which had become hives of industry. Other reports stated that large armed formations had been seen marching towards the south. They were mixed formations consisting of regular troops wearing the khaki uniform of the old Turkish Army, Circassians, Lhazes in their gay national uniform, carrying scimitars and silver-inlaid pistols, brigands in mufti, carrying rifles, and armed peasants in local dress.

Several men were wearing Prussian Grenadier trousers and, above them, sky-blue French tunics—abandoned by their original owners in the Great War. Others were marching in shirts and trousers, for Anatolia was poor, cut off from the world, still blockaded.

At night sections of artillery lumbered over the plains, making a wide detour of the villages and settlements in their line of advance.

These reports from the occupied territory in Anatolia aroused considerable excitement in Constantinople. The Allied High Commissioners, who imagined that the forces in Anatolia had been demobilized and disarmed, frowned, but transmitted the reports to Paris and hinted at various obscure dangers and possibilities. Rubbish ! said the Big Three : Turkey was in no position to make trouble !

Well, look out for the Grey Wolf !

·   ·   ·   ·   ·   ·   ·

The scene was a small café situated not far from the Galata Bridge in Constantinople.

Rendered almost invisible by a dense cloud of blue-grey

cigarette smoke, and seated on a small platform at the end of the room, were three Russians wearing Tsarist general's uniform, their chests smothered with orders and medals. They were playing music. The fiddler, who was minus one sleeve, held his bow at the end of a bare arm, while the arm which held the fiddle was still encased in green uniform cloth.

They were playing those soft, melancholy gipsy airs, which seem to have neither beginning nor end. The melodies spoke of the Russian steppe, and of the musicians' longing for their native land.

No one listened to them. Music in this café performed a similar role to the cigarettes: it was a drug for the nerves. People were conscious of it, but paid no heed to it.

Most of the men occupying the small tables were officers—Turks and a few Russians. Those who were present in civilian dress were typical representatives of the Levantine race. Spongy, yellow faces, with piercing, black eyes, oily smiles smeared on their lips and protruding, suspicious, receptive ears. Despite their insolent expressions, there was still a look on their faces of the old, inherited fear of the soldierly figures, who sat with their heads together, talking in whispers.

The tired flames of the mosque-lamps, which fought a hard battle with smoke-filled atmosphere, flickered shyly as the door opened. A cloud of smoke slipped quickly through the opening and lost itself in the air outside.

The newcomer, a Turkish captain, took a seat, and in an instant was surrounded by friends, from whose faces the look of boredom, inactivity and hopelessness suddenly vanished.

"In South Anatolia the Kemalists have soundly defeated the French troops of occupation. Marash and Urfa have been hastily evacuated by the French."

The new arrival imparted this information in a quiet, almost indifferent voice, at the same time maintaining a vigilant eye on the Levantine gentlemen.

The musicians struck up a lively tune. The eyes of the fiddling general with the missing sleeve were moist; he was far away, somewhere on the Don or the Volga.

A dozen questions were fired at the Turkish captain. His

listeners found it impossible to believe that the French had even been attacked, let alone defeated.

The captain rested his hands on the table.

"Eighty volunteers captured a full-strength French battalion, and for the benefit of doubters poilus in their sky-blue uniforms are now being exhibited throughout Anatolia. Later on they are to be made to work. In Anatolia every hand is needed."

He lowered his voice almost to a whisper.

"The British have evacuated Eski Shehir—much to Mustafa Kemal's satisfaction. He means to transform the railway depots into munition factories. Moreover, Eski Shehir is an excellent place from which supplies can be dispatched. Work is proceeding day and night on the shells which were captured from the French, readapting them for use by our Krupp guns."

"You say the English have left Eski Shehir?" asked someone incredulously.

The captain laughed.

"A Kemalist envoy paid a visit to the English commander and demanded the evacuation of the town. The Englishman smiled, whereupon the other led him to the window and pointed to the hills surrounding the town. The Briton cursed as he caught sight of the muzzles of guns protruding through bushes and when he was informed that the place was surrounded with Kemalist Free Corps. He was further told that a steady stream of reinforcements was on its way through the mountains. The English officer, overawed by this numerical superiority, and not wishing to be blown to pieces by the guns—which he could see for himself were already in position—departed in haste. On the following day two hundred volunteers marched singing into the town and showed the local citizens the iron pipes which they had posted to represent guns."

An old major, having recovered from his laughter, ordered a round of cognacs, took the tray and first offered the drinks to the Russians, whom he was obliged to consider as guests of the country.

A yellow-faced Levantine in the corner then observed how the captain and a number of officers quietly slipped through a small door behind the service counter.

"Here we are," said the captain in satisfied tones, after they had reached the bottom of a narrow staircase. He opened a door. A shaft of light fell along a dark cellar passage-way. They entered the room.

Seated behind a small table loaded with document files was a lieutenant. At other small tables orderly-room clerks were busily at work.

" The secret recruiting-office."

The captain bent over the table and spoke to the lieutenant.

" My friends want to get to Anatolia as quickly as possible."

The subaltern eyed them thoroughly and then said:

" Gentlemen, I'm afraid I shall only be able to get four of you across. To-morrow an Italian steamer leaves for Samsun. I can get four men taken on as trimmers, but no more. Some of you might be able to get jobs loading the vessel and then slip aboard unnoticed and chance your luck as stowaways. The Italians are not too sharp, but recently the French have been sending secret police agents aboard the steamers, and I shouldn't recommend anybody to fall into their hands."

Later, when the captain and the other officers returned unostentatiously, one by one, to their places in the café, they saw seated at a table near the exit a captain of the British Military Police.

He appeared to be absorbed in a copy of *The Times*.

The Levantine signalled with his eyes.

· · · · ·

The valleys of the Taurus mountains, in the far south of Anatolia, echoed with the sounds of rifle and machine-gun fire.

Isolated French detachments, ignorant of the country, were trying to find their way through the difficult mountain terrain. Their main-bodies were in flight across the passes, endeavouring to reach the sea. All were striving to reach Adana, the last-remaining French base in Kilikia.

Hard on the heels of the fugitives followed the Kemalists. A wild, motley collection of soldiers. The swarms of horsemen might have been taken for a fantastic vision, a charging Fata Morgana, their infantry columns for uncanny, masked processions. They turned up at the most unexpected times and places and launched themselves at the French soldiers, who tried to escape, or sought cover behind rocks, returned the enemy fire, and then bolted again towards the south, not knowing whether they would be fired on again on reaching the next pass, or whether, when they were least expecting it, the Anatolians would suddenly rise from behind cover on the hill-sides and charge down on them with fixed bayonets.

The officers had difficulty in maintaining a resemblance to discipline. Their men, who had come to Kilikia with the thought of leading a paradisaic existence, simply could not believe that war had started again. They had just made themselves at home in a land where Nature's generosity knew no bounds. At Adana the cafés-chantants had shot out of the ground like mushrooms, the officers and N.C.O.s had been joined by their families from France, and a veritable miniature Paris had been established only a few miles inland from the Gulf of Alexandretta.

The officers, in their brilliant blue uniforms, swaggered between the rows of dazzling white houses, and flourished their riding-whips. Their men were not slow in copying their example. Soldiers belonging to the Armenian Legion knocked the fezes from the heads of pious Mohammedans and tore the veils from the faces of the women—the worst insults that a Turk could suffer.

From the various cafés and low music-halls came the metallic din of a French hurdy-gurdy hammering out the latest Paris popular melodies.

Such was life in lovely Adana.

The feelings of horror and surprise when a number of torn and bleeding poilus made their appearance at this scene of ease and luxury may well be imagined. Once more the ghost of war raised its hideous, terrifying head; and in this case the attackers represented a downtrodden, fleeced, exasperated nation, who were now releasing their pent-up anger against oppressors. There was no quarter—as the survivors, shaking from head to foot, reported. They told of the horrors in the ravines of the Taurus, of the wild, headlong flight and the relentless pursuit.

During the retreat the garrison of Urfa were slain to the last man, and only a few of the soldiers from Marash succeeded in escaping with their lives.

If this continued—God have mercy on Adana!

General Gouraud must send reinforcements from Syria.

That evening in the cafés the officers shouted and bawled more than ever; they were not anxious for people to notice their nervousness.

After darkness had fallen, bands of armed Turks crept along the streets and pounced upon French and Armenian patrols, who were not seen again. In the bazaar and cafés there were numerous scenes and brawls. Turks thrashed Frenchmen.

No reinforcements had yet come.

. . . .

The British High Commissioner had made his quarters in the mansion which was formerly the Austro-Hungarian Embassy. In his study were assembled a number of captains of English ships, in addition to the C.O.s of certain land units.

The High Commissioner handed a list to the senior officer of the Military Police.

"Here you have a list of the names and addresses of the Nationalists who are to be arrested. It has been prepared by the Sultan's secretaries, and the Sovereign himself has checked it and made certain additions. So we owe his Majesty our gratitude. The arrests must be made to-night—*en masse* and suddenly. Unfortunately, the rebel has received news in Angora of the intended coup. If only his spies were a little less efficient!—but for that matter he might have guessed from the idle talk in the House of Commons that something was in the air. On the other hand, we may thank God that his deputies are so comfortable here that few have obeyed his instructions to depart. However, despite the elaborate precautions taken by the Allied authorities, several of the most dangerous men have already succeeded in escaping to Anatolia. The Minister of War, Fevzi Pasha, and his Under-Secretary of State, Ismet, are among those who have got away. I would rather have seen them in a prison camp at Malta. Gentlemen, I think that the situation is now clear to you. The important thing is that the Allies can no longer tolerate being made fools of in Constantinople. The crowning act of insolence was perpetrated only the other night, when some rebel officers raided the Allied munition depot, which was intended for the White Army in Russia, looted it, and shipped its contents across to Anatolia. It is high time that we stepped in and restored order. It is confidently expected that the Sultan will be granted permission to despatch an army to Angora. The gentlemen in London are slowly re-discovering their common sense. They now hold me responsible for seeing that this disciplinary action is carried through in such a manner that it will be a lesson to others. The deputies are to be placed immediately in chains and taken aboard the ships; and we are also falling in with the wishes of the Sultan, who wants us to mix a number of convicts with the political prisoners. Is everything clear? Then that will be all, gentlemen."

As the first sun's rays descended upon Constantinople, English marines began their march from the harbour. While, in their rear, fresh detachments were being disembarked from the warships, they advanced through the streets of Stambul, in extended order and with bayonets fixed.

Out on the Bosporus, moving gently with the waves, was the ship in which the Nationalist prisoners and convicts from the Constantinople prisons had been embarked.

The marines doubled forward in silence, led by their officers. They were sturdy, reckless men, who as they advanced drove the people from the streets with the butts of their rifles and fired at the windows.

Turkish military posts and police stations were stormed, as though in a war, and their occupants, startled out of their sleep, were promptly put in chains. Everything was done at lightning speed.

The city was taken completely by surprise.

In the Shachsade Bashi quarter machine-guns opened the way for the troops to occupy the Government buildings. Once they were inside, everything was turned upside-down in a frantic search for incriminating, treasonable documents.

The Ministry of War, long a thorn in the eye of the High Commissioner, was one of the Government premises thus occupied.

One of the clerks, Monastirli Hamdi, remained in the telegraph room of the Ministry of War and sent messages to Angora. All the other clerks had departed in haste.

Outside, the rifle and machine-gun fire continued while Monastirli, imperturbable and faithful to his duty, continued to send out his messages.

Over in Angora Mustafa Kemal stood in the telegraph office and took down the messages, word for word, as they came through from far-off Constantinople.

". . . the British have invaded the city. . . . The military posts were taken at dawn. . . . In Shachsade Bashi 6 people have been killed and 15 wounded. Still more troops are advancing through the streets. . . . At this moment British marines are approaching the War Ministry . . . they are now entering the building. . . . The Nizami Gate has been taken. . . . Troops now approaching. . . . Impossible to continue the messages. . . . They are here. . . ."

Mustafa Kemal read the report without moving a muscle. He had expected something of the kind. Now it was his turn to act.

The Grey Wolf now showed his claws. In a short time orders were being despatched to all parts of Anatolia.

All Allied agents and control officers were to be rounded up and detained. All troops of Occupation were to be driven out.

Anatolia was forthwith to elect a National Assembly, which was to sit in Angora and exercise the powers of Government. The assembly would be called at the commencement of May, in order that Anatolia might be given a new constitution.

Mustafa Kemal's orders quickly began to bear fruit. English, French and Italian troops from all parts of Anatolia began streaming to the coast where they would be under the safe protection of the ships' guns.

Mustafa Kemal and his followers again visited the villages and markets and spoke with the people.

Under a bright sun-awning stood a general, on a slightly-raised platform, in order that all might see him. He began to speak, and the crowd listened in rapt attention. They had climbed on to roof tops and up telegraph-poles in the hope of seeing and hearing the saviour, the Messenger of Allah. His voice, though seldom loud, had a penetrating quality, and his words and forceful personality held and fascinated his hearers.

Occasionally the crowd broke out into cheers, but most of the time there was tense silence. Mustafa Kemal was speaking to the people.

Long after he had left the town, the enthusiasm which his visit had provoked remained with the people, who copied his erect bearing and movements and endeavoured in every possible way to imitate him. Gradually the nation was being regenerated. All eyes were on one man, the outstanding leader.

CHAPTER X
SÈVRES

NOTICES posted in the principal streets and squares of Constantinople proclaimed a State of Siege. Damad Ferid had for the second time assumed the responsibilities of the office of Grand Vizier. Shouts echoed through the streets. The Sheikh-ul-Islam called for the death of the rebels. Who would gain paradise must kill the Nationalists, who had been declared outlaws and on whose heads a high price had been set by the Padishah.

Zubeida Hanum heard the news, and her heart almost stopped beating. For a long time she had been without news of her son. Now he was an outlaw. One division after another was being sent over to Anatolia to crush the rebellion. Mustafa was lost. Her only son, who at one time came so near being one of the Sultan's leading advisers, and for whom the highest honours were within grasp, would end his life on the gallows, as a rebel.

Suddenly the rumour got about that Mustafa Kemal was dead. The message passed from mouth to mouth, until it was known in every street and square of the capital.

It was stated that the Caliphate Army stood within gunshot of Angora. All true subjects of the Padishah had risen against the traitors, and Mustafa Kemal had been arrested. A sentence of death had been passed upon him, and he had been executed. The rebel was no more. Praised be Allah! Long live the Padishah!

Zubeida Hanum was prostrate with grief, but who cared about the mother of a traitor? She might count herself lucky that she had not been hanged.

Grief brought the old semi-blind woman to the verge of insanity, but she was too strong to break down.

She prayed without ceasing. . . .

Anatolia was aflame. Risings occurred in all parts of the country. The Sultan's emissaries spent liberally of the English money with which they had been furnished, and they had no difficulty in finding deluded people who could be persuaded to fight for the Sultan against Mustafa Kemal. In addition, the summons of the Sheikh-ul-Islam was not without effect. Nationalist troops were despatched to all parts of the country, but owing to their weak numbers and the vastness of the country they were unable to quell all the outbreaks.

SÈVRES

Anatolia was in a state of civil war.

Angora itself was a huge camp. People from all parts streamed into the little city, which was unable to accommodate even a small fraction of their number.

Generals lived in stables and deputies slept in the open. When their day's work was done, they wrapped themselves in their overcoats, stretched out on the ground, and slept as well as the cutting steppe wind would allow. All differences in rank had vanished; the common emergency made all persons equal.

The National Assembly, which represented the revolutionary party, sat in the building formerly occupied by the Young Turk Committee of " Union and Progress." The assembly room was a long, narrow apartment with the Turkish flag hanging from one of its walls. The deputies, officers and civilians sat on plain wooden chairs. The President's chair, in front, was occupied by Mustafa Kemal.

This was the centre of the revolution, where work never ceased. During the evenings and nights two mean parafin lamps provided necessary, though inadequate, illumination.

The Executive Committee of the Great National Assembly was the Revolutionary Government of Turkey. Mustafa Kemal was its President and Dictator.

Among the many persons who reported to the Dictator in Angora there was a short, unprepossessing man in the uniform of a colonel, but when Mustafa Kemal recognized him his delight was evident. Quickly the news spread through Angora that Colonel Ismet, after an adventurous journey from Constantinople, had arrived at the headquarters of the Nationalist Government.

Who was Ismet? A newcomer, an unwritten page. At the Ministry of War he was supposed to have been working in secret for the revolution. Mustafa Kemal had long talks with the little colonel and aroused a great deal of astonishment by entering Ismet's name in the list of Ministers of the Revolutionary Government.

Then it was announced that he was to receive command of the entire army.

A storm of protest broke out. Old friends of Mustafa Kemal were furiously indignant. Arif scowled, but held his peace.

Old, deserving and trusty soldiers, like Marshal Kiazim

Karabekir, Ali Fuad, Jevad, Refat and many others, rebelled at the suggestion that they should serve under a young man, recently arrived, who had had no previous experience in Anatolia.

The appointment gave rise to a number of fierce arguments and angry scenes.

Arif had the temerity to point out confidentially that it was a mistake, and was sent away with a sharp rebuff. Mustafa Kemal insisted on his decision, and was determined at all costs to establish the authority of the new man, even though it meant going against the advice of his oldest and truest soldiers and many of his best friends. The moment he met Ismet in Angora he realized that confronting him was the man he had been seeking, a man who appreciated and understood his aims, who was ready to make any sacrifice to achieve them, and who, despite his unimpressive appearance, was the possessor of outstanding talent as a military leader. And that decided him. His closest friends would have to yield and provide an example of discipline to others, showing them that ability came before seniority and friendship.

And there the matter was left.

Arif was conscious of a feeling of bitterness. He scoffed at himself: he jealous? That meant possessing sentiments, and Arif knew no sentiments, and did not want to know any. Devil take them!

Another who also found his way to Angora was no less a person than the ex-Minister of War, Fevzi Pasha, a big man with dark, faithful eyes. Arif soon realized that this newcomer also possessed a great measure of the Grey Wolf's confidence and that the latter at times discussed with him matters which he never mentioned to the others.

But Arif had to admit that there was not the slightest change in the relationship between himself and Mustafa Kemal. Mustafa still continued to treat him as a brother and best friend, with whom he would discuss any personal matter. They spent hours in each other's company. At such times Mustafa would think of his mother, to whom he was unable to send news and who probably considered him as dead. He wondered, too, how his sister was faring. Arif, when left to his own thoughts, remembered the old bear, with whom he had not wrestled for such a long time. Was the old fellow still alive, and was he enjoying life? Did he get his daily ration of honey, which he liked so much? And Ayesha, his good old housekeeper, how was she?

Although they saw as much of each other as before, Arif could not help noticing that there was a well-defined demarcation line between personal and official matters. In the latter sphere both Ismet and Fevzi took preference over Arif.

Was he jealous on that account? Was he a climber, a career-maker, or was he a friend, a comrade, a brother?

Arif when left alone would ride far into the steppe, gripping his horse's sides until he nearly broke its ribs and laughing diabolically to himself the while.

When in those moods he was distinctly unpleasant both as a man and as a superior officer, and it was a good thing that Mustafa Kemal kept him on a short lead, instead of letting him loose in Armenia, or some other part, at a population that showed any tendency to be refractory or hostile.

Arif knew that very well for himself. It was his fate always to be held in check. It was so during the War; it was so now. Despite that he remained a true friend and set a fine example of disciplined conduct to others.

The future was obscure and the revolution might bring almost any kind of developments. It might one day place Arif in a position where there would be more scope for his particular talents.

Mustafa Kemal about this time was unfortunate enough to develop a severe attack of malaria, an illness from which many in the district of Angora suffered. In addition, he was surrounded by a numerous body of paid assassins, spies and traitors who were only too eager to play the part of a Judas. There was practically no one whom he could trust. The Sultan's agitators found their ways into the side-streets of Angora and tried to influence the minds of the people. To fall into the hands of the Caliphate's troops meant a painful death.

At night, when the heat was stifling and sand clouds obscured one's vision of the sky, the assassins were never far away. Already they had poisoned his favourite watch-dog Karabesh.

Mustafa slept only when Arif was there to keep guard over him. At nightfall Arif settled down to sleep for a few hours, while

Mustafa rose and watched over him. When the chilly hours of dawn approached, Mustafa again retired to bed and Arif, with a loaded revolver in his hand, again stood guard. He first tasted each dish of food and each drink before passing it on to his friend. When Mustafa's fever rose, he placed the tablets between his parched lips, until he was fit enough to stand up and apply himself again to his work. Wherever he went he was guarded by Arif, whose suspicious eyes were everywhere.

Ismet wandered restlessly up and down his work-room. At work in the next room was Fevzi, who at regular intervals paused to brush a lock of black hair from his forehead.

" Succeed or perish ! " was the watchword which Mustafa Kemal was continually uttering as he sat at his desk and issued his orders.

Sultan Vahideddin had not been idle. Further batches of Imperial troops had been sent over to Anatolia, and while the Kemalists were well occupied in quelling the risings which had broken out in all parts of the country, the Caliphate Army was steadily approaching Angora.

Vahideddin was within sight of the day when he would again be master of the land and in a position to establish his tribunal of vengeance.

At Sèvres, near Paris, the Allied Supreme Council had arrived at its decision regarding the peace conditions. Eighteen months had elapsed since the conclusion of the Armistice, and for eighteen months the Turkish people had existed in cruel uncertainty of their fate.

Now they were to know. The victors had come to an agreement, and the dictated peace waited for signature.

As May of the year 1920 drew to its close, the Big Three published the conditions of the Peace.

Even Sultan Vahideddin turned pale on being informed of them.

Constantinople and the Straits were to be placed under international control, and the Sultan, as Head of the Mohammedan religion, was to remain at the Golden Horn and reside under the eyes of the English. South Anatolia, Kilikia and its capital Adana were to fall to France, Italy was to receive the territory of Adalia, and Smyrna was to become Greek, in which instance the Greeks would be acting as stewards for England. Cut off from all access to the sea, Turkey was to have central Anatolia and Turks were to live in what may be described as a sort of Indian reservation. The Arab provinces were to be placed under British and French mandates. A new Armenian Republic was to be created in the Eastern Provinces and along the Black Sea.

It was Mustafa Kemal's special care that every peasant was made aware of the conditions of this dictated peace, which in vindictiveness and madness exceeded all others.

All at once Anatolia grew calm, and the noise of fighting ceased throughout the land. Soldiers of the Caliphate Army held their rifle-butts aloft as a sign that they wished to fraternize with the Kemalists, and marched to Angora to place themselves under the banner of the Grey Wolf.

The risings suddenly died down. All eyes turned to Mustafa Kemal, the man who had predicted what would happen and the man who summoned them to resist the victors and the traitors in their own land.

The remaining loyal Imperial troops fled back to the Straits, hotly pursued by the Kemalists. Near Constantinople, on the Asiatic side of the Sea of Marmora, the British had dug themselves in. The loyal troops made for this position. The Kemalists, without a moment's hesitation, opened the attack. British soldiers were roused from their life of ease in the capital and hastily dispatched to reinforce the position at Ismid on the Sea of Marmora, where fierce fighting was already in progress.

The Kemalists were the first at their destination and reached the coast before the British were able to arrive. Soon shells were flying across the Bosporus, several of them falling on the headquarters of the British High Commissioner. In the rear of Constantinople, in European Turkey stood a Turkish army corps that had gone over to Mustafa Kemal. It was set on the march. The British thus found themselves caught between two fires, held in the two arms of pincers. Stambul cheered itself hoarse, while in Pera the houses were hastily shut and barricaded.

After a few days the fright was over.

Mustafa Kemal had been merely staging a demonstration. The main force of the Nationalist Army was still in the centre of Anatolia, where a big task still confronted it.

But the Allies now knew what they might expect—and they had hardly expected such an answer to their dictated peace!

The Grey Wolf was now very much on the alert. Everything depended now on what Sultan Vahideddin would do.

Vahideddin actually had little choice. Either he bowed to the revolution, subjected himself to the will of the hated rebels, or he complied with the wishes of the victors. A decision was not difficult. England at least guaranteed him his throne. What would the Grey Wolf be prepared to guarantee him?

The Sultan laughed bitterly. He knew precisely the goal at which Mustafa Kemal was aiming. Victory by the Grey Wolf meant the last of the throne of Osman. Did the Anatolians realize what goal they were fighting for?

Punish everybody, leaders as well as followers! declared the Sultan. Put an end to this state of affairs, this Empire without territory, whose power did not extend beyond the limits of its own capital!

Only England could now bring salvation from the Nationalists. England!

Vahideddin signed the Peace Treaty.

He had now played his last card. It was the Grey Wolf's turn to show his hand.

All Anatolia shouted and cheered when Mustafa Kemal pronounced the Grand Vizier, Damad Ferid, a traitor and deprived him of Turkish citizenship.

The Grey Wolf was wise enough not to aim his blow directly at the person of the Sultan-Caliph.

The Allied Supreme Council in Paris were placed in a position of considerable embarrassment. In particular the French were seriously alarmed. It was no longer a secret that General Gouraud had been obliged to approach the Grey Wolf for an armistice in Kilikia, and that he had been forced to enter into negotiations with the Angora people just as though they were a regular Government. France cursed the whole East. There was war in Africa, war in the mandatory territory in Syria and war in Kilikia, while the bulk of the troops were in station on the Rhine. It was an unenviable position.

The Peace Treaty was ready and had actually been signed.

SÈVRES

Treaty? At the moment it was worth little more than a scrap of paper. In the circumstances there seemed little likelihood of being able to enforce its conditions.

There was only one way of enforcing them, and that was through the use of military persuasion.

Lloyd George was the first to draw this unwelcomed conclusion.

The French shrugged their shoulders. England had had the pick of the booty, then let her pull the chestnuts out of the fire! To France the treaty was not worthy a new war in the East. They had already had a foretaste of the joys of mastery in Kilikia. Italy was in no position to furnish an expedition. What was the position of England?

Lloyd George found himself in a somewhat awkward position. The army at home had just been demobilized, and it was hardly to be expected that the men would relish being summoned to the Colours again.

Then there came to his rescue a country to whom the Treaty was well worth an expedition:

Greece burned for a chance to extend its conquests in Anatolia—and Greece was ready. Venizelos had not allowed grass to grow under his feet. In Smyrna and in the Province of Aidan Greek armies were already there, prepared to march.

Lloyd George, thrilled and delighted, seized the offer with both hands and showed that he was both grateful and generous. England would assume the responsibility for equipping the Greek troops: money was no object. The Greek army was to have the very latest equipment for the campaign and English officers were to be attached to the staff. All Venizelos had to do was to find the men, 200,000 of them, eager, fresh soldiers, who had not had a world war behind them.

The British Fleet was to open up the way.

Great grey hulls again ploughed the waves of the Bosporus.

Sultan Vahideddin prayed to Allah. Neither God nor the devil could save Mustafa Kemal now.

Nationalist troops hurriedly climbed the passes on the mountains east of Aidan and dug themselves in. Some were volunteers, bare-footed and in rags, while the others were soldiers of the Regular Army, in an almost equally miserable condition. Many had no rifles, and most of the remaining men had weapons of ancient pattern, which were heavy and of practically no use. Field telephones and such luxuries did not exist. Each unit was more or less left to its own resources.

The commanding officer, Ali Fuad, did everything that lay in his power.

When the Greek attack burst upon their positions the Nationalist forces were flattened out like sand-hills under a steam-roller.

What remained of them assembled short of the Anatolian railway line, far in the interior of the land.

What could Mustafa Kemal do now? He was ruined: the power of the Kemalists had been swept away as though it were a soap-bubble. The High Commissioners and Sultan Vahideddin rejoiced and wondered why they had allowed such an empty nightmare to disturb their slumbers as it had. . . .

In Angora there was panic.

The mean apartment at the old " Committee " premises, in which the Great National Assembly sat, witnessed some tumultuous scenes.

" We went too far."

" We demanded and attempted too much."

" We ought to have been satisfied with reasonable claims."

" Let our policy be one of reconciliation and discussion."

" Quickly, before it's too late ! "

These and similar shouts rang in Mustafa Kemal's ears.

The Grey Wolf looked straight above the heads of the deputies, and peered into the distance, the future.

To all protests and questions he replied with the same, uncompromising formula :

" All or nothing ! Freedom or death ! "

With calm assurance he set to work to stem the tide of defeat.

Ali Fuad was relieved of his command of the West Army, and Ismet was appointed in his stead. The older generals moaned, and the deputies looked askance at the youthful colonel. There were many men who had done greater service to the cause of the revolution.

Granted, but special talent and military genius came first, Mustafa Kemal decided. Ismet duly became officer in command of the troops in the west.

SÈVRES

In a few weeks Mustafa Kemal accomplished marvels. First the Free Corps were disbanded and their members drafted into the regular army, then recruits were enrolled. Each block of twenty houses, in villages and towns, had to provide a recruit and furnish his equipment.

The National Assembly, which was still thoroughly apprehensive, gradually began to regain its lost confidence.

In the autumn of 1920 the campaign was opened in the Eastern Provinces.

A month later the last remaining Armenians were in flight across the Caucasus to Russian Armenia.

The Great Armenian Republic, that pet child of the Treaty of Sèvres, was trampled under the feet of the Kemalist battalions.

Compensation for the defeat in the west had been made. Mustafa Kemal now had only one front to defend.

Anatolia trembled under the beat of hammers. Primitive factories sprang out of the ground and war material—wretched, patched-up stuff for the most part—was manufactured in feverish haste.

Bullock-carts lumbered over the passes of the Anatolian mountains transporting material that had been captured from the French in Kilikia to the west front—whole depots of the most precious supplies.

The Anatolian railway in the west groaned under the weight of troop trains and munition wagons.

At intervals of about two hundred yards the trains were forced to halt while the axles cooled. There was not an ounce of wheel-grease in the whole of Anatolia.

Transport officers cursed and saw that progress was hopeless, and yet—by some power of magic—the trains managed eventually to reach their destinations.

Everything was impossible, hopeless, yet in the end everything got done.

It was due to the resolute determination and tremendous energy of one man, who accomplished the impossible himself and who fired others to do the same.

No orders were impossible of execution. Those who loafed or refused to obey were kicked out—there were no arguments in Anatolia!

The men at the front were now beginning to recognize their new commanding officer. He was to be seen riding a superb horse at the head of a brilliant cavalcade, appearing first at one point and then at another, with unexpected suddenness. He examined positions, ordered new works to be prepared, reconnoitred all the important strategical points, organized, and had every man on his toes. A soldier's life in Anatolia at this time was no joke. There was no time for sleep. When the men were not engaged in field exercises they were digging and strengthening their positions, and when that was done they had to supply the work of the armourers and sappers. Then, by way of a change, they would raid the Greek depots and supplement their own stores. The enemy was their only war contractor—and a very unwilling one, as they discovered!

Meanwhile, in Angora, Mustafa Kemal, after a hard struggle, managed to get his way, and a definite constitution was approved. The whole power of state was vested in the nation, while the task of government was entrusted to the Great National Assembly on its behalf.

Sultan Vahideddin trembled. When he was the least expecting it the rebel had ousted him from the saddle. The sovereign passed through an anxious time. And to add to his cares, the Allies demanded that he should proclaim the Peace Treaty throughout the country. After a bitter struggle with himself he resolved, powerless though he was, to yield once more. At the same time he set another trap for the Grey Wolf.

The latter laughed scornfully and demanded absolute subjection to the will of the nation.

The Greeks now prepared for a new offensive.

Tortured with anxiety, the Sultan awaited the outcome of this new battle. The Greeks, in greatly superior numbers, launched a great blow at the Turkish positions near In Eunu.

In the Yildiz Kiosk, in Paris and in Athens there were days of horrible uncertainty. Then the news came through.

Ismet had beaten off the main attack.

The High Commissioners began thoroughly to dislike the situation. The Kemalist army was becoming a little too uncanny; the whole country was becoming uncanny.

The Grey Wolf had his claws at the Allied throat, and it seemed

SÈVRES

impossible to shake him off, save at the cost of terrible bloodshed. The Allies decided that it would be better to try methods of gentle persuasion. Perhaps he might come for a few morsels of bait thrown down to him. And finally, they reasoned, he was a man of sense, and would not welcome a fight to the death.

The Allies assembled in London to a conference and attempted to come to a settlement between Turks and Greeks.

A few concessions and modifications were to be made to the Aidan frontier, and the Turks in return were to recognize the Treaty of Sèvres.

The Imperial Government was invited and Mustafa Kemal was instructed to send delegates.

He replied that there was a government at Angora, but none in Constantinople. The Big Three made the best of a bad job and despatched a formal invitation to Angora, which was equivalent to recognizing the revolutionary Government.

The conference in London was still sitting when the Greeks began a new offensive in Anatolia. Furious fighting raged in the neighbourhoods of In Eunu and Afiun Kara Hissar.

Behind the backs of the London conference the French established secret communications with the Turks. Briand flattered the heroism and patriotism of the Kemalists and signed a pact with Turkish plenipotentiaries by which France agreed to suspend all hostilities, to relinquish possession of Kilikia and to regard Turkey as a friend. In consideration of this France received economic preferences.

Mustafa Kemal read the pact, tore it up, and relieved the plenipotentiaries of office. There could be no discussion of proposed economic preferences in Turkey.

The National Assembly stormed and protested, but he took no notice of them.

At Afiun Kara Hissar the Turks were beaten and the town and railway were lost.

In the north, as in In Eunu, the fighting still continued. There the Greeks fought under the eyes of their own King Constantine.

With the support of a few staunch adherents Mustafa Kemal in Angora managed to hold the National Assembly, which again began to waver, in check.

The amount of work that remained to be done was enormous. The administration had to be reorganized; the civil service had to be reconstituted; corruption had to be stamped out; national resources had to be mobilized and the army had to be supplied with indispensable stores. During the whole of this time, too, a stiff battle had to be fought against the Opposition, against cowardice and despair—sleep was impossible.

From the front came news that Ismet had repulsed the Greek offensive at In Eunn after a fearful struggle, and had forced the enemy to relinquish his gains in the south. Afiun Kara Hissar and the railway were evacuated by the Greeks. Refat badly let Ismet down by not arriving to assist him in time and so make it possible for the victory to be consolidated. In Angora voices were raised saying that a deliberate intention lay behind this. It was known that there had been disagreements between Refat and his old friend, the Grey Wolf.

In any case, Mustafa Kemal severely reprimanded Refat, and a friendship that had long been weakening finally broke. Refat angrily retired to the Forest of Kastamuni. Officially it was stated that he had been granted sick leave.

The big military pashas protested. The Grey Wolf's régime was too strict. His methods of punishing army commanders for each failure went too far.

But the Grey Wolf's hold of the army and the National Assembly grew stronger from day to day. Mustafa knew that the least sign of weakness would have fatal consequences to the nation's cause. He had no time for feelings or personal considerations; all that counted with him were figures, facts, geographical data and unconditional sacrifice for the sake of victory.

He did not spare himself, had never done so. Despite his kidney trouble and malaria he was at his post day and night.

Even Arif at times shuddered at his cold-bloodedness, and that unbelieving scoffer was often secretly horrified when he saw how Mustafa Kemal, without a second's hesitation, sacrificed his best friends, if they happened to supply the slightest hindrance to his plans. Arif was beginning to wonder which came first—his friendship for the great taskmaster, his hate or his admiration.

He had not been promoted, and he had been kept out of the battles.

GENERAL ISMET INEUNU

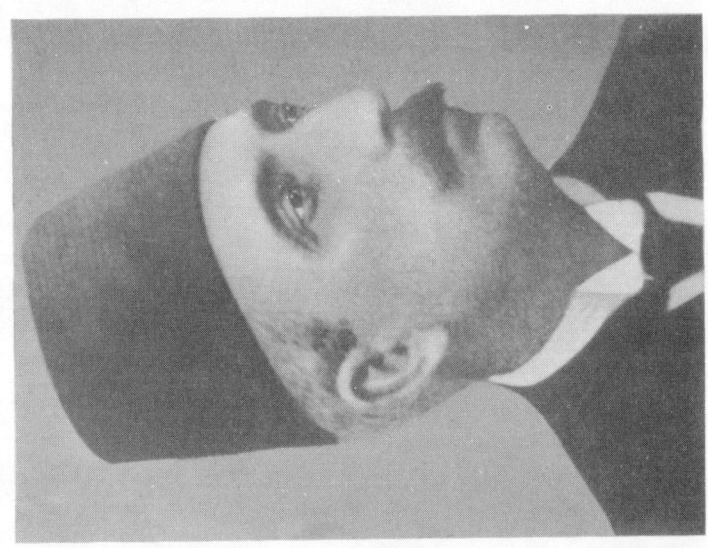

MOHAMMED VI
SULTAN OF TURKEY, 1861–1926

Mustafa Kemal needed his presence just as he needed cigarettes and cognac to stimulate his energies. He needed a man with whom, in moments of leisure, he could philosophize. In Arif's company he liked to pick to pieces the characters of their closest collaborators, exposing their weak points with merciless candour. And so Arif must be at hand always. Arif, though, burned with ambition and desired a more active field for his labours.

Often, when standing behind his friend, watching him while he slept, his hand would start. He knew every detail of the Grey Wolf's plans, knew his innermost thoughts, and knew his ambitions as well as his methods and ways. He was tempted to press the trigger and put an end to him, the steppe-wolf, the man-eater! Many would rejoice. Then he, Arif, would assume his mission, carry it through to a successful conclusion, and take the credit for it.

Suddenly a change would come over Arif: he turned pale, his eyes bulged, he trembled, looked at the masklike countenance of the other man and realized with deep emotion that Mustafa Kemal was his brother, friend and comrade—an infinitely greater man than he.

When Mustafa opened his eyes he saw Arif laughing, and laughed himself at the biting witticisms in which the colonel then indulged.

Nevertheless, Arif was a powerful man. As the intimate friend of the great Kemal he was much sought after and flattered, and great store was set on his favour and friendship. At the same time he knew well that a single false step—an offer of wrong advice, an omission, an ill-considered action—would bring him the severest reprimand and destroy him for all time.

An envoy of the "Indian Committee of the Caliphate" arrived at Angora authorized to offer on behalf of the Indian Mohammedan community a contribution of several million pounds to help the Kemalist cause. The money was on its way.

Sagir was received with great honour. He was an enthusiastic admirer of the Grey Wolf, and took advantage of every opportunity to be with him. In a very short time he was on friendly terms with all the leading men.

He enjoyed Turkish hospitality to the full. Angora resembled a disturbed beehive. Several hundred thousand people had crowded into the little town. A few hundred of them were lucky enough to have a permanent roof over their heads. The rest camped where they could find room—in tents, bivouacs and temporary shelters.

In the circumstances it was no easy matter for the police to keep a check on all persons of interest.

Nevertheless, one day a hand descended silently and heavily on the shoulder of the Indian, Sagir. Wheeling round, he found himself looking into the inscrutable faces of several secret police agents, who immediately placed handcuffs on his wrists.

At the police station he was shown a bundle of letters.

" We have been indiscreet enough to take an interest in the correspondence which you have been having with the British Intelligence Service in Constantinople. Unhappily for you, we have also succeeded in rendering invisible ink visible. It's an old trick. You will not remain long in ignorance of your fate."

Sagir capitulated and made a confession. He had been employed by the British Secret Service to assassinate Kemal, and was to receive a hundred thousand pounds as the reward.

Mustafa Kemal shook his head when this was reported to him.

" I had no idea that my head had such a high market value."

Sagir expressed one wish. He desired that, out of consideration for his family, his name might be kept a secret. The wish was respected.

A gallows was erected on a small platform.

With a smile on his lips, Sagir walked to the platform, sat down on it, and calmly waited for his execution.

The executioner politely pointed out to him that, in the circumstances, it was necessary for him to mount the platform.

Sagir bowed and smiled.

" I beg your pardon, but I have not been in a similar situation before. . . ."

The burning summer of 1921 descended upon the rocky deserts of Anatolia.

Everyone had a feeling that the decisive hour was fast approaching, and that events would presently reach a crisis.

Work was feverishly carried out on the heights of Dumlu Punar. Farther to the north the chain of mountains near Eski Shehir was fortified.

In the Turkish camp it was known that the cranes were working day and night unloading great quantities of war material from the ships in Smyrna harbour. Numerous British officers had arrived, fresh transports of soldiers were being disembarked and the front was being reinforced.

Greece and England were preparing to launch the final, crushing offensive. Between them they had nearly four times as many men as the Turkish National Army. They had artillery, munitions, aeroplanes and supplies in abundance.

The other side had nothing.

Constantine gave the command: " Forward to Angora ! "

PART THREE
THE VICTOR

CHAPTER XI

SAKARIA

ABOUT fifty kilometres west of Angora, between swampy banks, the Sakaria flows northward on its way to the Black Sea. Fever germs infest the air, and when you breathe you inhale a devilish poison. A merciless sun almost blinds you. The rocks are like oven-plates. To touch the ground is painful.

The grinning ghost of malaria thrives and lurks in the heat. Many thousand men were cast into its clutches, for suddenly this lonely, accursed land became filled with soldiers. There were two hundred thousand Greeks and about sixty thousand Turks. What a meal for the yellow ghost!

For the moment they were farther west, beyond the fever zone, fighting on the far side of the Anatolian railway, whose track groaned and shrieked under the burning axles of Turkish goods-trucks.

Often, whilst a train was in motion, flames would spurt from one of the cars. The axles caught fire, and the flames spread to the bone-dry wood of the truck. An irreplaceable load of munitions blew up.

For ten days the rocks had been trembling under the bursts of shells from the Greek heavy artillery, and the wild, yellow hill land was ablaze with the flashes of gunfire. Aeroplanes blackened the summer sky. Concealed machine-gun posts spat fire at the death-bringing birds, and more than one crashed in the wild ravines. Anatolian soldiers rushed forward, extinguished the flames, and hauled the machine to the base, to Eski Shehir. There waiting mechanics patched it up and made it more or less airworthy.

Turks who had been airmen in the Great War then proudly (and courageously) donned a flying-helmet, clambered into the " appray " (Turkish for *appareil*), often succeeded in getting off the ground and, in rare cases, making a safe return.

The enemy supplied them with everything—even with a small air force. As it happened it consumed more pilots than it was worth. But that did not matter!

These " apprays " could not be utilized as bombers, but they were of some service as scouts. Starting from Eski Shehir, or from Afiun Kara Hissar further in the south, they flew over burning villages which pointed the way to the front. But what was a fire in that hell?—why, the sun's rays almost put it to shame!

Below khaki-clad men sprang to their feet and dashed forward over rough ground. Shells screaming over their heads prepared the way for the advancing infantry.

Suddenly the advancing lines met with resistance, like waves beating against rocks. Flashes of bayonets could be seen, and patches of red-stained khaki tunics.

To save ammunition the Anatolians invariably waited for the enemy to approach, and then engaged him in shock action. Generally there were three Greeks to an Anatolian.

In the north at Eski Shehir the line held, but it grew thinner and thinner. From the air it could be seen how the Turkish regiments steadily grew smaller.

Everything had to be observed without waste of time, because it was never long before hostile 'planes made their appearance. And an " appray " was in no shape to engage in air battles.

A captured machine flew south, to Afiun Kara Hissar.

There no Turkish line could be seen, and the Turkish pilot suddenly awoke to the grim fact that the enemy had burst through.

Thousands of corpses littered the battlefield. The Greek had paid dearly for his victory.

Above Afiun Kara Hissar fluttered the Greek flag, and Greeks were busily shunting wagons in the station goods yard. On the Turkish side of the town and the railway they could be seen still advancing.

The railway was lost, irretrievably, as it seemed.

All at once came sounds of heavy firing, and it became evident that Ismet had rallied his men for a counter-attack. Artillery fire tore great holes in the Greek columns. Wounded men twisted in agony on the sun-scorched ground.

Now the Anatolians charged, in small but well-disciplined and determined formations.

The two foes met and wrestled and struggled in a furious hand-to-hand skirmish. Quarter was neither asked nor given. Prisoners were taken only for purposes of information. There was nothing to be got out of an Anatolian. He would rather be beaten to death a hundred times than allow one word to escape to a dog of a Greek.

From the west came reinforcements, and the Turks were encircled.

But again the Anatolians came forward, and for hours the

SAKARIA

hand-to-hand fighting continued. Finally it ceased, and the Greek companies, terribly reduced, clambered over the heaps of corpses and ran towards the east, in the direction of the Sakaria. Beyond the river lay Angora. The last Turkish reserves were now thrown into the battle. Arif, too, was there leading a division.

Ismet neither yielded nor allowed himself to be forced into a defensive position. But slowly his line was being shortened. Already the Greeks were beginning to extend to the north. They could afford to do so with their inexhaustible reserves, the dogs!

At all costs the railway must be held.

The enemy assailed their positions with increasing tenacity.

Where were the men for a counter-attack?

The enemy could make good his losses. Not so the Turk. No matter how hard he tried, he could break through nowhere. The wall was too thick, and the holes which he made in it were filled as fast as they were formed. In addition, there was the artillery superiority!...

But, however desperate their situation, they must hold out!

Ismet had a conference with his generals, who unanimously agreed that the railway must be held and, moreover, the lost sections regained. There were no two ways about it. Must was the watchword....

An orderly ran forward and announced:

" His Excellency Mustafa Kemal Pasha."

It was the Grey Wolf in person. He had come post-haste from Angora, and appeared, as Head of the Government, in civilian dress.

He asked for a detailed report, and after hearing it stayed silent. Although they could not tell what were his thoughts, the generals derived fresh courage from his presence, and new strength and new hope stimulated them to further efforts.

There was calm and confidence in the bearing of the leader—no trace of excitement or panic. The thoughts were active behind his strong forehead. His expression could not be read, but everybody had a feeling that, as always, he knew what he wanted.

His presence inspired new confidence, courage, hope.

Mustafa Kemal mounted a horse and rode to the first-line trenches. He was anxious to see the men, form some idea of what they were still capable of achieving, and to see for himself what was the position forward.

Not a muscle of his face moved at the sight of completely exhausted, half-dead, half-starved, wounded soldiers, who, when he gave the order, were ready at once to leap from their trenches and charge the enemy, though it meant certain death to do so.

The encircling movement was extending, and the position grew perilous in the extreme.

A decision had now to be made—a quick, irrevocable decision !

Delay, hesitation, dallying meant death.

At headquarters there was an embarrassed silence. Standing in the bare room, his voice hard and metallic, the Grey Wolf issued his orders.

They had expected to be told to hold out at any cost, until possession of Eski Shehir and the railway had been regained; but instead he ordered the baggage and stores to be taken to Angora, after which the army was to withdraw across the Sakaria. When this had been accomplished the men were to have a day's rest before digging in.

Withdraw over the Sakaria and leave the railway and many important towns in the enemy's hands?

They wondered if Mustafa Kemal had lost his nerve, or whether he had surrendered the Nationalist cause.

They wracked their brains for an explanation, but none was forthcoming. On the other hand, they had their orders, and these must be obeyed. Well, the army was to retreat across the Sakaria— it was madness, suicide pure and simple.

During the withdrawal Arif badly mismanaged his command. He led his division negligently, he made bad miscalculations, and in his hurry he arrived at many false decisions, for he had lost heart and had for the first time failed to understand the orders and failed to understand the Grey Wolf.

New armies were to be raised to replace those which had been annihilated, and press-gangs were to be sent out to comb the country for more men. Still enough men would be found to man the machine-guns, and afterwards history would not enquire how many had been sacrificed. All that would matter was who was victorious. So Arif argued.

SAKARIA

Mustafa Kemal's eyes flashed angrily when he saw him in Angora. One glance was sufficient to tell him that in the moment of greatest crisis the man had lost confidence in him.

He of all men!

In a cold but polite tone he enumerated Arif's mistakes and informed him that for the present he was to leave his command and hold himself at the disposition of the headquarters staff until he was needed.

Arif clicked his heels.

" Very well, sir ! "

A message came from the front by wire, in which Fevzi reported that the troops had dug themselves in on this side of the Sakaria.

" The position is encouraging," he said.

Mustafa Kemal praised the blind courage and faith of Fevzi the Giant and Ismet the Dwarf.

Arif bit his lips. Mustafa ordered him to attend at the National Assembly.

" Give me your arm," he said in a cool but not unfriendly way. Malaria again had him in its grip. Without comment, Arif obeyed.

They entered the assembly hall in their usual brotherly fashion, though their features were stiff and masklike.

The Great National Assembly were in a panic, and a heated discussion was being held.

On the fringe of the town were camped a great mass of refugees in an exhausted and pitiful state, having with them only such articles as they had time to rescue and carry with them. They represented the whole population of the surrendered territory and had accompanied the army on its withdrawal. Now they were clamouring for admission to Angora, which simply was unable to accommodate them. Meanwhile, the troops were digging their new trenches on the Sakaria.

The hall in the old Committee building was in a tumult. The deputies were beside themselves.

" Where will the army finish ? "

" Where will the people end up ? "

" There must be a man responsible for these events. Who is he ? "

" He's not visible."

" Where is the Pasha President ? "
" We will demand an explanation from him."
" He must take over the sole command."
" In that case many necks would appear to be in danger."
" No one will be harmed unless he is an enemy of the people."
" It looks as if the President's friends are at a loss to know what to do."
" The lukewarm were warned long ago."
" That's an insult . . ."
" Order ! Here is the pasha."

Mustafa Kemal had entered. His stick hammered the floor and his footsteps were heavy as he made his way up to the President's chair. Mustering the assembly with a calm eye, he said :

" In a month I shall have defeated the enemy."
" Listen to that ! "

The tense, awed silence was broken by peals of ironical laughter which rang through the room.

" The situation is encouraging."

He looked steadily at the Opposition. The latter challenged him.

" Is it incorrect then that the railway has been surrendered ? "

" I gave orders for our troops to withdraw across the Sakaria. The disadvantages of this manœuvre will automatically disappear in face of the successes which we shall achieve through it. It is bound to have certain moral disadvantages, but," he said, raising his voice, " we shall know how to deal with that ! "

" We'd like to see the man who really is responsible for the sorry position in which we now find ourselves at the head of the army. We should not be made responsible for circumstances which are no affair of ours."

" Quite right ! "

" The army ? " said a deputy, growing heated. " The army is defeated, and there is no further hope of retrieving the situation."

The Grey Wolf smiled.

" If it affords you any relief to bawl at me—do so ! "

Instantly the assembly calmed down. A deputy then rose and demanded that Mustafa Kemal should place himself at the head of the army. His words received universal approval. Mustafa Kemal went towards the speaker's desk.

SAKARIA

" I have given orders for a new front to be formed on this side of the Sakaria. The railway, Eski Shehir and other important points have been surrendered to the enemy. But what are the railway and Eski Shehir worth ?—nothing ! The army, on the other hand, is worth everything; and that is still in existence. At this very moment they are building the new line. In a month I shall have defeated the enemy."

The opinion of the majority of the assembly, promoted by a genuine feeling of confidence and gratitude, was that the President himself should take command of the army.

Mustafa Kemal thought quickly, and then confronted them with a demand for dictatorial powers for a duration of three months.

A vote was taken.

A short time later the Grey Wolf found himself absolute dictator and leader of nation and army. He spoke.

" The whole nation, with its feelings, actions and thoughts, must be mobilized if we are to win the war. This applies not only to those who actually are in the trenches, but the last man in the last village must be made to consider it his duty to devote his entire existence to the cause of victory. He must be convinced that the result depends upon his efforts. When this frame of mind has been established, then physical elements can be made to count. I order National agents to be appointed in each district with powers to requisition certain things. It will be the duty of each home throughout the country to furnish clothing as follows : a set of under-linen, socks and boots. With the promise of subsequent compensation, forty per cent of all foodstuffs, leather and textile goods are to be requisitioned for the army. Everyone is to be placed under an obligation to give his services, once a month, and with recompense, to carry goods needed by the army. When we speak of war we do not mean a struggle between two armies, but between two nations, both of whom are staking their very existences and who fight with every means they can find and with everything that they possess. There is all the difference between nations who seem slow in their sacrifices and those who are determined at all costs to achieve victory. Let us set to work ! "

· · · · · · ·

On the Black Mountain, close to the Sakaria, a field outpost lay behind some boulders and kept a watch forward. Weird-looking were the home-made iron spikes which, in place of bayonets, they had fixed to their rifles.

"I think I am slowly beginning to understand the Bash-Kommandan," said one of the men. "The enemy will take a damn long time to follow us here. It has taken him four weeks to arrive in the district."

"And, by Allah! we haven't got any weaker in those four weeks. The Greek dogs must have worked like slaves during that time, getting familiar with the unknown territory, establishing their bases and camps and organizing their supplies. That sort of thing uses up time and strength. Now do you understand the Bash-Kommandan's order? Now do you understand why it was we crossed the Sakaria?"

"Perhaps to-morrow or the next day I shall. That's when the shells will start falling. Wonder if we'll win?"

"The Bash-Kommandan has said we shall win. So we shall win. There—do you see? See them crawling along over there? They're here, the Greek dogs! Wish we could send them a few shells!"

"They're still a long way away."

. . . .

The guns thundered and echoed over the hills and vales as the Greek divisions on the west bank of the river advanced towards their goal. The batteries were in position and the whole war machinery had been set in motion. High above everything, on a prominent site, stood King Constantine's standard, which could be seen all over the country-side.

The last chapter of the glorious expedition was to begin.

"Forward to Angora!"

On the other side, close to the front line, in the little village of Alaghersh, stood the Turkish staff.

Wearing an ordinary private's uniform, without badges of rank, stood Mustafa Kemal, the Bash-Kommandan, with a number of his generals.

"Gentlemen, let us rid ourselves of the idea that our hopes rest upon any particular line of defence. Each unit is to fight its own battle, without regard for what may be happening on its flanks. Units may be ejected from their positions. In that case they will form a fresh front on the nearest rise. There are no lines of defence, but there is an area of defence, and that area is the whole country."

He mounted his horse and rode forward to inspect the positions. Enormous activity was apparent everywhere. Pleasure was written on the faces of the Anatolian soldiers as the Bash-Kommandan rode up to them.

A long procession of women, with children tied securely on their backs, marched to the front line carrying shells for the artillery. Farther in the rear were numbers of bullock-carts, in which the munitions had been brought from the base. On the fringe of the fighting zone they were unloaded by women, and from that point everything was carried by hand. No men were available for these duties.

The women marched along silently and bravely, bent under the weight of their burdens, often under fire and in danger of being struck by shell-splinters. The children, scared by the noise of battle, whimpered pitifully.

A nation was at war.

The wind drove hot sand into the eyes.

Mustafa Kemal turned his horse in the direction of the Black Mountain, the key position of the Turkish front.

Loose stone slipped from under the horse's hooves. Suddenly the horse itself slipped, lost its balance and fell on the rider.

Mustafa Kemal was picked up, and it was seen that he was very pale. His chest was extremely painful, and he found it impossible to move.

Faster than the wind the news travelled along the line that the commander-in-chief had broken a rib. It was necessary for him to go to hospital in Angora for treatment.

An accident to the commander-in-chief on the day before the big battle !

Heads drooped. It was a bad omen.

In Angora a man lay motionless while the surgeons examined him. If only they patched him up, they might torture him as much as they liked. He must get back to the front !

On the southern sector the Turkish front had already been

burst. It was very evident that the Greek was aiming at a penetration in the south with the object of cutting off the Turks from Angora.

There was now bitter fighting for every inch of ground. Soon the hot, parched soil was steeped in blood.

Slowly the Anatolians yielded. The Greeks pressed forward with redoubled energy. The hills crumbled under the bursts of the heavy shells.

The Black Mountain at the moment was still held by the Turks.

The word then passed from mouth to mouth that the commander-in-chief had returned.

"The Bash-Kommandan is back!"

The soldiers shouted the news from trench to trench. The message was hardly believed, but it was passed on.

"He's been seen at headquarters in Alaghersh."

The men were dubious. There had been so many rumours during the last few weeks. It was probably a trick to rouse their spirits.

A stimulant for their courage!

The Anatolian fire grew more intensive, their bayonet attacks fiercer. The Greeks began to notice that the opposition was increasing, that the enemy was no longer fighting with his back to the wall. Their progress grew slower, their losses heavier. The Anatolians were fighting like devils.

The Bash-Kommandan *had* returned.

The soldiers could scarcely believe their eyes. Had Allah worked a miracle? There he was, pale, riding with difficulty, his horse on a leading-rein—an ordinary soldier in a well-worn tunic devoid of all ornamentation. He visited the forward positions, issued orders, and by his very presence put new life into the men.

Mustafa Kemal was back at his command.

On reaching the Black Mountain he shouted to the soldiers:

"A sign from Allah! Here, where I broke my rib, we will break the enemy's resistance."

Duty had called the Grey Wolf back into the ranks of the fighting men. Wearing a temporary bandage, he had returned to the front to direct the battle. All the while he was suffering great agony, for the fractured rib had penetrated a lung.

· · · · · ·

KEMAL ATATURK WITH HIS WIFE, LATIFEH HANOUM

The thirteenth day of the battle.

Mustafa Kemal sat at a big table studying a map by the light of an acetylene lamp.

It was a bare apartment containing a camp-bed, hardly used, a couple of chairs and the big table with a map spread out on it. Those were his quarters.

Orderlies came and went, and on all hands there was evidence of great activity; Refat had returned to duty, and was performing wonders in organizing supplies and seeing that stores reached their destinations on time.

Evening in Alaghersh.

Reports came in. Mustafa received them without comment, though his hand appeared to tremble slightly as he took one of the little flags from the map and replanted it a few millimetres farther back. Every evening it was the same; the flags had to be set back a few millimetres.

Sitting on the camp-bed was Arif. During the day he had been touring the front to see for himself how the battle was developing. From time to time Mustafa fired brief questions at him.

Arif, who by this time knew every inch of the district, supplied the answers.

He then relapsed into silence, thought of the old bear at home and Ayesha, the aged housekeeper. . . .

He knew that although he might lose everything else, friendship, comradeship and the great plans which he had for the future, Ayesha would stick to him.

Mustafa turned round and faced him. They were quite alone.

" To think of the future for a moment—what is going to happen ? This time we can't take the line back as we did a month ago at Eski Shehir. On the other hand, shall we allow ourselves to be slowly driven back to Central Asia, where our nation once had its home ? "

The recently reprimanded colonel shrugged his shoulders and smiled.

" There are still plenty of men in the country who place very little value on their lives. We can hold out for a long time yet."

Mustafa said nothing. His face turned ashen. Arif recognized that their opinions were no longer the same. The man in front of him, suppressing a groan with difficulty, was tortured by the thought of the number of lives that had already been sacrificed. Arif was a war-monger. What did human lives mean to him?

Both men felt that they belonged to two totally different universes. They began then to speak about the past, of the early days in Angora when they watched over each other as they slept; and Mustafa mentioned that dark hour in Erzerum when their fates hung upon the decision of Kiazim Karabekir, on which occasion they had sworn to sell their lives as dearly as possible and to stick together to the end.

This last Mustafa said with special emphasis. It might have been that he was drawing a comparison between their present position and their position at Erzerum.

Arif looked at his friend with increased interest. Mustafa was the same as ever. There was nothing in his attitude which suggested that, only a short while ago, he had severely reprimanded his friend. Nevertheless, they were two distinct spheres, strictly separate from each other. Arif as a soldier was practical enough to realize that. But he must possess political influence over Mustafa, for he was in no wise prepared to subordinate himself to men like Fevzi and Ismet for whom he had nothing more than a contemptuous smile.

If in their present hopeless situation Mustafa were to summon him to attempt some bold, adventurous coup, he was as ready as had been the old Turkish generals in the past; and if there was no other way, he was prepared to force his way to the tent of the enemy commander and put him to the sword. With Mustafa at his side he would not fear death, and many a Greek dog would pay the penalty before he.

Mustafa appeared to have similar thoughts.

Soon, however, he was again immersed in his calculations; he had dismissed from his mind the past and future, and was concentrating on the urgent needs of the present.

Arif rose and quietly slipped out into the night. On the threshold stood a group of staff-officers whispering. Arif passed on without looking at them.

From the roof the Turkish crescent banner fluttered in the steppe wind. An artillery duel was in progress, and in between the reports of the guns could be heard the howl of a wolf, or cry of a jackal, as it prowled over the battlefield.

Mustafa Kemal dragged himself with an effort to the camp-bed, cautiously lowered himself on to it, but after a few minutes again stood up and wandered restlessly up and down the room. Every movement caused him acute pain, but he had to be doing something. It tortured him even worse to keep still.

Going over to the map, he reconstructed the situation for the thousandth time and again assessed the various possibilities.

But still he could visualize no way out of the terrible predicament.

He wondered whether to wait and see if the Greeks would gradually crumble against the incredible resistance which the Anatolians were maintaining. And he wondered, too, how much longer these brave fellows would be able to hold out.

The telephone rang. It was an appeal for more shells and small-arms ammunition.

Presently all sectors of the front began to cry out for munitions. There were no more to send.

Gradually one battery after the other became silent. In addition, all that might be termed reserves was a thin line of troops held a little in rear of the front.

The first grey streak of dawn appeared in the sky.

A lonely man breathed a sigh of relief and summoned his staff. Horses were fetched and the little group rode out to the forward positions.

They found bitterly determined batches of soldiers lying in blood and filth, firing an occasional bullet from their meagre supply, and chewing a few grains of maize between shooting. It was their first meal for a fortnight.

Many lay where they had lain yesterday. They would never stir again. But the enemy, in a three and fourfold numerical superiority, had not ceased to attack their positions—who, then, had time to attend to the removal of the dead?

Officers, almost at the end of their strength, rushed from point to point.

Everywhere it was the same picture, along the whole of the hundred-kilometre front. The army was slowly but surely bleeding to death. The enemy, too, had bled, but he could stand more of it. The resistance of the Anatolians had yet to shake him. Now his heavy batteries were hurling great masses of metal at the Turkish positions, who were practically unable to reply, let alone reply in kind !

Soon all munitions had been expended.

Another long night of torture and anxiety passed in the small farmhouse at Alaghersh. The faces of the staff-officers were tense and sullen. They were in despair.

" As long as the enemy fails to take the Chal Heights we need not fear the worst," said Mustafa Kemal, encouragingly. " But if they do fall into the enemy's hands, then we are in a trap and our line of retreat is cut."

He examined the map and then pointed with his finger to the spot where Chal-Dagh, the last key position before Angora, was situated.

Mustafa Kemal was then called away to the telephone.

He was very pale when he returned and informed his officers that the Chal Heights had been in the enemy's possession for some hours.

In the small, low-ceilinged room of the farmhouse there was no sound. The flapping of the flag on the roof began to get on their nerves.

A rapid decision had to be made.

Mustafa Kemal gave orders for the left wing to be taken back, so that the front formed a right-angle.

In the streets and public squares of Angora people knelt on the ground, touched the ground with their foreheads, and prayed for victory. Sounds of artillery fire were borne to them on the wind. The monotone singing of the prayers was punctuated by the sounds of shells bursting in the distance.

Another day and another night passed.

In the small room at Alaghersh staff-officers were discussing final possibilities. The situation was desperate in the extreme. A retreat meant certain defeat, while continued resistance meant probable defeat. Was there any alternative?

Not far from them, bending over the map as though hypnotized by it, was the commander-in-chief. For the last twenty-four hours he had been less worried and seemed to have regained a spark of his lost confidence.

The time was getting on for two o'clock. Nerves were threatening to give out.

SAKARIA

Suddenly the 'phone-bell rang. The officers roused themselves and strained their ears to catch the message.

They could hear Mustafa Kemal speaking, in a series of disconnected, unintelligible phrases, but . . .

Were they dreaming? Could it be true? Or were they the victims of overstrained nerves? What was it that the C.i.C. had just said?

Distinctly now they heard his cold, metallic voice:

" . . . The Chal Heights regained? The enemy at the end of their strength? . . ."

As well as his fractured rib would allow, Mustafa Kemal sprang to his feet.

" Gentlemen, this is the great turning-point."

There was a slight tremor in his otherwise cold voice.

" The enemy is beaten. When we withdrew our southern flank we confronted him with a task which was beyond him. We will dictate the next step. We must counter-attack at once ! "

A few minutes later he was in the saddle. A small group of horsemen disappeared into the night, trotting in the direction of the front line.

With an angry gesture General Papulas threw away his cigarette. Suddenly the Greek headquarters was being bombarded with appeals for help on the southern wing. What was wrong there? No one could rightly say. All that was known was that the Turks had taken their line far back and that they had been pursued as fast as the Greeks could follow. What happened after that remained to be discovered.

Gradually Papulas was able to put two and two together. His men, it appeared, had advanced rapidly and in their haste had failed to establish essential rearward communications. They were now in a waterless hell, cut off, without munitions and without supplies. Between front line and base contact had been severed.

Papulas swore furiously.

He was finding the enemy more than a match for him. Instead of launching his counter-attack in the south, where it was expected, the Grey Wolf now began to mass troops in the north. Air observers reported that behind the Turkish lines division after division was being moved to the north.

Bad news continued to arrive at the Greek headquarters.

Already the Black Mountain had been reconquered by the Turks. Mustafa Kemal stood on its summit and directed the operations from that point.

The Turks now began to exert pressure in the south, though airmen continued to report large-scale troop movements in the north.

Then the river bridge at the foot of the Black Mountain was lost.

The Greeks now began to retreat over the Sakaria. Papulas lost all control over the front; there was no holding his men now. The morale of the army, after long weeks of fighting in this Godforsaken land, had gone completely. But their enemy suddenly seemed to recover from his exhaustion. The Anatolians, sensing that victory was within their grasp, stormed forward—they were irresistible.

The battle dragged on for a further seven days and seven nights, but Papulas was not prepared to admit himself defeated. He was fighting under the eyes of his king. Moreover, the soldiers showed signs of recovering from their first shock.

At this time the situation in the north took a critical turn. The Turkish troops which had been massed on the northern extremity of the front now began to penetrate deep in the rear of the Greek lines. That deluded rebel general had taken all the men that could be spared from the fighting line and cast them on the north wing. Now a half-beaten enemy was encircling a three times larger Greek army and bottling it in.

Soon urgent appeals for aid came from the northern sector.

Papulas was lost; he could no longer avert his fate. Despite savage counter-attacks, to defeat the encircling movement, the line steadily receded, and in the north the enemy remained unshaken.

Only one course was open to him: retirement, and retirement without the waste of a single second.

On reaching the Anatolian railway the Greek army halted, faced about, and reoccupied its old positions. In Angora the National Assembly voted Mustafa Kemal the title of honour " Ghazi," and in addition awarded him the rank of marshal.

Peace reigned temporarily in the rocky deserts of Anatolia. Strongly entrenched, the two foes lay opposite each other. Winter laid its first frost on the parapets of the trenches. Soon all military activities ceased. The mouths of the guns stood facing and menacing each other, but they remained silent. . . .

Lonely and abandoned, Sultan Vahideddin stood by the tall windows of his palace, looked out over the Bosporus, and brooded. The gaiety and life that usually characterized the Yildiz Kiosk had disappeared, and in their place a gloomy, deathlike atmosphere had made its appearance. The gaiety now was confined to Angora, where the rebels were being decorated with the highest honours which it was possible for them to receive under the Crescent. Mustafa Kemal had now received the title " Ghazi "—Victor. In the whole course of Turkish history there had been only three sultans who were entitled to use this by-name.

Vahideddin silently and sullenly watched the progress of events. After the victory on the Sakaria, France had concluded a temporary peace with the Grey Wolf and had recognized him as *de facto* Head of the Government. France had also met the rebel's wishes and had ceded Kilikia without demanding anything in return for it.

In the gloomy solitude of his palace Sultan Vahideddin froze. Often he was visited by his brother-in-law, Damad Ferid. The two men on such occasions would gloomily consider what—if anything—was the best to be done.

They had one remaining hope: England. England had no thought of yielding. Lloyd George had categorically rejected all offers of peace made by the Grey Wolf and was not prepared to consider any sort of compromise. Greece, too, was willing to fight on. They still had a force far superior in numbers to that of the Kemalists, and their positions at Dumlu Punar, on the Anatolian railway, in the opinion of military experts were impregnable.

The British Commissioners were the only persons of note still seen passing in and out of the Imperial Ministries and who still paid homage to the Sultan. Anger consumed the despot when he thought of the others. Envoys from Mohammedan nations in all parts of the world now turned their steps to Angora. They assembled, too, in full force at Chankaya, where the Ghazi occupied a small country house, bringing with them costly presents, honours of all kinds and addresses, in which he was acclaimed as the Saviour of Islam and Liberator of all Mohammedans.

Was the history of 1300 years ago to be repeated ? Were all the faithful to rally round the banner of a new Mohammed ? Had a second Genghis Khan arisen ? The Islamitic world with one accord looked towards Kemal, worshipped him, and hailed him as a new prophet.

The time went on, and soon spring broke over Anatolia. Nothing happened. The two armies still faced each other and remained inactive.

Slowly the Greeks overcame the fright which they had suffered as the result of their defeat on the Sakaria.

Apparently, also, the Kemalist army had paid a very high price for victory, for as far as one could judge the Anatolians were about at the end of their tether.

England now attempted to tumble the Ghazi out of his saddle by diplomatic means. It was known that he desired peace, and accordingly it was decided to open negotiations. The Treaty of Sèvres was to be modified.

The London gentlemen were correct in their estimate. In the National Assembly in Angora the offer was received with joy and enthusiasm.

Mustafa Kemal vigorously opposed them, and resolutely declined to consider the offer, saying that there was no such treaty as that of Sèvres and that, furthermore, anyone who intended negotiations with the Grey Wolf would be well advised to leave the word " Sèvres " out of it. In addition, he refused to discuss peace with anyone until Anatolia had been completely evacuated by the Greeks.

England was not prepared for negotiations on so clear an understanding.

And so everything continued in the balance.

Summer would soon be upon Anatolia, but there seemed to be no prospects of an end to the State of War. In Angora there were long faces ; the Greeks were planted in Anatolia as firmly as ever. The chance of disposing of them through diplomatic negotiation had been frittered away by Mustafa Kemal's obstinacy. What were they to do now ? . . .

The President's villa in Chankaya now had a mistress. Shortly after the victory of Sakaria Mustafa Kemal had brought over his mother from Constantinople. Zubeida again saw her son, whom she had believed was dead, as a victor.

She was dressed wholly in white. A tall, dignified figure, she walked slowly through the rooms of the house and, in keeping with her character and usual custom, ruled the household with a rod of iron. Frequently she found fault, and not infrequently it was the Ghazi himself who was made to feel the weight of her displeasure. To-day she still expected obedience from him, and his exalted rank still did not alter the fact that he was her son.

She began gradually to have faith in his mission and in the course of time became reconciled to the fact that he had chosen a road that was so different from the one which she had intended him to follow. She became a fervent Nationalist, only disagreeing with her son when he evinced a disposition to be disrespectful and hostile to the leading representative of the nation, the Padishah. Mother and son lived side by side like two friendly great Powers. Each respected his own frontiers, but immediately showed his teeth if the other attempted to violate those frontiers. Both were fired with a determination to succeed, to achieve victory. Zubeida prayed; Mustafa calculated.

CHAPTER XII

DUMLU PUNAR

SEVERAL Greek officers were standing on the Dumlu Punar heights examining the Turkish positions through their binoculars. Owing to the heated atmosphere it was difficult to use field-glasses and they were not able to distinguish very much. Everything was in a haze.

" There seems unusual activity over yonder. The airmen report that large bodies of troops are being concentrated in the north. And apparently there is no little confusion there."

" The papers report a counter-revolution in Angora. Mustafa Kemal is said to have flown to Konia."

" Let's wait until they're all starved out."

" That's all right, but our Commander-in-Chief would be making a mistake if he did not, as a matter of precaution, reinforce the northern sector. It looks as if some despairing effort may be made there."

They laughed.

" Curse this heat! I wish we were in shady Smyrna."

" If you'd been lucky enough to belong to headquarters, you'd be there."

" Don't you think it's rather too far away? Having headquarters 300 kilometres from the front seems a little unwise."

" Let's make a four for bridge! . . ."

Being a soldier in Anatolia was not all joy. Year after year in the trenches, with nothing to eat, no proper clothing, exposed to winter cold and summer heat, and often covered by a screen of red-brown dust which obscured the sun.

Day and night there were field exercises, patrols and guards to be furnished and numerous duties which brought no laurels—it was all war training. For what purpose? The Ghazi still did not give the order to attack.

In addition to their ordinary duties, the soldiers had to supply the work of the various service and transport corps. Their only recreation was an occasional game of football.

The officers were no better off. They received not a penny more pay than the private soldier, their rations were the same, and they had to endure the same sufferings as their men.

In Angora the deputies, narrow-minded civilians, know-alls, grousers and pacifists, were continually causing trouble.

For that matter—the private soldier himself was beginning to lose faith in the Ghazi.

Although he appeared to have lost interest in his soldiers, leaving them very much to their own resources, he was busy requisitioning and hoarding all kinds of supplies and goods in readiness for the forthcoming campaign.

Meanwhile August had come. Only a few months to pass and then winter round again—another year gone. They would have to wait then until the following spring. . . .

About this time Enver re-entered the news. He was somewhere in Russia leading Turkomen against the Bolsheviks. It was said that he had been elected Emir of Bukhara, also that he had written to the Grey Wolf. The latter was supposed to have refused to permit him to return to Turkey.

Very soon after this it became known that the former Vice-Commander-in-Chief had died. He fell to the swords of the Red cavalry. That was in far-away Bukhara.

The soldiers talked about it in the trenches.

It was fate, Allah's mysterious will. What might there be in store for the Anatolians at Dumlu Punar? . . .

The Ghazi then visited the front. The men in the trenches stiffened their backs.

Near Ismet's headquarters there was a football match. All the army commanders were present to watch.

In the evening they assembled in a small hut; and on the next day it was reported that the Ghazi had left.

Now began the most exhausting period of service that the soldiers had yet known.

They marched all day under a scorching sun, heading for the north. When darkness came, they retraced their steps, at the double. This continued for days and nights. Greek observer machines flew in swarms over the Turkish lines watching this new activity.

Similar manœuvres were soon in progress on the other side, but the Greek troops instead of marching back during the night kept steadily on their way to the north.

On 25 August the word passed from mouth to mouth that the Ghazi was back at the front.

At midnight orders for the general attack were issued to all sectors of the front. At dawn the assault on Height 1310 began.

Chin-straps were tightened and rifles were given a final inspection. Batteries were ready to open fire on the word of command. Shells were grouped in small stacks in rear of the guns.

The first ray of sunlight, rising above the jagged ridge of the Dumlu Punar heights, pierced the darkness like a flaming arrow.

At that moment the earth shook under the roar of the guns and the force of bursting shells. Before the Greek soldiers had had time to rub the sleep out of their eyes, the Turks had charged their trenches and, despite their superior numbers, were ejecting them from their positions. At Dumlu Punar they were taken completely by surprise. In the north, near Eski Shehir, the assault had been anticipated and large bodies of troops were in readiness to receive it.

The Greek generals cursed and swore. In spite of the large number of troops that had been shifted to the north, they still had the stronger force at Dumlu Punar. What was the explanation, then, of the fact that the Anatolians were now storming this assumed impregnable position ? What was happening ?

What had headquarters to say ?

Nothing ! . . .

Communications with headquarters had been severed ; all that they could do was to establish feeling with the troops in the north.

This again proved to be impossible. . . .

The Anatolians with their first assault on Dumlu Punar had burst through the lines. The front had been torn into two parts.

From the Heights the Crescent banner waved. The fierce summer sun rose higher above it.

The gentlemen in Athens were beside themselves. The Commander-in-Chief, General Hadyanesti, who had spent the time enjoying himself in Smyrna, was recalled.

Trikupis, a general holding an actual command at the front, was appointed in his stead.

He attempted to restore order in his army, but his efforts were futile. The soldiers had only one ambition, and that was to reach the sea.

Trikupis then ordered that during the retreat they were to burn everything in their path—towns, villages, mosques. The civilians were to be driven into the flames with machine-guns—old men, women and children, without mercy.

Mustafa Kemal stayed on the Heights, a little in rear of his front line, saw the confusion below him and witnessed the burning country-side, from which the piercing cries of helpless victims echoed.

He issued the famous Army Order:

" *Ordular ! ilk hedefiniz ak denizdir, ilereu !* "

" Soldiers, your goal is the Mediterranean. Forward ! "

On the following day, 2 September, 1922, Trikupis and his army were captured at Chalkoi.

" *Ilereu !* "

The Anatolians stormed over the high plateau.

. . . Your goal is the Mediterranean !

The Greek front in the north, near Eski Shehir, collapsed.

Above the station buildings on the Anatolian railway, or more accurately above what was left of them, waved the Crescent flag.

Eski Shehir fell.

With that the Greeks abandoned the field, cast away their rifles, and fled wildly towards the west, towards the sea. There ships waited to rescue them.

A breathless six days' chase ensued. Anatolia was a sea of fire. The fugitives burnt everything in their road. Turkish pilots flew ahead of them and dropped warnings : let there be no senseless, cowardly destruction, no butchery of a defenceless populace !

All in vain !

The fugitive army left in its trail a desolate and terrible scene of ruin and frightfulness. No matter how hard the Anatolians pressed forward, the Greeks still found time for devastation and atrocities.

Shortly before reaching Smyrna, the Turkish army halted and re-formed. As evening drew on, General Kemaleddin Sami, subsequently Ambassador in Berlin, rode over the battlefield. A badly-wounded Greek lay there and cried out to him for water.

In Anatolia water is one of the most precious things. However, the general—incidentally he was wounded six times in the Great War—jumped off his horse, and held his water-bottle to the wounded man's lips, sacrificing his last drink. When he turned round to remount his horse, the man shot him in the back.

The Greek civil population, the Levantines and other foreigners, crazed with fear, fled back to the sea with the troops.

On the sixth day the Anatolian cavalry, which had ridden ahead of the main army, drew within sight of the Mediterranean.

The order had been carried out.

Below them lay the fair city of Smyrna.

The harbour was a scene of terror. The Greek soldiers were firing on their own civil population, driving them from the quays. The transports were for the soldiers.

The last steamer disappeared through the exit of the bay and continued out to sea.

On the quays, quaking with fear, were thousands of civilians. The spectacle was watched through telescopes from aboard the British warships which lay at anchor in the harbour.

Soon, from the east, Anatolian horsemen galloped into the city.

All warnings were now unheeded: the Anatolian soldier was not going to be cheated of his right to reprisals.

Along the Anatolian coast the Mediterranean swallowed Greek soldiers and civilians by the thousand.

Mustafa Kemal with his flying staff closely followed the army. He was on this occasion, as on all others, confident of complete victory, and for that reason he paid small heed to the numerous, often conflicting, reports which arrived at his headquarters. His calculations had been thorough and accurate. His mathematical problem was now solving itself as he had foreseen.

At Ushak, half-way to Smyrna, he made a halt.

The smiling province of Aidan had been transformed by the fleeing enemy into a smoking hell. Outside his headquarters assembled a howling mob of protection-seeking Greeks. These incendiaries and murderers of defenceless women and children were chased off with whips. To the Devil with them!

Mustafa took not the slightest interest, but quietly continued making his calculations.

The captured Greek commander and his C.G.S. Dionis shook at the knees when they were summoned to the Grey Wolf's headquarters at Ushak.

They thought of the burning villages, the devastated vineyards and of the blackened corpses of women and children that they had left in their route.

The two men who were responsible for these senseless, cowardly atrocities turned pale as they entered the presence of the Grey Wolf.

The Victor, the new Genghis Khan, stood before them. On his right stood Fevzi the Giant, on his left the small, wiry Ismet.

Mustafa Kemal coldly but politely shook hands with them, asked how they were faring and whether they had everything they wanted.

An orderly brought in coffee and cigarettes.

The two men scarcely dared to breathe. Mustafa asked them a number of questions and gradually there developed a discussion of the recent events.

He then glanced at his watch. Their interview was at an end.

" War is a game of chance," said the Grey Wolf. " You did what you could. Take comfort in that."

The two prisoners slipped out.

Mustafa, Fevzi and Ismet exchanged glances. Mustafa shrugged his shoulders and gave a short, scornful laugh.

Poor specimens !

Forward !

The route from Uif to Smyrna was one of the most moving journeys of triumph that ever a victorious general made.

The staff progressed towards the city in a long line of motor cars. At the head was Mustafa's car. All the vehicles were decorated with laurels. Great crowds of people lined the roads and children were held aloft in order that they might see their deliverer. For kilometres on end thick walls of people knelt by the roadside weeping and praying; then the procession passed more crowds whom the miracle had left speechless, people with tear-stained eyes, stretching out their arms towards the deliverer as he passed by. People with mutilations and terrible scars from burns ran alongside the car hoping to obtain a glimpse of the Grey Wolf and perhaps kiss his hand; his life-guards were powerless to interfere. The whole country-side echoed with the sounds of cheering. Over and over again the shout was repeated:

" Long live the Ghazi ! Long live the Deliverer, the Messenger of Allah ! Our lives for the Saviour ! "

Shortly before the city a cavalry escort was waiting, formed up on both sides of the street, with drawn swords.

In the city itself the horsemen clattered at the side of the car, sparks shooting from under their horses' hooves as they rode along. Tremendous cheering and shouts of " Long live the Ghazi ! " were raised on all sides.

On the quays of the harbour stood groups of Anatolian cavalrymen looking across the water and laughing scornfully at the British warships, whose officers and men, on the previous day, had been silent and awestruck spectators of the gruesome scenes which had been enacted before their eyes. There were no movements in the great ships ; England was checkmated.

The commanding officers swore under their breath as the triumphal procession slowly passed the quays. Mustafa cast a brief glance at the warships, powerless, fettered giants. A brief, contemptuous smile played on his lips.

A few days later half the city of Smyrna was on fire. Greeks were the incendiaries. The Christian quarter was reduced to ashes. Smyrna resembled a huge torch. In olive groves and amidst vines on the hills near Smyrna could be seen the camp fires of the cavalry, and from time to time there was a great explosion as an ammunition dump blew up. The streets resounded with cries and shots. Turkish troops were hunting for concealed Greeks, seeking the incendiaries and those dogs who had cut all the fire-hoses.

Standing on the balcony of a country house at Burnabad, on the hills, was Mustafa Kemal, watching the terrible, awe-inspiring scene at his feet.

" It is a sign," he said, " a warning sign that Turkey will be cleansed of traitors and foreigners. Turkey belongs to the Turks ! Turkey for the Turks ! It is accomplished ! "

In Europe people had not had time to grasp the significance of recent events.

Envoys hastily despatched from England, France and Italy set out on the journey to Smyrna.

ANGORA
Kemal Ataturk's villa in the grounds of his model farm.

Only the French envoy, General Pellé, succeeded in reaching the Ghazi in time and in learning what were his demands.

He then vanished from Smyrna and the Allies suddenly found themselves confronted with an entirely new situation. The National army had left Smyrna for the north and was proceeding with the utmost haste towards the Straits. Volunteers for the victorious army came from all parts. Pride and enthusiasm among Turks were boundless.

Their solution of national problems was to drive the British into the Sea of Marmora and then march on Athens.

Enthusiastic congratulations from India, North Africa, from America and even from France and Italy arrived in Angora.

But Mustafa remained cool and clear-headed, cooler than his army and cooler than his people. He demanded free right to march through the Straits Zone for the purpose of expelling the Greeks from European Turkey.

Impossible! The Allied Powers would in no circumstances permit any infringement of the neutrality of the Straits Zone.

Mustafa Kemal advanced on Chanak. Seven years had passed since he had defended the Straits and Chanak against the British; now Britain was defending the Straits from him.

The Constantinople garrison, in full war equipment, marched towards Chanak. Above the barbed wire in front of the British positions Allied flags were hoisted as a warning.

Mustafa Kemal did not allow that to disturb him.

The advance-guard of his army crossed the Straits and set foot on Gallipoli.

Neutrality had been violated. It was an open challenge.

Behind the backs of the British soldiers stood the rebellious population of Constantinople, cheering the liberators, who were now crossing the Straits battalion after battalion.

"Yield! Evacuate the positions! Otherwise we shall be thrown out of them," wired General Wilson to London.

A few days later and the British troops would have been completely surrounded. The Turkish generals and their men were getting hard to hold. The Ghazi was bombarded with appeals to give the order to attack and drive the British and Greeks into the sea and then march on Athens.

But the Grey Wolf still held back, and repeated his demand.

He wanted a free right-of-way or immediate evacuation of Thrace by the Greeks.

Hours of unbearable tension dragged on. It was touch and go. The British High Commissioner, General Harington, did everything in his power to avoid a clash and ordered his soldiers to exercise the greatest self-control. Kemalists and British were perilously close to each other. Shouts passed between them.

One slip or misunderstanding and the fat would have been in the fire. Kemalist rifles were on the point of being discharged at any moment.

Mustafa, for his part, impressed on his men the need for extreme caution, but at the same time, and despite all protests, continued to advance.

Lloyd George sent forth a battle-cry and called the nation and the Dominions to war.

France hurriedly withdrew her troops from the Straits. Italy did the same.

Finally England was left alone, to deal with the situation on her own responsibility.

From the Dominions Lloyd George received polite refusals.

The obstinate Welshman was ready to burst with anger; he ordered the Fleet to proceed to the Straits and had troops sent from Malta and Egypt. Fresh formations of Kemalist troops advanced from Anatolia.

It was at this time that France decided to intervene and make peace between the two enemies. M. Franklin Bouillon went to Mustafa Kemal's headquarters and proposed an armistice. He undertook that the Allies would prevail upon the Greeks to quit Thrace.

The generals gathered at Mudania. Ismet demanded not only the evacuation of Thrace but also the withdrawal of the Allies from Constantinople.

General Sir Charles Harington had no authority to grant this.

Mustafa Kemal then ordered the advance to be resumed. Guns were pointed against the warships.

But France again interposed, and England this time agreed to a compromise. Constantinople would be evacuated, but by stages, in order that Allied honour and prestige might not be damaged.

Mustafa Kemal consented to this.

Sultan Vahideddin sustained a rude shock on learning that Constantinople was to come forthwith under Kemalist administration, that the Army of Occupation was to remain invisible and eventually depart altogether.

The National Pact had been realized. Flags were flown all over Anatolia. The Grey Wolf had gained his goal, had accomplished the impossible, had turned defeat into victory. As a victor enjoying equality of status, Turkey was to meet the Allies at Lausanne and discuss a new peace, a peace with honour.

The Yildiz Kiosk grew even quieter and lonelier. The Seraglio was now a great gilded prison. Like a shadow, the Sultan, dressed in black, wandered alone through the luxurious, high rooms of the palace. His hands played nervously with the inevitable *tespi*, the prayer-chain. He muttered quietly to himself, prayers and half-uttered thoughts. Outside, in the streets of the capital, the people cheered frantically. Crowds filled the streets, which were festooned with flags, bunting and flowers.

" Long live the Ghazi ! " shouted the people.

A soft breeze continued to carry the sound across to the Yildiz Kiosk. Pera was desolate, abandoned. All non-Turks had left the country in panic. One and a half million Greeks, with their belongings, marched along dusty roads leading in the direction of Athens. Deported !

Vahideddin was unable to grasp the significance of the new situation. He refused to believe that all was lost.

" Long live the Ghazi ! "

No, it was no dream. The cheering outside grew rather than diminished. The Sovereign, Allah's Messenger on earth, sat alone and forgotten in his palace. Nobody asked about him ; nobody seemed to be aware of his existence. The new Governor-General of the capital had already arrived ; Refat took charge of the administration, turned everything upside-down, and set to work at such a pace that the easy-going inhabitants were completely bewildered. For the first time, the flabby citizens of Constantinople made acquaintance with the more vigorous methods of Angora. Ismet Pasha, on his way to Lausanne, broke his journey in the capital, and spoke at the University. Sultan Vahideddin was ignored. Only his English friends remembered him and sent him an invitation to attend the Peace Conference. The former despot smiled bitterly.

Pale and distraught, he stood by the window and looked in the direction of Anatolia. Situated many hundred miles in the Anatolian plain was Angora. Probably the Sultan had little inkling that, at that very moment, the Grey Wolf was forcing through new legislation in Angora. The National Assembly, although surprised and a little shocked, gave it their sanction.

Immediately the telegraph wires carried the news round the world.

What the Great National Assembly had decided was that, " The Sultanate now belongs to history."

Mustafa Kemal had spoken in very clear terms.

" Sovereignty is not passed on, it is gained by conquest. Formerly it was seized by the House of Osman; to-day, the nation has secured it."

Vahideddin's pent-up wrath exploded. His curses echoed from the high walls of the Seraglio. He was determined not to stir an inch. He was not only sultan, he was caliph, too, Pope of all the Mohammedans. England with its numerous Mohammedan subjects would never permit them to dethrone the Sultan-Caliph! England!

The British High Commissioner was called.

General Harington respectfully regretted that he was powerless to do anything and tendered the advice that his Majesty should abdicate and leave the country forthwith. An English warship was in readiness to convey the Sovereign in safety to Malta.

Vahideddin was amazed; he had not envisaged this possibility.

Abdicate? Never! He was Allah's Chosen Representative. He could not dare to contemplate such a thing.

An anxious, disturbed night passed. In the Yildiz Kiosk persons came and went all through the night. The telephones were in continuous use. Messages were received and despatched.

Absorbed in melancholy thought, Sultan Vahideddin sat curled up on his ottoman. At his side was his son Ertogrul.

An elderly Pasha-in-Waiting slipped noiselessly into the room. His eyes filled with tears as he haltingly whispered:

"The rebel has proclaimed that he intends dragging the Padishah before a national tribunal as a traitor. . . ."

Vahideddin suppressed a cry, stood up, and placed his arms round Ertogrul. Trembling, he said:

"Allah, grant me my life! Anything! but not my life."

A dozen hands hastily packed the Sultan's luggage. The Padishah wandered ghostlike up and down his apartment.

As day broke, he left the palace by a small side-door. At the quay an English naval pinnace was waiting to bring him to the warship that was to take him into exile.

CHAPTER XIII

LAUSANNE

THE representatives of some dozen States stared coldly at the small, slightly-built man in the frock-coat, who appeared in the doorway of the conference hall.

So that was Ismet Pasha, Count Palatine to the Ghazi, the great soldier.

Mussolini's expression was openly hostile, Poincaré's was no more encouraging, and England's representative, Lord Curzon, was obviously at some pains to emphasize an attitude of reserve and so make clear to the Turk that they did not recognize him.

In order to accentuate the inferiority of status, the Turkish Delegation had been provided with ordinary chairs, while the other delegations had arm-chairs.

Ismet glanced round the room, and his eyes came to rest on the chairs. He understood their significance.

Why were there no arm-chairs, he desired to know?

There was a certain amount of embarrassed coughing, after which it was explained that owing to the shortness of time it had been found impossible to procure more arm-chairs.

Good, said Ismet, then we'll return when the omission has been remedied.

Lord Curzon bit his lip. In the twinkling of an eye the arm-chairs were in their place.

Ismet's determination not to be hoodwinked and brow-beaten had passed its first test.

The Peace Conference was then officially declared open, and Poincaré and the other delegates addressed the assembly.

They expressed satisfaction that at last they were able to come together and confer on certain modifications of the Treaty of Sèvres.

Ismet politely and quietly objected.

They could not proceed on that assumption. The Kemalist Government would have nothing to do with a Treaty of Sèvres. Negotiations could only be pursued on the basis of the Armistice of Mudania, which, as they were aware, he had concluded as victor. The first, unalterable condition was discussion on terms of perfect equality—or . . .

LAUSANNE

This bombshell took the Conference members completely by surprise. But whether they liked it or not they were obliged to submit. Since the days of Mudros the situation had entirely altered. They were not dealing now with an Ottoman Empire defeated in the World War, but with a Kemalist Turkey that had been victorious in the Anatolian mountains.

Could they adjourn the Conference before it had begun?

That would have been a leap in the dark.

England wanted to reach a settlement, and Mustafa Kemal wanted to reach a settlement. It was decided to preserve a sense of realities and to attempt to come to an agreement.

Ismet saw that he had not deceived himself. His bold front and resolute attitude had made an impression. His faith in the political wisdom of his most powerful and most important partner in the negotiations had proved justified.

Lord Curzon gave proof that he possessed that leading virtue of a statesman—the ability to acknowledge reality, no matter whether it happened to be agreeable or disagreeable.

The Allies continued to stress the unity which existed among themselves.

Ismet, who was slightly deaf, on this occasion displayed a pair of uncommonly sharp ears. He heard immediately the slightest discord, which from time to time disturbed the harmony of the discussion, and took these rather over-emphasized allusions to unity for what they were—an admission of the contrary.

On the face of it his position may not have appeared a very favourable one, but as a Kemalist he knew that an individual was more than a match for a multitude. In numerous instances this had been proved in history.

Once more they attempted to overawe him with the methods which were used all too often and with extreme thoroughness at the Peace Conferences in 1918. They desired morally to drive Turkey into a position of defence and began to cast up the question of War Guilt.

The small, rather deaf general immediately opened a counter-attack. It was a question, he complained, which the victors were constantly putting to the defeated, and he refused categorically to enter into any discussion about it. In order to arrive at any definite decision about the matter it would be necessary to review in all details the history of the last thirty years, and the Turkish Delegation had neither the time nor the inclination to enter upon such academic and practically worthless discussions.

Their demands were equally as clear as they were simple and just. They desired for the new Nationalist State complete independence in political, economic and military matters.

The Turkish Delegation pointed out that the Allies themselves had gone to war simply and solely to secure self-determination for the nations.

Two years ago it would have been impossible for such words to be used, but at this Conference Right was once more a powerful weapon, for in this case the justice-seeking had fought for, and secured for themselves, a position of might.

In the first phase Ismet was victor.

Now began the main part of the Conference. Clearly it was a straight issue between the two protagonists, Ismet and Curzon. The rest receded into the background, had only secondary roles to perform.

Turkey and England were anxious to establish a new relationship that was to be free of all ambiguity and sources of conflict. First the numerous misunderstandings, which had been accumulating for centuries, had to be cleared out of the way. On both sides there was suspicion, mistrust, contempt, hatred.

Ismet introduced a new tone to the proceedings, displaying a candour to which diplomacy had hitherto been a stranger. Every nation had its right to exist. When governments were prepared honourably and unreservedly to recognize this principle, there should be no great difficulty in harmonizing the various interests.

Kemalist Turkey had no ulterior motives to serve. It had not the remotest intention of making war on any other nation. All it demanded was justice and recognition and assurance of the liberty which it had just secured, at the cost of great sacrifice, with the sword.

Ismet knew that it would not be easy to convince Conservative England of the genuine non-aggressive intentions of the new Turkey. Not two years ago Mustafa Kemal had been described in

London as a bandit. This had not been forgotten in the Kemalist camp.

Days, weeks, months passed. The Conference was still in session in Lausanne. It was not so much a conference as a fight, a hard-fought duel between Ismet and Curzon. The others were merely spectators, go-betweens. Ismet was no diplomat of the old school. He had no desire or intention of tricking his partner in the negotiations. England was to be satisfied. The legitimate interests of the Empire were to be respected. A Peace was to be concluded that was acceptable to both parties.

At the same time, the small, deaf general—he made a habit of having everything repeated in order to gain time to compose a ready answer—drew a well-defined boundary where all concessions ceased.

The defeat in the Great War was fully acknowledged. As the price for that, Mustafa Kemal was prepared to pay over all non-Turkish provinces. It was a high price, and the fact that Mustafa Kemal paid with a light heart, without reserve or ill-feeling, made it no less valuable to England. On the contrary, England had no need in future to worry about interference from the Kemalist side.

Soon the vexed question of the Straits was occupying a prominent position in the negotiations. Hardly had the name " Dardanelles " been mentioned when spectres of the past made their unwelcome entry to the scene. For a good two hundred years the Straits had been one of the chief danger points in European politics. The problem was rendered even more complex by the confusion of treaties which had been formed round it. Old, unforgotten grievances and threats were reawakened.

It was almost as though the men who died on Gallipoli might be heard uniting in the chorus: Enough of this interminable wrangling! Solve the question once and for all; free Europe of this source of peril!

In the treatment of this question of the Narrows Soviet Russia had been admitted to the Conference to have an opportunity of stating its case. The scene underwent a change. The real opponents now were Tchitcherin and Curzon.

Tchitcherin demanded that Turkey should acquire full and absolute sovereignty over the Straits.

The Straits are free. Turkey is the sole prophet of Freedom.

That was the claim made by Soviet Russia.

Curzon now had an opportunity of confirming that Ismet was a statesman of no mean ability.

The Turkish general subjected his zealous Russian ally to a sharp scrutiny. As a Nationalist this solution of the Straits Question was very acceptable to him, but he knew that it was not to be achieved at this Conference, that it would not be achieved at Lausanne.

England returned an unconditional " No ! " to the Russian demand. England intended to continue to occupy the Straits and could afford to be unyielding.

If Ismet adopted the Russian standpoint as his own, the Conference would break down and the situation would remain obscure and pregnant with dangers. Peace would recede farther than ever. Sooner or later guns would fire again.

That might suit very well certain, far-aiming Soviet Russian plans. But Turkey's urgent need was peace. England discovered herself in a similar position.

Much to everyone's surprise, Ismet ignored the Russian demand. Turkey certainly was not willing to act as door-keeper of the Narrows for the Russians. She did not wish to become a Russian pawn in the game against England.

Turkey was pursuing an essentially independent, national policy and was not going to allow herself to be taken in tow by any foreign Power.

And so Ismet accepted the compromise which England offered.

Freedom of the Straits and demilitarisation of its shores.

That meant abandonment of sovereignty over one of the most important areas of the Nationalist State. The Turkish nation had bled for complete independence. Had not Ismet given away too much at Lausanne?

Already grumbles were heard in Angora. There were many men in close association with the Ghazi who had taken a distinct dislike to the small, semi-deaf general, and they knew, too, of the extent to which he enjoyed Mustafa Kemal's confidence. It was a risky thing to attack the Grey Wolf. On the other hand, there was nothing to prevent people from attacking Ismet.

It was spread about that Ismet, in respect of the Straits Question, had let his country down at Lausanne.

In far-off Angora Mustafa Kemal placed himself before his paladin and defended and approved his attitude.

Turkey desired and must have peace. She had to pay the price of it to England. Politics was the art of doing what was possible. Granted, it was intolerable that they should have a demilitarized zone and that they should not be in a position to defend Constantinople against possible violent measures undertaken by a foreign Power.

But had Constantinople the same crowning importance to the new Turkey that it had possessed for the old Ottoman Empire?

Constantinople, said Mustafa Kemal, was no longer a Turkish city in the strict Nationalist sense. Constantinople was an international city. It had revealed itself to be the chief centre of reaction. The curiously mixed population, consisting for the most part of elements who were bitterly opposed to the new order of things, at the present time could not be relied on and had no claim to any sort of confidence. Through the removal of the Russian danger in the East the Straits had lost a great deal of their significance to the new Turkey. But for England the question remained as urgent as ever. England could not, and would not, make any concession. Her obstinacy was aimed not so much at Turkey as at Soviet Russia. They must learn to distinguish the upper from the lower notes in the political concert.

In this case it was shrewd statecraft to show a certain willingness to yield.

The Conference in Lausanne continued. In general there were no great difficulties in coming to an agreement concerning the frontiers of the Nationalist State. That was not to be wondered at, since Mustafa Kemal had already as good as drawn them with his sword.

However, a definite decision with regard to the Turkish-Irak frontier led to some sharp disagreement. Both Ismet and Curzon claimed the Province of Mosul.

England demanded the union of Mosul with Irak, not simply on account of Mosul oil but, principally, for strategical reasons.

The Vilayet of Mosul was the doorway to Irak. Suddenly the world became filled with suspicion of the men in Angora.

Would Mustafa Kemal, after a short breathing space, summon the Arab peoples to fight against England? Was his ultimate goal the revolutionizing of all Mohammedans?

The echo of his victory had reached the Islamitic world, where it had had a tremendous effect. He was being called the Messenger of Allah and a second Mohammed. All the hopes and all aspirations towards independence on the part of the Eastern peoples were inspired by the man who had seized unto himself the sword of Osman and who had employed it so successfully against the Christian world.

People suddenly began to ask themselves, did he meditate uniting the Eastern races in a new invasion of Europe? Western imagination, excited and overstrained in the Great War, feared that the spirit of Genghis Khan had risen from the plains of Central Asia and descended upon the leader of New Turkey.

The atmosphere in the Conference room was charged.

Ismet was not willing to give up claim to Mosul. The majority of the inhabitants of the Vilayet were Turks. The position from the point of view of Right was perfectly clear.

Quite so—said Curzon—perfectly clear. England was *de facto* possessor of the territory by reason of her victory on the Palestine front.

There was not one right for victors and one right for defeated. There was a single Right, and that was on the Turkisk side. The inhabitants of the Vilayet were Turks and by reason of the National Pact should have their place within the new Nationalist State. Moreover, the territory was not occupied until after the conclusion of the Armistice of Mudros.

So Ismet argued.

Curzon contradicted.

The Vilayet was populated by a Kurdish majority. The Kurds were not Turks.

Ismet grew indignant.

For centuries the Kurds had lived side by side with the Turks. They were a brother race. It was impossible that they should be given to Arab Irak. Furthermore, two years ago they took up arms against the British.

What did that prove, Curzon parried? Had the Turkish Government never been called upon to deal with revolts in their occupied territories?

On both sides tempers began to rise and it became evident that there was no prospect of an agreement on this point being reached.

Was the Conference to collapse on a part-question?

Ismet again gave proof of his qualities as a statesman and of his sense of responsibility. He accordingly proposed leaving the Mosul question entirely out of the programme of the Conference for the present. The interested parties might then have an opportunity later of coming to an amicable arrangement. Until such time the *status quo* would be binding on both parties.

No less serious difficulties were caused through the Turkish demand for an exchange of populations with Greece. About two million Greeks lived in Anatolia, although a large percentage, admittedly, had fled with the defeated army.

Mustafa Kemal was determined to make Anatolia a purely Turkish land. The foreign minorities must be uprooted and expelled, unfortunately by a violent process. This would entail great misery and suffering to those concerned, but history knows no mercy when her hand is forced.

But consider how much misery this motley collection of races brought to the East! In them lay one of the chief causes of the disaster of the old Ottoman Empire.

Turkey for the Turks!

On this question Ismet was unyielding.

The Conference agreed in principle. The materialisation of this sole instance in history of a mass deportation was to be the subject of discussion at a later date.

The negotiations grew more dramatic as the Conference proceeded.

Presently came the trickiest and most difficult question of all— that of the capitulations.

Ismet demanded the complete removal of all privileges which had formerly been granted by the sultans to foreigners in consideration of loans. The *Dette publique*, the International Debts

Administration, the real ruler of the old Ottoman Empire, must disappear, and with it all the many forms of control, concessions and restraints.

Away with the inextricable tangle of treaties and contracts, through which no man could possibly find his way!

The desire was to clean the slate of the past centuries, Ismet explained.

This matter affected the Allies' most vital interests. The system of capitulations was a convenient and certain method of maintaining a control over the Ottoman Empire. Now this was to come to an end, the Turk desired to be master in his own house.

The Ottoman Bank, which held the exclusive right to issue notes, was controlled principally by French capital.

Such conditions were intolerable to the Kemalists.

The Allies endeavoured to make it clear to Ismet that Turkey without the help of the European Powers simply could not exist. The country had been bled dry, was backward and devastated; what could it do without external aid?

The financial experts drew horrible pictures of what might be expected if Turkey carried her independence to this stage.

Turkey could only survive with the assistance of loans. But—the delegates smiled coolly and sarcastically to themselves—who would be willing to grant loans to an economically ruined land?

No one need worry himself unduly about that, retorted Ismet, New Turkey would defend herself as tenaciously against foreign money as she had done against foreign soldiers. She would work for her own recovery entirely with the means at her disposal.

The people in Angora were wished luck, but at the same time it was pointed out to Ismet that Turkey lacked everything that, in a civilized State, was essential as the *prima facie* basis of economic independence. The country not even possessed a proper legal code; all it had was the Sheria, the ancient Islamic ecclesiastical code.

Ismet wore a superior smile. They would very soon alter that.

A bitter struggle continued. No concession was to be got out of Ismet, not the slightest foreign privilege, not the merest suggestion of the old capitulations—they were a disgrace, worse even than ruin!

LAUSANNE

In the face of this heroic attitude on the part of the war-seasoned soldier all legal and commercial arguments lost their force. They automatically collapsed.

But Curzon and his allies were not willing at once to admit themselves beaten. In particular, the French were unwilling to give up all hope. Poincaré, the representative of close-fisted petty *bourgeoisie*, saw a danger to French savings.

An endeavour was made to reach a compromise.

Ismet again stated that his decision was irrevocable.

Curzon now became ruffled and threatened to take his departure.

Ismet shrugged his shoulders. If his Lordship was prepared to take the responsibility on his own shoulders . . . !

It was eight in the evening. Lord Curzon drew attention to the fact that his train left at nine. So Ismet still had an hour in which to reconsider the matter. He hoped to be able to take pleasant memories back to London with him.

The two men bowed to each other.

Ismet left and returned to his hotel, which was immediately invaded and overrun by the French delegates.

The French implored the Turkish general to accept the compromise. There was still time. The train had not yet left the station.

Ismet expressed regret. He could not consent to any sort of compromise nor tolerate any veiled capitulations that were irreconcilable with the honour of an independent State.

The Frenchmen attempted fresh entreaties, then flattery.

Monsieur Bompard reminded him that Marshal Foch had elected to conclude an armistice with the Germans rather than march to Berlin. Ismet Pasha, too, was a great soldier.

Eh bien, said Ismet, and at Mudania I acted in very much the same way that Marshal Foch acted at Compiègne. What was there to stop the Nationalist army from marching to Athens, or for that matter to Constantinople?

Lord Curzon waited on the platform, watch in hand. Already the train had been held up half an hour.

His Lordship then lost patience, but decided to wait a few more minutes.

No signs of Ismet.

Curzon stepped into the train, the door slammed, and the train slowly set itself in motion and vanished into the darkness.

The Conference had broken down. Uncertainty and peril again cast their shadows over the East. Would war break out again? Was mankind to suffer still more misery?

In Angora a bitter debate in the Great National Assembly continued for nine days.

Everybody who had been angered by the dethronement of the Sultan, and all those who were jealous of the personal power of Mustafa Kemal, pounced on Ismet. He was treated as a man who had been defeated. Clumsiness was the mildest of the terms which were applied to him.

Mustafa Kemal allowed the storm to subside, again showing that, despite being a man of action, he could wait when necessary.

With the present Parliament no work could be done. The Opposition had nothing better to do than drag out the debates, argue about matters which were of no concern, and produce greater confusion.

Mustafa Kemal, the Victor, had only just begun. His next great task was reconstruction of the State. This implied ruthless destruction of many ancient Turkish traditions and, in their place, the creation of new traditions: it was a leap from the Middle Ages to the twentieth century.

It was a fight that could not be won while there were individuals working at cross-purposes with the Government. As at Sakaria and Dumlu Punar, all national forces had to be mobilized and a united national will formed.

The path to this unity was to be paved by the creation of a Party sworn to give unconditional support to the aims and policy of the Ghazi. Moreover, it was to be a Party representing the will of the entire nation, not a particular group of parliamentary deputies.

While the Opposition was still hurling abuse at Ismet, Mustafa Kemal launched his blow. He dissolved the National Assembly. It had functioned for three years. Meanwhile, the situation had radically changed. It was now right that the people should be consulted.

Mustafa Kemal went into the country as a preacher and was given an enthusiastic reception by the people. He mingled with

KEMAL ATATURK ATTENDS A SCHOOL HOUR

Anatolian peasants, listened to their needs and wishes, induced awestruck people to talk and express their opinions—most of them had never in their lives seen a real pasha at close quarters, let alone a Chosen One of Allah—explained the situation to them, canvassed, and organized them.

In little, out-of-the-way villages local groups of the People's Party were formed, on strictly military lines, which owed allegiance to their President.

The election for the new National Assembly ended in a sweeping victory for the Ghazi. Not a single member of the Opposition gained a seat in the Assembly. Unity of will had been achieved. The creative work of State reconstruction could begin.

At the commencement of April Ismet went again to Lausanne. The Peace Conference resumed its deliberations.

In the place of Curzon Sir Horace Rumbold appeared as head of the British Delegation.

Ismet stuck to his old tactics—as far as possible satisfaction of British desires for the purpose of establishing a frictionless relationship between the two countries.

Sir Horace, a calmer and more diplomatic man than Lord Curzon, approved of his efforts. Between Turkey and England there were no longer any disagreements which made the prospect of an amicable settlement impossible. The question of the Straits had been solved in a manner satisfactory to Great Britain. It had meant a great sacrifice to Turkey, but that sacrifice had been made. Regarding Mosul, they were to arrive at a settlement after the conclusion of the Peace Conference.

In the matter of the exchange of population England acceded to the Turkish demands; and to relieve the Straits Pact of some of its bitterness, a concession was made. Turkey was accorded the right to maintain twelve thousand soldiers in the Straits Zone.

France was chiefly interested in the economic questions.

The same France who, at the critical hour, had placed the trump-cards in the enemy's hands, and who, dissatisfied with the early stages of the Conference, had encouraged Ismet to be unyielding. Poincaré, at the time fully occupied with the Ruhr adventure, now found himself facing an England that had settled its account with Turkey and who had no further interest in French requirements.

Ismet's clever tactics now became apparent. With the aid of France he had acquired from England practically everything that Turkey demanded, in order to have a satisfied England with which to checkmate France.

England pressed for a conclusion of the Conference and had not the remotest intention of sending a single soldier to champion the interests of the French *rentier*, whose part Poincaré now began to take—admittedly, with a considerable display of anger and with extremely little skill.

And so Ismet, by agreeing to a few, negligent limitations, was able to prevail with the Turkish claims on the question of capitulations.

In Lausanne, on the afternoon of 24 July, the bells began to peal.

Peace at last, peace after nine years' terrible war !

Ismet, as the representative of an independent State enjoying equality of status, signed the Treaty.

England showed an attitude of cool contentment. France felt that she had been cheated and was exceedingly downcast.

Italy too was disappointed. Garroni and Montagna had given themselves great pains to please Ismet and had seldom failed him with their support. He had made use of it in the same way that he had employed the French help.

Ismet, it must be admitted, was extremely suspicious of his friends. He knew that Italy expected to earn a rich reward for her services. But in that she would be disappointed. Turkey was certainly not going to permit any extension of foreign economic interests.

Would Italy remain on amicable terms when she saw that her hopes had been deceived ?

The Conference concluded without excitement or ceremony. Only one speech was made and that by the Swiss Federal President Scheuer, in his capacity as host, who addressed a few words to the delegates. He made reference to the fact that in Lausanne a peace had been concluded by peaceful negotiation, not by dictatorial methods. Now was the time, he said, for these peaceful principles to be extended over the whole world, in order that humanity might be relieved of a grievous burden. No nation should be denied the right and duty of contributing to that end.

The incredible had been achieved, Mustafa Kemal had carried his programme through. Turkey was free. Military limitations were no longer the subject of discussion at Lausanne, and political and economic shackles had been shaken off.

The victory was complete.

The nation worshipped its deliverer, called him Saviour and Messenger of Allah. The whole Islamite world was stirred. From near and far deputations pilgrimized to Angora, bringing costly presents and paying homage to the man who was considered as the new champion of Islam, as an instrument of the one true God, who sent Mohammed into the world as his prophet.

Osman's throne was vacant. Silence reigned in the rooms and apartments of the Yildiz Kiosk. The servants had departed and vanished.

Officials appointed by the Kemalist Government were now in occupation of the administrative offices. Refat Pasha was Governor-General and energetically engaged in restoring order in the capital.

The Army of Occupation was preparing for its departure. By the terms of the Peace Treaty the capital had to be evacuated by the autumn. There was still time for the troops to feel a breath of the fresh breeze which blew across the Bosporus.

The new masters indeed had nothing in common with the masters of yesterday. There was no trace in them of the peaceful lassitude and laziness of the Oriental. They lived at twentieth century pace. They applied themselves to the practical work of administration with the same fanatical zeal that their earliest ancestors had shown when they descended upon the people of the East and the Christian world with their scimitars.

Would they be successful?

The tasks which Mustafa Kemal, which history set them were so gigantic, so unprecedented, that any experienced professional civil servant would have capitulated at the outset.

These young men, leaders of a nation of illiterates and of a country still existing in medieval primitiveness, completely exhausted by an eleven years' war and ruined by the maladministration of centuries, set to work. Not with the courage of despair, nor with the rapture of Oriental visionaries, but with sober minds and amazing energy.

They knew the difficulty of their position, but they possessed two qualities which were absent in the well-nourished, venerable nations of the West: they had the faith of youth and the iron determination of the seasoned soldier.

They were not accustomed to recognizing the word " impossible," but they were accustomed to carrying out their orders.

In Angora people were now urging Mustafa Kemal to put an end to a state of uncertainty. The Sultan had been dethroned. There was no Head of the State.

A solution of this problem was easy. The entire Moslem world was ready to acknowledge Mustafa Kemal as Sultan-Caliph. The era of the Osman Dynasty was past. The era of the Kemal Dynasty could begin.

Mustafa Kemal had evolved in his mind a bold plan that was to produce a completely new situation. He had the solution of the question that was troubling many minds and which was impatiently awaited. No one had knowledge of it. He both knew how to keep silent and how to wait. But now the psychological moment had come.

The President's house at Chankaya was a moderate-sized, fairly comfortable stone house surmounted by a tower. It stood on a hill and had formerly belonged to a wealthy Armenian.

Adjoining the study on the ground floor was the reception-room, which resembled a winter-garden. It contained very little furniture, but was rich in wonderful carpets, valuable *objets d'art*, vases, pottery and many flowers. In the centre of the room a fountain played. It was a bright, light and airy apartment. The study next door was very similar. Its principal article of furniture was a large writing-table, which, save for its inevitable two vases of flowers, was usually empty.

It was the home of a modern man of the world.

Assembled in the winter-garden one October evening were several of the Ghazi's chief colleagues, who had been invited to tea— Ismet Pasha, Fethi Bey, Kiazim Pasha and Kemaleddin Sami Pasha.

Throughout the afternoon the Party Committee had been

endeavouring to solve the Government crisis. The National Assembly were unable to agree among themselves, and to complete the confusion several of the leading men had deliberately obstructed progress—on orders given them by Mustafa Kemal.

His voice was perfectly calm, almost indifferent, as he quietly informed them:

" To-morrow we will proclaim the Republic."

His followers were not surprised. Knowing the Grey Wolf, they realized that, with his nature, personality and world-ideology, that solution was bound to come.

Until late in the night he and Ismet sat at work planning the new legislation that would be necessary.

The measure was so incisive, so bold and daring, that it could not be allowed to become the subject of a long-drawn-out conflict of opinions. That would have been tantamount to condemning it to failure from the very start.

Mustafa Kemal acted as a soldier would have been expected to act. His principal adversaries, among them Refat and Kiazim Karabekir, were absent.

The Party meeting was taken by storm, and all opposition crumbled before this unexpected assault.

On the following day Mustafa Kemal admitted the deputies of the National Assembly to the Party debate, and then allowed them to discuss the new turn until they wore themselves out. Kemaleddin Sami then rose and proposed that the President of the Party should be entrusted with the solution of the crisis.

The proposal was accepted. Mustafa Kemal went to the speaker's desk, unfolded a sheet of paper, and invited them to vote on the legislation which he and Ismet had prepared a short while before.

" The form of State is a republic."

No serious opposition was raised. A little later the National Assembly met.

Late in the day the deputies proceeded to elect a State President. Ismet announced the result of the vote: the Deputy for Angora, Ghazi Mustafa Kemal, had been unanimously elected Head of the new Nationalist State for life.

A salute of a hundred and one guns proclaimed the news to a rejoicing nation.

And so the great change came about without the shedding of blood or shock of any kind. Mustafa Kemal had allowed the counter current no time to rise.

The eyes of all the world were upon him. He had now placed his cards on the table. The proclamation of the Republic was an unpleasant surprise for the entire Moslem world.

However, the pilgrimage to Angora still continued, and deputations from the peoples of India, Arabia and North Africa continued to arrive. The Russians sent a legation, in the belief that they could play him against their great opponent, England. They kept dinning into his ears that he should constitute himself Deliverer of all the Oppressed.

"There are no oppressors and no oppressed," replied Mustafa Kemal, "but there are nations which allow themselves to be downtrodden. The Turks are not one of those nations. They know how to help themselves. The others should do the same."

The Moslem deputations experienced a similar disappointment. The mere thought of making himself Sultan or Caliph caused Mustafa Kemal to laugh. They had finished with such gewgaws.

The caliphate especially was to him an exceedingly perilous institution. For many centuries it had burdened the Turkish nation with tasks, for which that nation had no direct interests. Its policy of necessity brought them into conflict with the Powers of the West.

"As British or French subjects are you in a position to carry out my orders as Caliph?" he asked the deputations.

"Then the Caliph is nothing more than a bugbear."

The non-Turk Islamite races had to accustom themselves to the fact that they might expect no help from New Turkey. Mustafa Kemal had no intention of embroiling himself in unnecessary conflicts with England, who was ruler of the great majority of Mohammedans.

Islam was, both according to its origin and its nature, imperialistic. Mustafa Kemal, however, was an implacable foe of all imperialistic aspirations. He was a nationalist. He had no ambition to be a conqueror. More than anything he desired to discard his military tunic and settle down to the peaceful, constructive tasks of civilisation.

He desired not conquests but modern civilisation.

The Western world could not understand him. He grew more puzzling to them day by day. They found it impossible to bring themselves to believe in the genuineness of his motives and honesty of his ideals.

They wondered what ulterior plans he might be fostering. To be on their guard seemed the most advisable course.

Mustafa Kemal attached little value to the opinions of the rest of the world. In ten years' time they would no longer find him a mystery or see in him any longer a second Mohammed, Saladin or Genghis Khan.

Prejudice could not be removed with words, deeds alone could dismiss it.

No matter how much the tempter may have assailed him, he had that rare strength of greatness not to budge a single inch from his chosen path. Neither glory, nor fame, nor romantic visions held any attractions for him. His goal was to make the Turks into a nation of sober, twentieth-century men of action. An aureola or place in history for himself was not what he desired.

He was no more than the first and truest servant of sovereignty by the people, and he hoped by stages to bring the people to the point at which they might govern themselves.

That was the essence of his authoritative system of government.

When at the height of success and celebrity, he was suddenly left alone.

At the commencement of 1923, when his greatest effort was needed to check the mutinous National Assembly, Zubeida died. On 26 January he stood at her grave-side at Smyrna.

Hers had been a hard life, and her son had made it into a martyrdom. Now she was able to die peacefully, for she had seen and recognized the purpose for which she had endured so much. She had heard the thunderous cheering in Angora and Smyrna, and had witnessed the parades and processions, tumultuous scenes of rejoicing and the homage; and she had experienced the unique joy of being the mother of a man who had now reached one of the highest positions in world history.

She was a typical soldier's mother, and to the very last maintained her strict régime in the household, before which even her son, the

Ghazi, had to bow. She now lay buried in Smyrna soil. Her last command to her son was: " Reconquer Salonika—for me ! "

During the last days of her life she constantly desired to return to Salonika, where, many years ago, she had lived with Ali Riza and where she had placed a golden twig in little Mustafa's hand and dressed him in a white robe when he was to be admitted to the ecclesiastical school.

Mustafa forcibly cast from his mind the memories of the Salonika days.

He now had only the nation, the brave, sturdy Turkish nation, of whom the deceased had been such a worthy representative.

It was not granted to him to enjoy a private, personal happiness. He was not made for it.

When he was on the hill-side at Burnabad watching the fires in Smyrna, standing at his side was a woman, a young woman with strikingly brilliant eyes.

In the intoxication of victory he took her to him.

This woman was seen at his side during inspections of troops and on the long tours of the devastated territory, but no one asked questions, and no one seemed surprised when, during conferences, she intervened in the debate and with her cold logic and skilled criticisms put her opponents to flight. It was known that the whole of the diplomatic correspondence with England passed through her hands and that she translated it.

She was the Ghazi's principal secretary.

Latifeh's home was Smyrna. Her father was the head of a local shipping company. She had studied in Paris, had enjoyed an all-round education, and was a woman of handsome appearance.

When the Greeks were in occupation of the city she had transmitted intelligence to the Turkish high command. Her life had hung on a thread.

After Mustafa Kemal had made his official entry into the city, and was casting round for suitable quarters, she had come to him with the offer of her parents' country house on the hill-side at Burnabad.

That for a Mohammedan woman was more than bold. But nothing pleased Mustafa Kemal better than boldness !

One day the secretary became a wife.

But Mustafa Kemal remained the grey steppe wolf. Only when he was alone, and entirely dependent upon himself, did he feel happy and strong.

He was a man of solitary nature; his whole strength was gathered from himself; he was uncommunicative to others; he allowed no one to read his heart.

The marriage was not altogether harmonious. Latifeh had an equally determined nature and possessed abundant self-assurance. Between husband and wife there was a tension, similar to that which had existed between Mustafa and Zubeida, which robbed their union of much of its happiness.

Here again fate had decided that Mustafa must fight.

Notwithstanding their conflicting natures he found this woman indispensable. Moreover, he admired herself, her "masculine" energy, her knowledge of the world, her shrewd judgment of affairs, her industry and her rare intelligence.

In Latifeh all the energy that had been bottled up in the Turkish woman for centuries seemed to find an outlet. She was a glutton for work and hurled herself into many spheres of activity, which were the exclusive province of men, and mastered the tasks which she set herself, with a sovereign—all too sovereign—assurance.

At Mustafa's side there arose a second will, a strong, ambitious will, that was armed with dangerous shrewdness and considerable knowledge.

Latifeh was the First Lady of the Republic, an autocrat by nature.

If only she had confined her energies and charm of personality to those provinces which are the business of a woman rather than of a man!

Mustafa Kemal had no time to reflect on the *problématique* of his private affairs, of his marriage.

He was victor. His most urgent present need was to consolidate his victory. Dangers from all sides threatened the soldier who had now undergone transformation into a reformer.

CHAPTER XIV

MOSUL

CONSTANTINOPLE was a city of the discontented. Constantinople, the Queen of Cities, could not grasp the fact that she had ceased to be the State metropolis.

Mustafa Kemal had promoted Angora to be the capital.

Angora was a paltry, God-forsaken hole situated in the barren steppe about four hundred miles from the Anatolian coast. There were no roads, no buildings, no parks, no squares. It lacked everything that a city should possess. The soil was hard and stony.

There were many towns in Anatolia with far better claims to be the seat of government. However, Mustafa Kemal insisted on Angora.

Angora, indeed, was the symbol of New Turkey. Angora from the very start had been the headquarters of the revolution. Strategically, Angora was favourably situated. Even a vastly superior army would have difficulty in carrying its invasion to this capital. But that was not the deciding factor. The choice had been made for sentimental reasons.

Angora was a city with a raw climate and a raw soil. The Turkish nation in raising it to be their capital were, in so doing, dedicating themselves to a hard, uphill struggle for survival. Mustafa Kemal proposed to wring from this soil a city, systematically constructed with the aid of the latest scientific and technical knowledge, which would be a credit to the twentieth century.

It was to be a far-reaching plan of immense range. Kemal was fired with an ambition to be a great architect, a ruling passion of nearly all great leaders.

The maze of miserable little houses called Angora was still hemmed in between swamp and desert. The marshes exhaled malaria, and from the desert came clouds of dust. In summer there was a burning heat, in winter a bitter cold.

Mustafa Kemal proposed defeating tricky, hostile Nature. The will to be a new pioneer of civilization was awake in him.

The Old Order was still not fully destroyed. Plots and conspiracies still flourished in the shadow of the ruins.

The sultanate had been abolished, but as yet Mustafa Kemal had not attacked the caliphate. Abdul Mejid, Vahideddin's brother, still resided in Constantinople as Caliph of all the Mohammedans.

That was considered only as a temporary solution. Too much could not be attempted at once. At the same time Mustafa Kemal was perfectly well aware that the Caliph's palace was the main focus of activities hostile to his régime.

Secret reports were received daily. Mustafa Kemal quietly took note of them and held himself in readiness to pounce when the time came.

The Caliph himself, a *grand seigneur*, had not the slightest desire or pretence to be a conspirator. He was happiest when left alone with his paintings. From him there was nothing to fear. But a dangerous game was being played with his person and office.

Among the squad of discontents were several familiar faces. It was a group that hardly took the trouble to disguise that its real object was to supplant the Ghazi.

Kiazim Karabekir was one of the malcontents, having a feeling that by Mustafa's actions, in particular by his removal of the sultanate, he had been betrayed. He had fought shoulder to shoulder with him for the liberation of the sultan! Now the result of their struggle was the creation of a republic after the European pattern.

Refat Pasha, Governor-General of Constantinople, ostentatiously paid homage to the Caliph, as much as to say, " He is the coming man."

The people were still in the grip of the old notions. The Caliph was still the representative of God. A word from the Caliph was still capable of rousing the faithful in Anatolia. Abdul Mejid was the strongest card in the conspirators' game.

The quiet old gentleman, who had quietly submitted on being ordered from Angora to appear at the official ceremony on his succession in a frock-coat, now found himself urged from various quarters to play a part which he had no desire to play.

The Young Turk Committee suddenly sprang into prominence again. In Constantinople, under the chairmanship of Javid Bey, formerly Minister of Finance in the Said Halim Cabinet, a secret session of former important members of the Committee was held.

How the Young Turks, the band of adventurers whom he had known so well in the past, how they hated Mustafa Kemal!

The " Union and Progress " Party had been banned and the Young Turk régime thus officially condemned. Suddenly it had revived. It looked as though the two principal opposition groups, the reactionary pashas and the members of the Committee, had reached a temporary agreement between them for the purpose of destroying the Republican Government, after which they undoubtedly would return to fighting each other, as they had always done in the past. It looked as though the country would never know peace.

Mustafa Kemal still hesitated. Several of the men were his best friends a short time ago, men who in the hour of greatest need had fought at his side for their country's delivery, but who to-day had turned his enemies.

In their ranks he recognized one who had enjoyed his confidence to the full—the only man whom he had ever called his friend. Arif!

Since the time of Eski Shehir there had been an estrangement between them. Arif had continued to become more reserved. Something malicious, something underhand, seemed to master him. The probability was that the two men were so much alike in their natures that it was impossible for them to agree in the long run.

Mustafa was aware of the reason of Arif's resentment.

Arif felt that he had been thrust aside and ignored; he was jealous, envious and offended. Then he began to get bored. And in such a condition such men are dangerous.

It was difficult to know how to proceed with such war-mongers and careerists.

At Eski Shehir Arif had been a failure; and Mustafa Kemal had no further use for a man who let him down at a critical time.

People like Arif were excellent comrades and friends. In their way they were clever, but they lacked all the qualities which were needed for the practical work of peace-time. They were unfitted for regular, systematic work, useless as politicians and of doubtful value as regular soldiers.

In the adventurous and chaotic conditions which existed during times of revolution they were of inestimable value, while for steady, conscientious, constructive work, with its numerous irritating little details and obstacles, which could only be surmounted with patience and industry, they were completely unfitted. For such tasks men like Ismet, Fevzi and Kiazim Pasha were needed. . . .

Arif had passed through terrible times. He found it absolutely impossible to settle down to the new life. For more than two decades his spheres had been war and revolution. Now, all at once, there was peace in the land. The revolutionary, Mustafa, the destroyer of the old régime, had now become the architect of the new State; the repudiator of the old authorities had become the champion of a new authority--one which claimed implicit obedience.

He would rather perish than play the part of a dutiful deputy in the Great National Assembly, where his only task would be to pronounce confidence in Ismet and his vassals; and he had no intention of wearing the flesh off his bones doing garrison duties anywhere!

When the malcontents tried to raise him on a pedestal and to persuade him that he was in truth the great man, whom Mustafa had treated with ingratitude, their flattery left him cold. It was rubbish, and he at all events would not be its dupe. He was the restless, eternal revolutionary, the possessor of a mind which could only destroy. He thoroughly despised all those who clustered round him, some because they were too stupid and too obstinate to acknowledge Mustafa's great reforms, and the others who had not received the appointments for which they had hoped. He despised them all, knowing that hardly one of Mustafa's friends had escaped a reprimand during some part of his career, and knowing, too, that any failure on the part of one of his friends aroused the Grey Wolf's anger more than anything.

Now the Committee had come to join them—the corpulent Javid, a Salonika Jew, and his confederates. He was now in fine company!

Arif laughed bitterly and ironically.

This elect company consisted, among others, of Refat, an idle braggart with a grievance, who now desired to see a return to the old Ottoman splendour, Kiazim Karabekir, a man of limited intelligence, and Rauf Bey, who, having been idiot enough to allow the British to imprison him in Malta, imagined that he had earned for himself a species of martyrdom, and who now shot with poisoned arrows at a man who was too big for him.

That is saying nothing of the others, of whom Javid and Dr. Nazim, in particular, were no more than political schemers.

Arif was firm in his belief in Mustafa Kemal, but his pride had been injured, and all that remained was the memory of a bygone friendship.

An evil spirit in the man was urging him to rise and distroy the one man whom he admired, and the only man in whom he had ever had faith.

The day would come when Arif would ally himself to the Devil and crush everything that was dear and of value to him, laughing scornfully the while, knowing well that he was behaving as a despicable cad.

Mustafa Kemal saw danger approach, but still the time was not ripe for the decisive action. First of all the conspirators' dummy, the Caliph, had to go.

Mustafa Kemal set himself to the task of explaining to the National Assembly the necessity for changing the present intolerable state of affairs. He had stated to the European Powers that he would not adopt a foreign policy that was in any way associated with the religious interests of the other Moslem peoples.

But how could the Powers accept this statement when in Constantinople, now as before, a caliph still existed as the representative of Turkish pan-Islamic aspirations. The very presence of the Caliph must give rise to constant suspicion. It would be argued that the caliphate, if it indeed fulfilled its purpose, must be an eternal source of international conflict. On the other hand, continued the Ghazi, if it was merely a cloak and a pretence—then have done with it once and for all!

Mustafa's reasons were unanimously acknowledged and his arguments accepted. The National Assembly, too, recognized that they were members of a movement in which there was no turning back. In the Grey Wolf's school the deputies had already learnt that half-measures were poor measures.

The Republic had now been proclaimed. They had decided for the twentieth century. They must, therefore, complete their work.

The caliphate was abolished.

And all members of the Osman Dynasty to leave the country! Mustafa Kemal quickly added.

The opposition greeted this decree in silence. Perhaps it will be just as well, they told themselves, if we give the dictator, the usurper, an opportunity to overstretch the bow. Then the storm will break! The people will recognize where his path is leading them to, they will rise up and fight for that which he himself once held sacred and inviolable.

The storm did not break. The people remained completely unmoved by the abolition of the caliphate; they had expected nothing different. Mustafa Kemal's authority was stronger than the magic lustre of the caliphate.

Kemalist propaganda was beginning to bear fruit. Kemalist enlightenment had been borne into every town and every village. Everywhere there were local representatives of the People's Party who taught their charges that a sound policy could only serve national interests, that the preservation of national honour and the increase of national well-being was its first and foremost task, and that not a single soldier would be sacrificed for senseless ideals. How many of the best Turkish regiments and how much of the nation's strength had been frittered away in the deserts of Arabia—and for no better reason than to satisfy the vain, imperialistic aspirations of the caliphate, of Islam.

What was Islam to the Turks? Their forefathers had not known it. It had been taken over from the subjected nations, and Turkish decadence had dated from that time.

That was what the Kemalist agitators were preaching. The simple Anatolian peasant, who was by nature a philosopher, pondered their words. At the back of the new doctrine he saw the figure of Mustafa Kemal the victor, the man who at the peak of the crisis appeared like a messenger of Eternal Providence, who accomplished wonders, and whose tremendous personality had gripped and held the people.

He had shown himself to be stronger than the united Western world. He had shown that he was stronger than the ancient gods.

With a rare, inexplicable indifference, the Turk turned away from the past and waited in confident expectation of what the future would bring.

Mustafa Kemal conceived that it would be wise, before giving effect to his various reforms, to educate and prepare public opinion beforehand. But for that, their success would have been extremely doubtful.

Now a decision was taken by Parliament—and a world crumbled.

On 3 March, 1924, the National Assembly met to pass new legislation.

Three decrees, which implied the foundering of the Old Turkey, were passed: The Ministry of Religious Affairs was abolished; schools and the responsibility for education were taken over by the State; the mosque schools were closed. The caliphate had ceased to exist and members of the Osman Dynasty were obliged to leave the country. A certain period of grace was allowed in order that they might have an opportunity to settle their financial and private affairs.

The National Assembly then proceeded to the next item of parliamentary business, which concerned a treaty of friendship between Germany and Turkey and the conclusion of a temporary Consular Pact with the German *Reich*.

Relations with the old ally in the Great War, which had been severed by decree of the Allies, were to be resumed.

On the following day the Caliph was escorted over the frontier. It was high time that he took his departure, for the Reaction were ready to launch their blow.

The road to construction was not yet clear of obstacles. At the moment the greatest peril came from the Army. Since the days of Abdul Hamid the officers had been accustomed to taking an active part in politics, and with the help of their battalions had spent much of their time in holding a pistol at the Government.

The Army was commanded principally by generals who were in sharp opposition to Mustafa Kemal's reforms. They were men of high reputation and of incontestable merits. In addition, they had seats in the National Assembly, and in this way constituted a twofold danger.

Unless something was done quickly the worst was to be feared. Revolt was in the air. How were these rebellious, arrogant soldiers to be got at?

Mustafa Kemal conferred with several corps commanders, on whose loyalty he could rely, and persuaded them that it was essential that politics be entirely rooted out of the Army. He insisted on the principle that a man could not be a soldier and a

THE GIRLS' HIGH SCHOOL IN ANKARA

deputy at the same time. Each must decide for himself whether he would resign his seat or resign his commission.

Mustafa Kemal's friends, as might have been expected, without hesitation pronounced in favour of soldiers resigning from Parliament.

The triumvirate, Kiazim Karabekir, Refat and Ali Fuad, expressed the opposite opinion.

Mustafa Kemal took a note of the fact. He now knew where he was with those gentlemen. Marshal Karabekir had been commander-in-chief in the Eastern Provinces. Now, at a time when the first signs of storm were appearing in the east, he deserted his post.

Political agitation and reactionary fanaticism had brought one of the best and most loyal officers to this stage !

Indeed, the reports from the Eastern Provinces were anything but reassuring. In the wild mountains of Kurdistan the sheikhs and native princes were summoning the people to take part in a holy war against Angora, and were assembling their followers under the green banner of the Prophet for the purpose of putting a sudden and violent end to the enemies of Islam, the revolutionaries and reformers.

Their threats, at first glance, did not appear very alarming. An insurrection of Kurdish feudal princes could have been crushed with relative ease. However, Mustafa Kemal saw this Kurdish manœuvre in a quite different light.

At the Lausanne Conference when, in the interests of peace, he had agreed with his principal opponent, England, to defer the discussion of the Mosul question until a later date, he was assuming that when the time came he would have to resign himself to the loss of that territory. The Vilayet of Mosul possessed no strategical importance to Turkey, who had renounced all imperialistic policy where Arabia was concerned. The inhabitants, the majority of whom were Kurds, were an unpleasant company, utterly useless for the tasks fo civilization. In the old Ottoman Empire off-handedly described as Turks. In the new Nationalist sense they had no place at all in the Turkish family. Turkey could do without them.

Meanwhile, in the Mosul territory a lively Kurdish nationalist movement had begun. The Kurds themselves, to whom all patriotic thoughts and feelings were entirely foreign, certainly were not the originators and promoters of this movement. The Mosul was occupied by England, occupied without right—having been seized after the signing of the Armistice of Mudros.

No doubt about it—England was using the Kurds in the Mosul territory to stir up trouble in Turkey. The rising was bound to have an effect on the Kurdish population in the Eastern Provinces. Probably England desired that.

Excitement in Angora became intense. The Mosul question should have been dealt with at Lausanne, people shouted. Negotiations would now begin, with Turkey in an infinitely less favourable position. It was evident that England did not intend to release the Mosul at any price.

As a gateway to Arabia the Mosul was of supreme importance to Empire interests. On the other hand, Turkey had right on her side, and in any case she could not tolerate a hearth of unrest to be created and to exist on her south-east frontier. The illusion of a Kurd national state must automatically lead the one and a half million Kurds in Anatolia into rebellion against Angora.

And so the Mosul negotiations began in Constantinople. Both parties displayed an unbending attitude. At the end of a fortnight the conference at the Golden Horn broke down. England was in the favourable position of already possessing the territory in dispute.

War on account of Mosul?

England made it clear that in the case of need she was prepared to go to any extreme.

In the highly perilous and extremely intricate situation of foreign politics Mustafa Kemal suddenly found himself obliged to deal with a strong domestic opposition that was ruthlessly advancing to its goal—his fall.

Was the whole of the work, that had only just been commenced, to be destroyed? Was the new Nationalist State, hardly born, to fall back into the ruins? Was the old game to be allowed to start all over again? One *coup d'état*, one military dictatorship after the other?

Civil war now would signify the collapse of the State. In the mountains in the east, in Kurdistan, certain events were moving. The sheikhs and feudal princes, who lived and ruled there as their forefathers had lived and ruled in the Middle Ages, received the Government officials with carbines whose safety-catches were released.

So they were no longer to be masters in their own house? They were to submit to a government of heretics; respect laws; pay taxes; send their children to school? To secular schools, where they would be taught the Grey Wolf's false doctrine?

To the Devil with the arch-enemy of Islam! Away with this Anti-Mohammed, this infidel god, who had even had the temerity to call the Prophet an ignorant desert sheikh!

These were the words of the sheikhs, and their subjects interpreted them as meaning that there would be tumult, robbery and pillage—a holy war whose reward was Paradise.

Things could no longer be allowed to take their course.

Mustafa Kemal had no intention of being forced into the defensive. A revolution only remained successful while it was active, while it was on the offensive.

That was his principle, and he acted accordingly.

His opponents said that as Head of the State he could not be Party leader simultaneously. He should resign the leadership of the People's Party.

Mustafa Kemal journeyed to the Eastern Provinces, to the hearth of unrest. He broke his journey to Erzerum at Trebizond, where he made a big speech.

He recognized no neutrality, no political aloofness in the Democratic-Parliamentary sense. The People's Party was for the Republic and for spiritual and social progress. It was unthinkable that there should be a single Turk who did not desire those goals to be attained. The programme of the People's Party was the affair of the whole nation. There could be no rival parties or counter-programmes.

The opposition took up the challenge. They would show him that there were rival opinions! The Constantinople Press announced the foundation of a new party. It was a sword drawn in the name of Democracy, wrote the *Tanin*.

The name of the party was "Republican Progress Party."

A blind! shouted the Kemalists. Reaction and the destruction of the Republic were the aims of the Republican Progress Party.

In the hour of national danger Kiazim Karabekir had relinquished his command in the Eastern Provinces to take the chair of the new party. That was significant.

There were many malcontents. Mosul grousers, who feared a Grey Wolf dictatorship; those whose personal hopes or whose ambitions had been injured; those who rebelled for the love of rebellion—all these united and added their not inconsiderable numbers to the new party.

And in the background, their presence becoming increasingly prominent, were the Committee of Union and Progress men, the Young Turk stars, who believed that the time for them to rise was again drawing near.

There were many incidents during sessions of the National Assembly, and debates began to degenerate into personal and private quarrels. Arguments were transferred to the corridors and conducted at revolver-point. The deputies challenged each other to duels, and in the course of one of these encounters a colonel was mortally shot.

Even those deputies remaining in the People's Party lost all discipline. They voted against Ismet and they voted against Kiazim Pasha, Mustafa Kemal's most loyal supporters: in other words, they voted against him.

Mustafa Kemal fell back; Ismet resigned; and the less radical Fethi succeeded to the Premiership.

The Officer Commanding the Lifeguards, Colonel Tchopal Osman, decided that the Opposition had carried matters too far, and he determined to make an example of some of them that would show all enemies of the Grey Wolf what they might expect if they continued on their present road.

He picked on the most notorious obstructionist and invited him to lunch. While he was eating a rope was slipped round his neck, a Circassian guardsman gave it a sharp tug, and the man was dispatched.

About an hour later a detachment of military police, furnished with a warrant, came to arrest Colonel Tchopal Osman.

Osman, whom they called the "Lame," could not believe it. He to be arrested? He, who had just given the State President such valuable service? He, the true, fanatically-devoted dog? Was that his master's gratitude—an arrest warrant?

Had the world gone crazy? The Sultan would have quitted such a service with a high reward.

"Colonel, you are charged with murder; we arrest you."

"For sending a mangy jackal, one of the Grey Wolf's enemies, to hell, where he belonged?"

"Murder is murder. Hand over your weapons and follow us!"

The colonel at that moment saw red, and quickly turning to his Circassians, he shouted:

"Follow me!"

He tore like a madman to Chankaya and rushed to the President's house, holding a revolver in his fist.

He was received with rifle-fire. There was a short, fierce encounter in the course of which Colonel Tchopal Osman, the Lame, was shot dead outside his master's house.

These events took place at a time when the Mosul dispute was reaching its most critical stage.

Meanwhile, the conflict was being debated by the Council of the League of Nations with all the customary formalities, in the various committees and to the accompaniment of much heated controversy. The Turkish proposal of a national plebiscite was turned down, the Council having decided to base its decision on the material supplied by a special commission of enquiry.

The Special Commission arrived in Angora and were received with genuine Turkish hospitality. But the gay and friendly spirit which prevailed at the official banquet given in their honour could not quite dispel the feeling that the air was charged, and that any moment the storm might break.

Mustafa Kemal received the gentlemen from the League of Nations at Konia. Then began their journey of inspection to the territory in dispute.

The Commission had to admit that no doubt existed that the Mosul Kurds preferred union with Turkey to union with Iraq. The desire for autonomy had not been born in the people themselves, to whom nationalist thoughts were entirely foreign.

King Feisal in Bagdad strove his utmost to impress on the Commission that the very existence of Iraq depended on possession of Mosul.

At this time, in the neighbouring Province of Hakkiari, the

Turkish Governor was kidnapped by Nestorians. But the Hakkiari, according to agreement, was neutral territory—No Man's Land. Ignoring this, Turkish troops marched into the province to restore law and order. By their draconic disciplinary measures they aroused considerable local indignation, and the Nestorians fled to the Vilayet of Mosul. The Turkish troops, whose blood was now up, pursued them, having little regard for demarcation lines or frontiers of any kind.

Soon English bombing 'planes were filling the air with their droning, and—as at Constantinople in those critical autumn days of 1922—everything hung on a thread.

Immediate withdrawal past the Demarcation Line! demanded England menacingly. In Angora fists were shaken in reply.

At this most critical stage the Council of the League of Nations intervened and established that frontiers had been violated by both sides. The Turks were to evacuate the area recently occupied by them, and the British were to withdraw from Suleimaniye, which they had subsequently occupied. A new Demarcation Line was fixed, and at the eleventh hour the danger of war was averted.

Scattered bands of Nestorians sought refuge in the Turkish Eastern Provinces and the wild, inaccessible mountains of Kurdistan.

The Kurdish sheikhs received them with open arms. Their hour, too, was not far off. The Nestorian revolt was only the prelude. Sheikh Said, Sovereign of the Order of Nakishbendi, of the "Enemies of Laughter," preached against the Anti-Mohammed of Angora, and marshalled his fanatical followers under the green banner of the Prophet, to restore with fire and sword the dominion of Islam and to destroy without mercy all Kemalist sons of dogs who dared to oppose them.

Kemalist *gendarmerie* combed the mountains of Kurdistan for fugitive Nestorians. The Kurds received them with rifles at the ready.

What did that mean?—resistance of State authority?

Death to all enemies of Islam! Death to all slaves of the thousandfold accursed Anti-Mohammed! yelled Sheikh Said.

The rifles went off, and the banner of revolt was hoisted. On hard-pressed horses the insurgents tore over the passes and through the ravines, towards the cities. The Angel of Death preceded them.

The weak garrisons were swept aside, and soon the banner of the Prophet waved above the cities of Charput, Butlis and Marash. The Sheikh's proclamation was posted on the walls:

Restoration of the Osmans! Back to the Old Order! To hell with the reforms and the Anti-Mohammed of Angora!

It was winter. The Turkish divisions slowly advanced through the deep snow which covered the roadless, mountainous country. In vain they sought to lay hands on the insurgents. The latter concealed themselves in inaccessible parts and conducted a gruesome, tricky guerilla campaign. Meanwhile the revolt had spread to other provinces.

Mustafa Kemal then shook the mailed fist.

What was the Kurdish revolt?—a mere episode! Sheikh Said? a fool, a dummy! Far more serious were the forces which hovered in the background of these events, those men who, directly or indirectly, were in league with the Kurdish rebels and who hoped to gain some advantage from the revolt.

Mustafa Kemal first intended to deal with those elements. Constantinople was the meeting-place of all counter-revolutionary currents; and on the eve of the Kurdish revolt a local section of the "Republican Progress Party" had been founded there.

In his mind Mustafa Kemal passed in review the leaders of the Opposition. In addition to the marshals, there were certain sinister individuals, politicians of the second grade, adventurers and soldiers of fortune, incorrigible revolutionaries and—worst of all—numerous survivors of the Young Turk Party, among them the corpulent Salonika Jew, Javid Bey, Enver's former Minister of Finance, a glutton and pursuer of women, Dr. Nasim and many others. Mustafa Kemal knew the men and their methods only too well. He knew these sinister schemers—the Freemasons, politicizing priests and the rest—who cast their nets in the dark and whose agents were in all lands.

He had been obliged to defend himself from these forces for far too long. It was high time that he put a finish once and for all to these remnants of a liberalistic past. In the Nationalist State there was no room for them. Was Turkey again to be torn asunder by international interests? Was it for that that Anatolian sons shed their blood?

Deal with them mercilessly !—even if many of them were old friends and war-time comrades.

The Grey Wolf was fully roused.

But he did not rush, he did not lose his temper. He dealt his blows with cold deliberation, pitilessly. He no longer was the slow-moving chess player, who skilfully and painlessly out-manœuvred his opponent in a series of carefully thought out moves. He was a vigorous and determined defender of the menaced Nationalist State.

Uneasy in mind, the deputies of the Great National Assembly answered his summons and gathered for a special session.

Before releasing his sword, Mustafa Kemal wanted to settle accounts with the traitors, eye to eye. He meant to pick out his men from among the leaders of the " Republican Progress Party."

He proposed giving them a last chance—leave the country. Many of them were old friends.

The mutineers knew that their hour had struck.

None made use of the chance to escape. They appeared boldly and defiantly, for in this sort of situation they were in their element.

A veritable bombardment of charges was directed against the Minister-President, Fethi. The Kemalists were his attackers.

The Premier had failed miserably to put down the Kurdish revolt. Important cities had fallen into the hands of the rebels. Military operations were stagnant. Did the worthy Minister-President think that mild measures would accomplish anything against these barbarians?

Why weren't military operations proceeding as they should?

The new commanding officer was only appointed a few days ago, and he was still unfamiliar with the conditions in that accursed part of the country.

Hear that !

In view of those facts could the Minister-President explain the circumstances in which the Inspector-General, Marshal Kiazim Karabekir, came to lay down his command?

There was an uproar in the Assembly.

Not a word against the marshal's soldier honour ! many shouted.

The Kemalists scoffed.

Then revolvers flashed. Bullets whistled through the room,

struck the masonry, and bored holes in the red flag with the white star and crescent that was draped on the wall.

The smoke cleared. No one had been harmed.

Mustafa Kemal then went to the speaker's desk.

Immediately there was silence. His voice sounded hard and metallic.

Somewhere on the benches Arif was sitting. The eyes of the two men met. Scorn and defiance were written on the faces of both adversaries. Forgotten now were Erzerum, the nights in Angora and the nights in Alaghersh during the great Anatolian battle.

Now it was a duel to the death.

The Grey Wolf began.

Every child knew who was behind the Kurdish revolt. Arm in arm with the Dervishes and Reactionaries stood an international clique which drew on help from across the frontier. Every child knew who was the usufructuary of their domestic disunion—the foreign enemy, England, who did not want to release hold on Mosul. Was it a coincidence that this revolt broke out at a time when there was danger of a new war with England? Who were the men who at this very moment were stabbing their own countrymen in the back? How differently they might have set to work in Geneva, and how different might have been their attitude to the League of Nations and England if only they had been united! Was it a coincidence that Marshal Kiazim Karabekir left his command on the eve of the revolt and abandoned his troops in the Eastern Provinces without a leader, then to place himself at the head of a party hostile to the State? And did it mean anything the when leader of the " Republican Progress Party " maintained a correspondence with the Kurdish Sheikh Said?

He held aloft a letter.

Immediately there was commotion in the Assembly, and a number of voices demanded the appointment of a Tribunal of Independence.

A gesture from the Grey Wolf silenced them again. Mustafa Kemal had not yet finished.

The State was in peril. The opponents of progress, who had the temerity to call themselves republicans and progressionists, had played into the hands of Turkey's enemy, England. It was known precisely in what sinister traffic these people, who had once sworn unconditional loyalty, were dabbling in a deliberate attempt to betray the freedom and existence of the nation. Anyone who raised a hand against the new State was a traitor.

Nothing could have been clearer than that.

The Assembly was completed captured by Mustafa Kemal's forceful personality, and gave him enthusiastic applause. Loyal deputies were seen to increase the space between themselves and the representatives of the Opposition. The latter, pale, but defiant, sat in sullen silence.

Mustafa Kemal now directed his attack against the Minister-President Fethi. He had shown a lack of sufficient energy and no longer enjoyed the confidence of the nation.

Fethi saw that he had no choice but to offer his resignation.

Ismet was entrusted with the task of forming a cabinet.

Events now began to move quickly. Mustafa Kemal and Ismet purposely drove matters to a head in order to clarify the situation. They were determined to put a finish to the undermining activities and to destroy the seeds of civil war, which in the east had already sprouted into open rebellion. They determined to finish with everything which was gnawing at, and exhausting, the nation's nerves.

The nation, and the peasant in particular, expected trenchant reforms of a social and economic character. It had had enough of the constant quarrels and political disputes. It desired to have nothing to do with a band of adventurers, powerful men of yesterday, who refused to acknowledge that a new era had dawned. Only those might rule who were prepared to devote all their energy and strength to the service of the nation. For particular ambitions and special interests there was no room.

Ismet formed his cabinet. On the same day the banner of the Prophet was hoisted at Arghana. Sacking and slaying, Sheikh Said's hordes entered the city, where they established a terrible tribunal of vengeance to condemn all who professed allegiance to the heretic government of Angora.

The cries of the martyrs could be heard above the fanatical yells of champions of Allah.

Sheikh Said foamed with rage. At Chankaya the Anti-Mohammed had at a single stroke of the pen destroyed the whole of the previous system of the universe.

From time immemorial it had been the custom for the peasant to surrender one-tenth of the produce of his work to his masters.

Recently the tithe had been abolished. The decree was proclaimed in Angora. The peasant was free. Agriculture was to be completely reorganized on modern lines.

Already Sheikh Said saw himself as victor in Angora, as restorer of the old order and as stern judge of all enemies of the Faith.

From the National Assembly Mustafa Kemal had secured exceptional powers for a period of two years. Supported by these powers, he intended to carry through the Nationalist revolution to the very last and to establish the foundations for construction of the new State system. His opponents had played into his hands. In face of the Kurdish revolt and in face of the attitude of the big Opposition generals at a time of serious domestic and foreign crises no one could deny the necessity for special legislation. The National Assembly acknowledged this by a large majority.

A few days later there was fighting near Diarbekr, and immediately afterwards shots were fired in the streets. Sheikh Said had to flee to the mountains.

For another month he kept his liberty, during which time he was pursued from one hiding-place to the other. Hot on his trail were the soldiers of the Ghazi.

Finally he met his fate. He was led into Diarbekr as a captive and placed on trial before the Tribunal of Independence.

The verdict was—death by hanging!

"I do not hate you," said the sheikh to his judge. "You and your master are under God's curse. We will settle accounts on the day of the Last Judgment."

The judge smiled, then nodded to the executioner.

Sheikh Said dangled in mid-air. Vultures hovered over the scene of execution. There had been forty-six hangings. The proclamations which had been posted on the dark basalt walls of Diarbekr were torn down. There remained no one in the city who in future would dare to speak of preservation of the rights of Islam through the "Kiazim Karabekir Party," or of restoration of the Osmans.

The Opposition had been crippled and made no attempt to parry the blows which the dictator now directed at them. The blows were hard and merciless. The "Republican Progress Party" was dissolved. Sentences of banishment were now pronounced by the hundred. Soon one hundred and fifty undesirables had been escorted to the frontier and exiled for all time.

Many took to flight. The Opposition newspapers were banned.

Mustafa Kemal was now undisputed master over life and death. No one dreamt of resistance. His victory was complete. However, he was wise enough not to overstrain the bow and, therefore, left the important generals alone. Marshal Karabekir's reputation, for instance, was still considerable. To the general public he was still the man who had defeated the Armenians, the man who had saved them from the Armenian peril.

He and his friends retreated, leaving the field to the Ghazi. Had he at last seen that he had been acting contrary to the interests of the State?

The defeated had very little time in which to ponder their defeat, for Mustafa Kemal soon launched a new attack. The Special Laws for the Restoration and Preservation of Order were an uncommonly powerful weapon. With their aid the reformer set to work, at twentieth-century tempo, in reconstructing the whole public life of the country.

On one November morning in 1925, standing at all street corners were policemen, who removed the fez of each passer-by. What did that mean? Rapidly the news spread through the cities that, from that day, it was prohibited to wear the fez.

Our fathers wore it, and it is the symbol of Islam, of the faith which unites us all—the people shouted.

The Ghazi says it is the symbol of ignorance, superstition and backwardness, answered the policemen.

A wave of indignation surged through the land. This time it was the nation, the man in the street, who rebelled. The latest decree affected him personally. The change of attitude towards old-fashioned conceptions now became clear to him.

Everywhere there were heated arguments—fezes or hats?

Jerseys and baggy breeches or jackets and trousers?

The question of dress was promoted to the status of a political problem, and once more brought the State authority in jeopardy.

Mustafa Kemal in person led the campaign against the national dress. At Dadai near Kastamuni he made a big speech. His audience were horrified to see him appear in a hat.

"The Turk," he said, "must adopt international civilization. That, too, must be apparent in his external appearance. In future we must regard international, civilized dress as the only form worthy of us."

The Dervishes and reactionary priests scented their chance. They started to agitate the people, and this time found willing listeners. Revolts flamed up everywhere. No one was willing to accept the dress reforms.

A few days later a bill was introduced into the National Assembly which sought to make the wearing of hats obligatory. Nureddin Pasha, an elderly general, made a maiden speech—against hats. He was at once expelled from the Assembly.

The Dervishes desired to make the most of the opportunity. Unfortunately for them, they overdid it.

Mustafa Kemal succeeded in convincing the National Assembly that the time had come for the nation to be freed of these men.

"Can you look upon a nation as civilized when it allows itself to be taken in tow by a horde of sheikhs, dedes babas and emirs? When it entrusts its fate and existence to a multitude of magicians, sellers of charms and quacks of all types?" he shouted.

Were they to lock them up, martyr them, and so cause the people to cling to them all the more tenaciously?

The very reverse was done: they were locked out. The National Assembly published a decree closing the Dervish cloisters and the monasteries of other religious bodies.

The Dervish friars found themselves robbed of their livings. They could no longer live at the nation's cost, and were faced with the necessity of earning their daily bread, like any other person.

This afforded the people an opportunity of discovering that these alleged miracle-men were in reality very ignorant and helpless individuals—drones, in fact.

They were disenchanted.

A number of examples were made, and they were not without their effect on advocates of the old national dress. A big propaganda campaign was then opened and all at once people began to vie with each other in their eagerness to become civilized. None wanted to be backward. Civilisation meant prosperity and progress. Each wanted to share in these. Civilisation—it was the new faith, which now transplanted the old.

Jerseys and baggy breeches were discarded. People began to storm the shops. Everyone wanted a European suit and a hat. As will be perfectly obvious, the shopkeepers were quite unable to meet this unprecedented demand, and so anything in the way of headgear, provided it was furnished with a peak or brim, was eagerly bought. Indeed, men were seen proudly strutting through the streets in out-of-date women's hats which they had dug up in one of the Armenian shops. For lace shoes, waistcoats, trousers and jackets there were, literally, free-fights.

The sword of the Special Decrees hung over the whole revolution, while in the background of events stood Kel Ali, Bald Ali, the Hanging Judge, with his travelling Tribunal of Independence.

A ruthless employment of force was necessary to transfer a nation through three centuries, from the Middle Ages to modern times. In Angora they could not permit themselves the luxury of democratic methods. It was a question of achieving what was considered essential, regardless of ways and means.

The women were more fortunate than the men.

The Ghazi left them alone, tactfully refraining from interference with the veil and headcloth. To force the veil from a Turkish woman, and so give offence to one of her most sensitive points, was more than he was prepared to do. But the veil must fall, on that he was determined. He preferred, however, that the woman should lay it aside of her own free will.

Mustafa Kemal himself made propaganda on this behalf. When meeting a veiled woman in the street, he would suggest to her that it was a pity to conceal handsome features or fine hair.

The women turned out to be less conservative than the men. After a little persuasion there arrived a new generation, which cast off veil and headcloth and began to use powder and lipstick.

The Turkish woman accepted her freedom naturally and was soon as at home in it as though it were her natural element.

In this great social revolution the last traces of the old Orient were made to disappear. What formerly had been considered impossible was now in the natural order of things. Government officials at entertainments and receptions were now accompanied by their wives, and those of them who were anxious to escape a disciplinary lecture made certain that they treated their wives as European ladies and allowed them to participate in everything.

A good ten years ago the women, then behind their veils, dreamed of an emancipator, of a romantic hero who would give them their golden liberty. The hero of their dreams was Enver, Enver the handsome, small-featured, eloquent advocate of progress. In appearance he was well suited for the role. With flashing eyes, a bold, military moustache and a vivacious manner, he was the ideal of the good-looking man of the day.

At that time no one had bothered to notice Mustafa Kemal, an abrupt, reserved, unsympathetic man with hard, impenetrable features.

To-day this face represented the ideal of every Turk and every Turkish woman. The days of soft effeminacy were past. Mustafa Kemal became the pattern which all tried to copy. People imitated his bearing, his walk, adapted themselves to his tempo, and they admired his strong, fighting nature. He was a good example of the type of man that emerged triumphant from the great test imposed by the Great War, a type of man who emerged with greater courage, increased energy and a firmer will.

The emancipation of women had been undertaken and completed in the short space of a few weeks by a man who was anything but a romantic hero. Moreover, it was achieved in a completely unromantic way—a way which only a mathematician could have chosen.

About fifteen years earlier a revolution failed in Constantinople because a number of women, having confidence in the Young Turk reform programme, walked over the Galata Bridge unveiled. That was in 1909. At the slightest attempt at Europeanizing, a storm of indignation swept through the country.

Since that time no one had seriously considered equality for women. The Sheria, the sacred Islamic Legal Code, remained inviolable. According to it, women were not to acquire civil rights.

At the same time the woman was not entirely without her own rights. In the house, for instance, she was undeniably the mistress.

However, modern ideas of emancipation had begun to find their way into Turkish households, and the Turkish woman was no longer satisfied to be mistress in a cage.

The Sheria placed very harsh restrictions on a woman's liberty.

The Anatolian war had made great changes in the woman's outlook. Women now accepted their liberty not as a generous gift, but as a hard-earned right. They won their right to social equality in those hard days when they stood under fire, shoulder to shoulder with the men, silently and bravely performing their duty. The Turkish woman was an associate of warriors.

To-day the war had been transferred to other fields of battle, to those of civilization, progress and work. Under the leadership of Mustafa Kemal the Turkish nation, as a disciplined and well-organized army, were to attack the big tasks of peace. All forces were to be mobilized to ensure success. In this struggle, too, the women were to be the companions of warriors.

That had been so in ancient Turkish history; to-day history was to be repeated. The ring was closing.

A big programme of work was set before the Great National Assembly. Outside the House of Parliament stood a notice-board, on which were the words:

" *Hakimiyet milletindir !* "

" Government is by the people ! "

Formerly a quotation from the Koran had stood there.

Tribal distinctions had been prohibited. Article 88 of the Constitution decreed that, " *All are Turks !* "

The construction of new railway lines was planned; an Air Association was founded; a tariff was imposed for the protection of home trade. Official uniforms were only to be manufactured of Turkish cloth; trade and friendship pacts were signed with foreign States; the European chronology was introduced.

The question of a legal code was then considered. The Sheria was abolished and the Swiss Civil Code, as the most modern, the simplest and the one least influenced by the Roman Code, was adopted.

A law passed on 1 March, 1926, decreed the employment of the Italian Penal Code. What Ismet had announced to the sceptics in Lausanne had been achieved. Overnight Turkey became the possessor of modern, European legal codes; and, in addition, the best and most suitable had been selected with infinite care. Shortly afterwards there followed the introduction of the Commercial Code, which resembled the German and Italian Codes.

Meanwhile, nationalization was being carried a step further. A Turkish Language Congress met at Baku, where it was decided to establish a Turkish Academy. In future Turkish was to be the only recognized language in the country.

Angora received a telephone service installed on the automatic exchange system. A great pipe line was laid through the desert to supply the new capital with water. Its construction met with great technical difficulties; but they were mastered. Simultaneously, work was begun with the object of draining the marshes.

During the whole of the time that this gigantic reconstruction of the State was proceeding, foreign affairs continued to give grave concern.

The immediate danger of armed conflict with England admittedly had been removed by the withdrawal of both parties across the Demarcation Line. But the dispute was by no means solved. The position remained unclarified and pregnant with danger.

In the days of high tension, when England dispatched an ultimatum to Constantinople, Mustafa Kemal had been determined, in the case of need, to go to war. His sharp rejection of the English demands should have left no doubt about that.

Firmly convinced that Turkey was in the right, Mustafa Kemal confidently awaited the decision of the Council of the League.

He was soon to be disappointed. It grew increasingly evident that the Council was not actuated by considerations of what was right, but of what the political situation required. Geneva had made up its mind in the first place to satisfy England. That could only be done at Turkey's cost.

In that case, the best move was to take up direct negotiations with the rival. In London the Turkish Chargé d'Affaires made a proposal that the disputed territory should be shared: the suggestion was that Turkey should have the city of Mosul and England retain the oil concessions.

Chamberlain regretted that he could not enter upon direct negotiations. England had decided to abide by the decision of the

League. On that basis, they would be willing to discuss, at a future date, the question of a resumption of friendly and neighbourly relations.

At Chankaya they now knew what to expect from a decision of the League of Nations.

The Commission's report confirmed that Turkey's claims were justified and the right of her position was fully established. Undertakings which England had given to Iraq, and simultaneously to the inhabitants of Mosul, were empty pretexts. England's demands were based on the suppositions of the Treaty of Sèvres. However, the military successes of the Kemalists had given the situation an entirely different complexion, which England had acknowledged at the Lausanne Conference.

The population itself did not know what it wanted. Its natural inclinations were towards Turkey; on the other hand it expected to derive economic advantages from the British Mandate of Iraq. Moral obligations to protect the Nestorians in the Hakkiari territory did not exist. Previous to the outbreak of the revolt the Nestorians had existed in definitely tolerable circumstances. The reprisals that they had suffered they had drawn upon themselves. And so England could raise no claim to the Hakkiari, which actually was in Turkish possession at the time.

If moral right clearly spoke for Turkey, England on the other hand had the full support of the political rights.

The State of Iraq, to which England as a Mandatory Power owed certain obligations, had a moral claim to exist. Without Mosul existence was not possible. To Turkey, this remote territory was of second-rate importance. A partition was not in the interests of the local population.

The only remaining possibility was cession of the Vilayet of Mosul to Iraq.

There could be no question of parting with the Hakkiari territory to Iraq.

Turkey, now represented by the new Foreign Minister, Tewfik Rushti, refused point-blank to accept the League decision and again sought a direct understanding with England. He failed.

England insisted that the decision of the League of Nations was binding. That had already been acknowledged at Lausanne.

MOSUL

That is a misconception—answered Rushti—it amounted to nothing more than a recommendation; it was not an arbitrator's award.

Then the matter would be referred to the International Court of Justice at The Hague. Rushti declined to agree. The Turkish Government was not prepared to acknowledge the decision of the Hague Tribunal.

Against the will of Turkey, the League of Nations Committee of Three referred the case to the Permanent International Court at The Hague.

The Hague judgment confirmed that the decision of the Council of the League of Nations was binding upon both parties in accordance with Article III, Section 2, of the Treaty of Lausanne.

On England's behalf, Mr. Amery gave an assurance that his country would submit to any decision of the Council.

Turkey denied the legality of the decision, and added that without her consent the Council could take no further action.

By an unanimous majority the Council voted for the contrary.

Mustafa Kemal then recalled his representative.

Meanwhile, a second commission travelled to the territory under dispute to examine the complaints which both sides had made concerning violation of the frontier and other excesses.

The Chaldeans related atrocious stories of Turkish tyranny. A satisfactory examination of these stories was not possible. However, Geneva decided to believe the Chaldeans, and feelings towards Turkey began to grow unfriendly.

On 16 December, 1925, the Council announced its decision. The Demarcation Line—the so-called Brussels Line—was to be the official frontier between Turkey and Iraq.

No Turkish representative was present.

Angora adhered to its obstinate refusal to acknowledge the decision. The dangerous situation continued. Baldwin then stated to the Turkish Minister that he was prepared to open direct negotiations on the basis of the Council's decision, in order to remove the tension and establish a tolerable relationship.

England was willing to build golden bridges and to make concessions. Turkey had certain misgivings regarding the Mosul Kurds. It was accordingly proposed that, within a stated zone extending on both sides of the frontier, both sides should agree to drop all propaganda. In addition, Turkey was offered a share of the proceeds of the oil concessions in the Mosul territory.

Mustafa Kemal hesitated. At that moment another danger arose, which again changed the situation.

Since the days of Lausanne, relations with Italy had grown steadily worse. Certain Italian hopes had not been fulfilled. Italy needed room for her superfluous population. Mussolini's eye had been on Anatolia. That great land, richly endowed with Nature's gifts, was relatively sparsely populated. What an eldorado for Italian mass emigration!

And how Italian colonists would be able to help the Turkish Government in the exploitation of Anatolian natural resources!

On more than one occasion such thoughts had found public expression. Each time Angora had flourished the sword in reply.

Italy, seeing that no progress was to be made by friendly overtures, began to issue threats. The old claims to Adalia, in Anatolian territory, were again raised.

Mustafa Kemal was filled with the deepest mistrust for Italy. He had not forgotten the invasion of Tripoli. What had been the position at that time? Italy had assured Turkey of her friendship, had solemnly denied all hostile intentions, and then, when Turkey was in the throes of domestic strife at the time of the Young Turk revolt, had taken advantage of the internal disunion to make war on her.

It seemed quite feasible that the present position of Turkey might encourage Italy to launch herself upon some Anatolian adventure.

The signs pointed towards it. They must be prepared for every eventuality.

The British Minister, whose residence was still in Constantinople, went to Angora to conduct negotiations on behalf of his Government. Britain had decided to finish with the Mosul dispute. Britain now intervened, offered concessions, took the first step, and held out the hand of reconciliation.

Mustafa Kemal, as it so happened, had signed a Neutrality Pact with Soviet Russia, but he had no intention of being drawn into a Russian, anti-English combination. This intention had already been made clear by Ismet, during the negotiations over the Straits.

Apart from Mosul, there were no points of friction with England.

It was improbable that the Turkish Nationalist State would have any need in future to fear danger from that quarter. England was a satisfied Power.

Not so Italy!

Politics is the art of achieving the impossible. In any case, the price of Mosul had to be paid.

Italy gave the final impetus to that decision.

In early April, 1926, Mussolini made a speech which appeared to give confirmation to Mustafa Kemal's fears regarding Italy's hostile intentions.

He did not keep him waiting for the answer. The order for General Mobilization was wired to all Anatolian provinces.

A few days later the Anglo-Turkish Mosul talks opened in Angora. Two months later the National Assembly ratified the treaty.

In consideration of Anglo-Turkish reconciliation, Mussolini returned his half-drawn sword to its scabbard. In his calculations for an invasion of Anatolia he had reckoned on England's aid. Alone, Italy did not dare risk opposing Mustafa Kemal.

As a wise *Realpolitiker*, the Duce buried his Anatolian aspirations and turned his attention to extending Italian influence in Albania.

The sky above the young Turkish Nationalist State slowly cleared. The time of serious crises had been surmounted.

To Mustafa Kemal it had also been a time of private difficulties. The marriage with Latifeh had proved a failure. Their similarity in character, which had at first blinded them and drawn them together, had been bound to lead to conflict. They did the only thing possible in the circumstances: they separated.

The Grey Wolf again returned to his natural sphere—solitude.

CHAPTER XV
ALHAMBRA

KEL ALI was a bald-headed gentleman with a jovial manner. His countenance was benevolent and sympathetic like that of an English country parson. He was first Vice-President of the Kemalist People's Party. On the eve of the Kurdish revolt he had mortally wounded Halid Pasha of Ardahan in a duel.

He was known as the " Hanging Judge." When sentencing a prisoner he was accustomed to smile and address him in a sympathetic, friendly tone. But there was no " getting off lightly " with Bald Ali.

For months he had been overwhelmed with work. With his Tribunal of Independence he had been travelling in the Eastern Provinces, going from town to town.

As soon as his tribunal arrived, the gallows automatically made their appearance. There was no doubt that Kel Ali was overworked. Often at the end of his day it was too late for a game of poker even ! When smiling Ali appeared, it grew very quiet.

In the Kurdish revolt area death sentences were executed without delay. In Angora they had first to receive the assent of the National Assembly.

Ali smiled and pronounced his sentences. If he had had his way Anatolia would have been a vast forest of gallows. That would not have added beauty to the country-side, but what Ali wanted was to rid the country of all enemies of the Grey Wolf, his adored master, and no means was swift enough for the zealous, bald-headed judge.

In Constantinople he had every house, whose occupants were suspect, searched from roof to cellar. In Angora he sentenced eleven members of the Reform Order to death. Constantinople journalists he handed with a meek smile to the executioner. Mustafa Kemal pardoned them in the nick of time.

All agitators and promoters of disturbances were morally outlawed. Still the authorities were not strong enough to bring a charge of high treason against the great military pashas, Kiazim Karabekir, Refat and Ali Fuad.

But, politically, they had already been executed. Their constituencies rebelled against them and demanded their resignation from the National Assembly.

Ali must have a little more patience.

Rauf and several of his friends fled the country.

Arif had no intention of copying their example. He was heartily glad to see the backs of this semi-pacifist fraternity—the erratic Rauf, Dr. Adnan and his wife, as well as the active Jewess Halide Edib, who has served as a corporal in the Nationalist Army, who wrote novels and who had now joined the ranks of the Opposition to vent her spite on a man who was too great for them all. Arif, although he hated him, still admired the Grey Wolf.

Once more he scented battle and felt that life again was worth living.

Arif knew that his game was one for life or death, of that no doubt existed. The two rivals, the former friends, had taken aim at each other. Now it was simply a matter of who pulled the trigger first.

The race began. Round Arif were gathered a small band of desperadoes, restless soldiers of fortune, men who were only happy when they were gambling with their lives.

Others then sought to join them—the rats, the Committee-men, Freemasons, Javis, Dr. Nasim, and their satellites.

Javid was Arif's rival in the race of secret conspiracy. He, too, had no intentions of running away. He had no need to. Who would dare to harm a single hair on his head? Behind him stood a great international combination, of which he was one of the leading members.

In the "Grand Orient" Lodge he met many powerful men. Sarraut, France's Minister in Angora, was his friend.

Mustafa Kemal knew this very well, and for that very reason the hemp for Javid Bey's rope had already been plucked. His influence as chieftain of the "Grand Orient" was his own undoing: that would not save him.

Mustafa Kemal as yet was not understood. Why, people asked, did he attack Islam? It was the same Islam that had been prepared to acknowledge him as its sovereign and raise him to undreamed-of pinnacles of power.

Was he an atheist?

No, it was not that—he wished to free the nation from influences which ran contrary to the interests of the State. The principal of these was Islam. In the second position, not very far behind, came those circles which with the help of former members of the Committee were attempting to regain influence. As a young officer Mustafa Kemal had frequented the Masonic Lodges in Salonika and Pera. He had never belonged to any particular lodge, but he had studied their methods. And to-day, as dictator, as creator of the State he was determined not to allow anything to grow that did not have its seeds in the national soil; anything that was bound first by international considerations he meant to stamp out.

He would be uncompromising in his fight against everything which stood in any connection with Masonry, and uncompromising in his attitude to religion, especially when it interfered in provinces which were the exclusive right of the State. In New Turkey Islam was a private matter for the conscience; members of Masonic Lodges were traitors.

The road of the Nationalist revolution was clearly marked out. The more powerful and influential the men, the sharper the sword which hung above their heads.

Mustafa Kemal's police agents had their eyes and ears everywhere.

The air was charged. Underground plots were fast maturing.

Why did Mustafa Kemal hesitate? Was he suffering from an attack of nerves? Were there doubts in his own mind?

The weeks passed.

Mustafa Kemal travelled from place to place, in all parts of Anatolia.

In early May he reached Adana in the south. A little later he was rushing northwards, in the direction of Brussa, where the new bathing establishments were to be built. At the beginning of June he suddenly made an appearance in the Princes Islands, in the Sea of Marmora. From there he went to Balikessir and then suddenly announced that Smyrna was to be his next destination.

Smyrna at once set to work to provide its deliverer with a fitting reception.

At dead of night a number of men gathered at Arif's house. Old Ayesha opened the door to them, eyed them suspiciously in

A SMALL SECTION OF THE SCHOOLCHILDREN OF
ISTANBUL
The mothers of all of them passed their lives in the harem.

HAREM LADIES OF ANATOLIA IN OUTDOOR COSTUME
BEFORE THE ABOLITION OF THE VEIL

the light of a lamp, guided them into the colonel's room, and then left them.

The men displeased her. What did they want in the house? On tip-toe, she crept to the door and listened.

What did all this mystery mean? What was the explanation of these night sessions and whispering? For some time past the young bey effendi had been causing her mental uneasiness. He looked pale and dissipated, and wore an ugly expression on his face. When he laughed, which was often, it made her blood freeze.

Why did they drag parcels into the house under cover of darkness? Parcels which no one was allowed to touch, Old Ayesha not excepted?

Something was afoot, something was amiss! . . .

Smyrna was gay with flags, bunting, triumphal arches and flowers. Thousands and thousands of little lights were suspended along the streets and on the walls of the houses. On the balconies of the windows stood baskets of flowers, which the women were to throw into the Ghazi's car as it passed below them.

The Prefect of Police secretly shook in his shoes. His agents were everywhere, scenting danger.

A simple, old man picked his way from the harbour to the Police Presidency and requested to see the Chief Constable.

That powerful man, who already had his suspicions, and fearing an attempt at assassination, nodded to his secretary.

" Bring him in."

The man was a simple Anatolian fisherman. In an awkward and embarrassed manner, he reported that three men had been to see him and had asked him to perform a small service for them.

The police officer raised his eyebrows. Well?——

He was to be rewarded with a sum in gold—the fisherman reported—if at a certain time on the morrow he rowed the men over to Chios, an island belonging to those dogs of Greeks. He was a poor fisherman and would gladly earn a few piastres. However, the sum which the three men offered was so high that he did not altogether like the business. He thought there might be something behind it.

The Prefect of Police lost no time.

Shortly afterwards three men waiting near the harbour were quietly surrounded. Numerous loungers, with their caps pulled over their eyes, lolling against the walls of houses and in odd corners, suddenly turned out to be police agents.

The three men were pounced upon, handcuffed and quickly removed. The life of the harbour continued as normally.

In the gaily-decorated main street a house was searched. A police inspector made an exclamation of satisfaction when bombs were discovered on the first floor.

The arrested men made a confession. They had been given the task of hurling the bombs into the Ghazi's motor car.

The telegraph wires buzzed, and in a very short time the whole police apparatus was at work.

As had been expected, the men transpired to be hired assassins. Rapidly the trail was traced back and the original source found. The Kemalist police got to work promptly and efficiently.

A certain Sia Hurshid was arrested. He had been a deputy in the first National Assembly. During the examination he broke down, admitted everything, betrayed everything.

All that was now needed were the names of the leaders of this secret society which so earnestly desired the violent removal of the Ghazi.

Sia Hurshid mentioned several names. Among them were those of three Ministers. Who was the ringleader?

Arif.

Not a muscle in Mustafa Kemal's face moved as he heard the name.

While he was receiving the acclamations of the people of Smyrna, Arif's wrists were being placed in handcuffs.

In Angora and Constantinople arrest warrants were issued by the dozen.

The hour of the great military pashas had now struck. Kiazim Karabekir was removed to the gaol for prisoners on trial. The events were made known in the columns of the *Agence Anatolie*. The excitement which the news produced in Anatolia was tremendous.

Mustafa Kemal issued a proclamation to the nation.

" One day I shall die, but the Republic will live," he said.

ALHAMBRA

On the following day a different sort of motor procession, coming from Angora, made its entry in Smyrna—Bald Ali and Nedshib, the Public Prosecutor, with their Tribunal of Independence.

Ali smiled in a friendly way and got to work.

Just at this time the new Penal Code came into operation.

Outside the *Alhambra*, Smyrna's biggest cinema, there collected a great mass of excited and indignant people. The planned attack on the man whom they idolized and worshipped had roused the whole populace.

The crowd joined in a chorus of curses against all enemies of the Grey Wolf.

Gendarmes, with loaded rifles and revolvers, held the crowd away from the entrance. The bold, glaring advertisements for the theatre had been torn down.

The film which was showing inside was grim, pulsating life.

Below the white screen, which gaped blankly at the audience, the members of the Tribunal of Independence had their seats.

Throned in the centre was Bald Ali, smiling as usual and looking at his audience, who sat spellbound.

It was a huge trial with a hundred prisoners, an army of witnesses and a packed public gallery.

Did ever the film-screen depict such a dramatic scene as was being enacted in the theatre at that moment?

The Public Prosecutor's voice echoed through the building; the bald pate of the Hanging Judge glistened under the lights. The whole scene was ghostlike, unreal, uncanny.

On the fifth day of the trial Marshal Kiazim Karabekir faced the judge, an imposing, soldierly figure, who listened in stubborn, bulldog fashion while the Public Prosecutor, Nedshib, described him as an enemy of the people and a parasite of the revolution.

His vindication of himself was brief.

He had no use, he said, for plotters and assassins. He was a soldier. Was it necessary for him to enumerate the various patriotic services which he had given to his country? He had fought for the liberation of the Sultan from the foreigners. Was he to blame for having been deceived? His honest soldier's brain was incapable of appreciating the political necessity for that deception and that deeds which make history are subject to different laws than are private morals.

How did he explain the letter which he was accused of having sent to Sheikh Said?

That was perfectly harmless, as might be seen from the contents of the document.

The Public Prosecutor jumped up. Who was to say that other letters had not been exchanged? And was not the bare fact of a connection with a rebel like Sheikh Said worthy of general condemnation and disgust?

The marshal shrugged his shoulders. He was not conscious of having committed any crime.

Bald Ali had made a careful study of public feeling and knew that there would be general relief if it were established that there was no case to be made out against the marshal. Kiazim Karabekir was exceedingly popular. Kel Ali knew that the man was no conspirator, but merely one who was unable to make the pace when worlds collapsed and others rose in their place overnight.

When, to the general surprise of the public, he announced an acquittal, the crowd standing outside the theatre called for cheers for the marshal and the Hanging Judge.

The film continued.

Marshal Ali Fuad was heard.

He had always held himself rather aloof, and Mustafa Kemal had never liked him. However, nothing could be proved against him, and his connection with the conspirators was not established.

He was acquitted and received an ovation.

But from that hour the military pashas were finished politically for all time. They retired into private life.

The drama now drew near the peak of its sensation.

Seated among a row of criminals was Arif, heavily ironed. At his sides and behind him stood giant warders. On his lips there was a smile of scorn.

There was absolute silence in the room. The Ghazi's friend! The head of the conspiracy! A veritable *sheitan!*

Kel Ali glanced at him. It might not be too easy to send this artful old fox to the scaffold.

Nedshib, the Public Prosecutor, had risen. Arif's smile irritated him. Ali returned the smile.

Colonel Arif Bey was accused of being an accomplice in an attempt to assassinate the Head of the State, Ghazi Mustafa Kemal. The men who were to carry out the assassination had been seen entering and leaving his house at night, and they had been given shelter there.

" That's a lie ! " exclaimed the accused, though he immediately afterwards resumed his cold, cynical attitude.

Ali nodded in a friendly way. If the prisoner were accused of that, it would have to be proved.

Arif wore the arrogant, self-satisfied expression of a man against whom nothing could be proved. The Prosecutor would have had the greatest pleasure in springing at his throat. There was an atmosphere of high tension in the room.

Ali now intervened to observe that they must hear the evidence of the only person who was in a position to say what visitors the colonel had or had not received—Ayesha, his housekeeper.

No one noticed the colour suddenly mount to Arif's cheeks, although the gendarme standing at his side observed how he dug his finger-nails into the flesh of his palms.

Old Ayesha shuffled into the room. Suddenly into Arif's eyes there came a look of tenderness. Memories of childhood returned to him. Ayesha—he would have liked to shout—how's our old friend, the bear ? Instead of that he continued to smile scornfully.

Had the prison atmosphere begun to get a hold on him, or why was it that he felt so uncomfortable when old Ayesha was led in ? When she was near he had always had a childlike feeling of security. However, he quickly recovered his *sang-froid*. His eyes wandered about the room, from Ayesha to Bald Ali, with whom in past days he had played poker, from Bald Ali to the Public Prosecutor, that raving idiot, and back from him to Ayesha.

Bald Ali leant forward sympathetically and addressed himself to Ayesha.

Did she know the gentlemen over there; would she mind looking at them attentively for a moment ?

Slowly the old woman turned towards the men who had been arrested at the harbour. She stood and examined them in silence.

A few seconds, which seemed like an eternity, passed.

Ali nodded encouragingly. The old woman turned slowly back to that kind, benevolent old gentleman, the Hanging Judge. Arif's eyes were fixed to her lips, which began slowly to open.

A movement passed through the room as, clearly and distinctly, she answered, " Yes ! " She knew the men.

Arif's eyes bulged in their sockets. He almost shouted : Ayesha !

Questioned again, the old woman repeated : " Yes."

Ali beamed. The Public Prosecutor crowed and triumphed.

Arif had collapsed. A momentary faintness had overcome him, but he recovered almost immediately. He regained full self-control and all his former bravado.

To hell with the trial and the court !

He scarcely troubled to listen to the rest of the proceedings.

Ali had already asked whether the worthy old *hanum* could say that the colonel had received these men at night.

Yes—Ayesha had replied.

Arif realized that he was finished.

Ali slowly rose, cleared his throat, and with his celebrated amiability pronounced the death sentence.

People in the hall and outside signalled their approval by clapping.

The pale, white light of electric arc-lamps fell upon the front of the prison and illuminated the faces of thousands and thousands of people who were jostling each other on the square and blocking the neighbouring streets.

Thirteen wooden scaffolds could be seen in the milky light, in which myriads of midges were buzzing merrily.

Each of the thirteen condemned men wore a white robe, rather like a nightshirt in appearance. Their hands were tied behind their backs. Round their necks was a rope.

Many thousands of people were present and yet there was absolute stillness. It was only with much difficulty that the condemned could be recognized. The white execution shirts had extinguished their personalities.

With a dispatch case tucked under his arm, Bald Ali stood in the centre of his staff. He looked for a moment at the sky and then gave the executioner the signal.

Each of the condemned—they were Ministers, pashas and soldiers of high rank—was allowed to address the people for the last time before meeting his fate. One recited a poem; another murmured a prayer.

That Arif departed this life without a word, with a scornful smile on his face, was what everyone expected.

Mustafa Kemal was waiting in his study at Chankaya. Bald Ali hastened to the telephone to report to his master.

Mustafa Kemal heard his statement without comment. When the name " Arif " was mentioned, he put his cigarette in the ashtray, extinguished it with his thumb, and went on with his work.

A few weeks later several influential representatives of the " Grand Orient " and of the big international finance circles were wearing out their shoes in Angora trying to secure a pardon for their brother in distress, Javid Bey.

He, together with Dr. Nasim and two former important members of the Committee, had fallen into the clutches of Kel Ali.

The French Minister, Sarraut, turned to Mustafa Kemal with a personal appeal, called him a brother, and pointed out that he himself once used to frequent the Masonic Lodge in Salonika.

He had never belonged to a lodge, replied the President of State.

M. Sarraut and his friends had to content themselves with realizing that any attempt on the part of foreign circles to exert influence on Turkish affairs only resulted in a manner contrary to that intended.

In the afternoon Ali pronounced the death sentence. In the evening the last four leaders of the once powerful Young Turk Committee were hanged in Angora.

The corpulent Javid made a grimace at the crowd before the rope silenced him for ever.

While, here, the last shadows of the old Turkey were passing, New Turkey was revealing its society face. Outside the city, at the Ghazi's country house, the second anniversary of the foundation of the Ish Bank was being celebrated. The ladies were in low-cut evening dresses, the men in tail-coats and stiff-fronted shirts.

The intimate, oily notes of the saxophones floated away over the dark, rocky Anatolian desert.

CHAPTER XVI

FATHER OF THE TURKS

AT Chankaya, half an hour's journey from Angora, situated on a hill, was the President of State's villa. It was not a castle, but a simple, moderate-sized country house with a tower. It had a well-tended terraced garden filled with many-coloured, sweet-scented flowers. Grouped round the President's villa were a number of hurriedly-erected pavilions, in which his closest collaborators lived.

The whole reminded one of a time long past and of an army camp of the Turkish nomads—in the centre the khan's tent; round about the tents of the minor leaders. Something of the ancient traditions of a warrior people, which was now experiencing its regeneration, seemed to make its presence felt at the home of its most recent chief.

In the lounge a fountain played. In addition, there were carpets and flowers; furniture was conspicuous by its absence. Nearby was the study, a bare, empty apartment, save for the big writing-table which occupied the centre.

Seated at this table was Mustafa Kemal. The conventional graciousness of manner, which his office had made it necessary for him to cultivate, had taken some of the hardness from his features. These softened features concealed the contempt which he felt for other men and disguised the aloofness of this lonely warrior, whose ruling passion was deeds.

Mustafa Kemal was victor, dictator, undisputed master in his own particular world. When he stepped to the window he saw Angora lying at his feet in the west. If he looked towards the east he could see the vast Anatolian country, which ended somewhere in the dim recesses of Asia.

He had no wish to be dictator. The dictatorship was to him a necessary evil, which would have to stay until the people were ready to govern themselves. At the same time, he was no friend of liberal democracy. A soldierly-disciplined, well-led national State was his creed. He saw in that the State form of the future.

The man who had been offered crowns and phantom empires, and whom they had wanted to surround with a semi-deistic nimbus, had not been swept off his feet. He had none of the human weaknesses of a Napoleon. When at the peak of his fame the victorious soldier transformed himself into a sober civilian.

Fame and glory—he despised them!

Mustafa Kemal had set himself a task which he intended to achieve with the cold logic of a mathematician.

It was that which made his revolution different from others. Throughout its whole course it had been the product of one will, of his will. It was a revolution without slogans, without ideals of humanity and without the emotionalism of other revolutions. It was also accomplished without bloodshed and without barbarism.

Blood had flowed, but in the fight against external enemies. You cannot find pathos in the revolutionary tribunals, however much you look for it. The Tribunals of Independence were not weapons of terror. They were called into action as a last resort in moments of the gravest national peril to counter the activities of enemies of the nation, who could not be persuaded to see the error of their ways. In consideration of the magnitude of the change and the extent and tragedy of events, the number of death sentences was extremely small.

This revolution was a disciplined march to freedom.

Mustafa Kemal was an enemy of violence. He himself brought forward a proposal for limiting his dictatorial powers, and on the day on which Javid and his associates were hanged he opened the door of the Mother Country to a number of exiles.

His foes were dead. Either they died, or they withdrew from the field. Constantine, his unlucky rival on the Sakaria, died three years before in exile. Hadyanesti, the Greek commander-in-chief, was executed in Athens. Sultan Vahideddin ended his life in San Remo. Of his rebel friends of yesterday, those who had not ended on the scaffold had been exiled for life and were refugees to whom no one paid any attention and who counted for nothing. His old enemy, Enver, was felled by the sabre of a Red cavalryman: he died in the deserts of Central Asia. And, finally, his doughtiest adversary—Lloyd George—was swept from the political arena by Bonar Law, only a few days after the Armistice of Mudania.

Mustafa Kemal had survived them all. Still in the prime of life, he was a victor, dictator, a man who had succeeded.

The President, a man in a simple lounge suit, now set to work to finish the equation which he had only half solved.

The business of civilization, of construction, now claimed his attention.

A new State had been created—a modern, totalitarian State. But the Constitution, the State form, was nothing more than a frame, in which the rough, medieval picture could not fit. In name New Turkey was the most modern State existing. In reality it represented an impoverished, backward, unexploited land with a population of ignorant, uncivilized, poverty-stricken and uncouth citizens, who lived on without the slightest feeling for time or progress.

In the War it had been possible to rouse them temporarily from their lethargy to provide an example of superhuman effort. Now they could not be permitted to suffer a relapse and drop back into the old pre-War dullness.

Mustafa Kemal attacked the new problems with customary energy. The picture of everyday life was to be so altered that it would fit the frame.

He would tolerate no half-measures, no piecemeal efforts. Nothing less than the latest European civilization would satisfy him.

Mustafa Kemal stood midway between Europe and Asia. Russia's arms were open wide. He was tempted to choose Asia. Asia after all was the great mother of the Turks, too. Asia, though, was in a chaotic, formless, uncivilized state. A nation which meant to count for something in the great human family had to place itself on twentieth century soil, had to recognize the principles of modern life.

Could a compromise be struck between Asiatic feelings and European thoughts? Civilization and technical progress would be a mere gloss. They would never advance past the stage of imitation. Compromises are always bad decisions.

Mustafa Kemal decided for the West. The Turk must learn to acquire European feelings and so receive Western civilization not as something foreign, something taken over, but as something in the natural order of events.

The smelting process had been made possible by the fire of the War of Independence.

Mustafa Kemal had fought bitterly to maintain for Turkey a foothold in Europe. He already regretted reaching a compromise over the question of the Straits. Constantinople now possessed even greater importance than ever. Not having sovereignty of the Straits territory, and not being in a position to defend it in the case of need, was an intolerable state of affairs.

Every Turk was conscious of this thorn in the flesh.

The nations of the West still hesitated to accept this new and bold candidate for admission to their circle; still they could not bring themselves to accept him as a European.

The experts were sceptical and refused to be persuaded that the experiment would be successful. Admittedly, it was a magnificent experiment, but it was being tried out on an unfit subject.

Realities would bring the reformer to his senses. Alone the lack of money would cause him to fail.

The Turkish Government found itself against a determined credit barrier. The international finance world regarded the Ghazi with undisguised hostility.

The credit barrier caused him no worry. If they had placed the money at his feet he would not have accepted it. At no price was he willing that Turkey should again become dependent upon international finance, on Western capitalism.

They would make use of their own resources.

An old principle was strictly adhered to: You can only spend as much money as you possess. Borrowed money is no money.

This principle was tenaciously respected. To achieve success by this means meant that all sources must be mobilized and guided from one centre. Turkey had very little money, but enormous requirements. The programme of construction cost tremendous sums. So there was no room here for private capitalistic, profit-making interests and just as little room for Communist experiments.

Mustafa Kemal maintained friendly relations with his eastern neighbour. But in Turkey Communists were hanged.

The road was clearly marked. The State would have to keep a strict eye on private enterprise and control it if and when necessary. The interests of the individual were to be subjected to the interests of the community. The (often) conflicting interests of capitalist enterprise were to be controlled and brought into harmony.

And so a national trade was built up that had Western liberalism beaten.

Mustafa Kemal had taken due note of the signs of approaching world crisis. He had not long to wait before world trade was struck a blow which rendered all former conceptions problematical.

Mustafa Kemal, so to speak, guided his nation past the crisis. Turkey stood outside the international net. The State controlled and governed, directly and indirectly, the whole of the country's trade, and kept it pointing in one direction—the welfare of the whole community.

Anatolia was a wealthy land, but its riches had first to be exploited.

The first step in that direction was the creation of an efficient railway system. The State acquired the existing lines, one after the other, and started to build new ones. In a few years the number of railways had been doubled. The separate industrial and agricultural districts were connected up. A second north to south line was put down, a third is under construction. Also a second line connecting the west with the east was constructed, affording a direct rail service from the Black Sea to the Mediterranean.

In addition to the principal lines, a number of branch lines have been, and are being, constructed, so that the country will have a complete and systematic network of railway communications.

The costs are borne by the State. If the State cannot provide the sums required, then the internal loan market is called in to help.

Hand in hand with railway construction there is road-building. The motor 'bus, as the most modern and practical means of transport, had been generally introduced and is popularly employed.

Industrialization is not to be carried beyond a certain, well-defined limit. Turkey is to be an agrarian State. In the centre of Anatolia there is a rich grain district, that could not be previously exploited on account of the difficulties of transport. Work is proceeding enthusiastically with the object of utilizing these natural resources in the cause of national prosperity. Transport lines are being laid; silos are being erected; arable land is being snatched from the steppe. Mustafa Kemal personally leads the campaign for modernizing agricultural methods of production. His private estate is an example of what it is possible to achieve. Irrigation systems are being created. Help for the peasant is provided by credit societies and co-operative societies. Seeds may be had free of cost. In Angora there is a first-class agricultural college.

The peasant has no fear of the profiteer. Credits are received through the State Bank of Agriculture.

The next goal is self-sufficiency. Up till now, and despite the immense possibilities for the production of grain, the needs of the big cities have had to be satisfied partly through imports.

But this is being rapidly remedied. In a short time Anatolia will be able to supply all the country's needs. And a little later Turkey will be able to make her *début* as a grain exporter.

Side by side with increased production improvement of the quality is proceeding apace. Seed-testing institutions are being established, and wheat-growing, which has been neglected in the past, is now receiving great encouragement. Germany, Austria, Belgium and Switzerland are the leading customers. Italy is the most important market for barley and oats.

In 1927 the wheat crop amounted to 1,333,000 tons. In 1933 it had risen to 2,712,000 tons.

The work is being carried on methodically; slogans and untested theories are not wanted. Things are done soberly and impartially, and only those things which are reconcilable with the needs and peculiarities of the country.

" Agricultural questions," said Shukri Kaya, who was Minister of Agriculture in the first Ismet Cabinet, " cannot be hidden under fine phrases and captivating arguments. They are a book written on the soil itself. The pages lie open there and any man can read them for himself."

Chiefly owing to the personal efforts of Ismet, a flourishing cotton and jute industry has been summoned into life. The State keeps a watchful eye on planting and cultivating.

And so the modernization and mechanization of agriculture is advancing in giant strides.

Land-areas which have been arid and barren for thousands of years are now being irrigated, and the earth returns thanks with its fruitfulness.

Wine-growing is also receiving a great deal of attention. Here the State has a monopoly.

The question of forestry has been tackled so successfully that to-day Anatolian forests are in a position to supply all the timber that is needed for home consumption. The giant forests which have still to be exploited are a potential source of wealth for the future.

The world is justly astounded at the success which Kemalism has had in the economic sphere. How was it possible? How were the men in Angora able to manage it?

The method was a simple one: they worked and worked, and left the talking to others. Unity and a strong leadership are the secrets of Turkey's success in trade. At the head of everything there is Mustafa Kemal, with his splendid sense of reality, his unfailing sharp-sightedness and his determination to carry through ruthlessly that which he has recognized to be right and practicable.

So New Turkey in a few years has travelled a course for which the other nations have needed many decades and, indeed, centuries.

Mustafa Kemal in his work of civilization is in a happy position.

Western civilization is something which grew gradually in the course of the centuries and which had to sustain many reverses. Turkey took over civilization in the form of a ready-made product and transplanted it in fresh soil. Turkey had all the advantages gained from past experiences and could start at once with a perfectly-functioning apparatus. The great crisis through which the Western world recently passed has been a timely warning. Mustafa Kemal does not build according to to-day's, but according to to-morrow's rules.

The criticisms of the world Press do not affect him in the least: the Kemalist system is not a real democracy, but rather a badly-disguised dictatorship.

History is not made with sophisms and dogmas, but is the product of realities. At the present time Kemalism is the only possible system for Turkey. Sooner or later other nations will find themselves obliged to adopt totalitarian methods, if they do not wish to be left behind.

The Grey Wolf is completely indifferent as to when and how.

He continues to create and perfect his work, which is a model example of modern statecraft.

FATHER OF THE TURKS

His cry, once heard over the battlefields of Gallipoli and Dumlu Punar, still echoes through the land : *Vitesse, vitesse, messieurs !* State manufacture is to be created. It will be limited to the production of manufactured articles for which the raw materials are already available and for which there is a home demand.

Manufacturing will be financed through a national bank known as the *Sumer Bank*.

At Kaissarie an aircraft factory run by the German Junkers Concern is already operating. Flying has been taken up with great enthusiasm, and the Air Fleet Association has the active support of the State. Electricity works and sugar factories have sprung up by the score. In poor districts industrial undertakings have been settled for the purpose of providing the local population with work and bread.

Textile factories are receiving the attention of the Government, and merino sheep are now being bred on a large scale to provide fine yarn for the mills.

Naturally, there are reverses, mistakes and blunders ; but these only stimulate the nation to redouble its energies.

Commerce, banking and finance, formerly exclusively in Greek and Levantine hands, are now being uncompromisingly Turkicized.

New Turkey's first banking venture was with the *Ish Bank*, the Labour Bank, which was opened in 1924. It has to-day some 42 branch offices. The deposits exceed 40 million Turkish pounds.

A year later the Bank for Mining and Industry, known to-day as the *Sumer Bank*, came into existence. The Agrarian Bank began its activities as early as 1924. With its 54 branches and 205 agencies it controls the entire agricultural credits system. It is the only banking undertaking that was in existence in pre-war days. The old Agrarian Bank granted in 1920 credit to the extent of 3,547,000 Turkish pounds ; in 1932 the new bank allowed credit to the extent of £(Turkish) 68,000,000.

The remaining, important banking venture is the Central Bank. It now issues notes—the right formerly exercised by the Ottoman Bank—and is a purely national institution. It is in reality the State Bank and works with extraordinary success.

In addition to these, there are numerous smaller banks of varying importance.

So the Turk has now also learnt how to be a capable man of commerce.

Stone by stone the great building is being constructed. The master-builder is untiring. One difficulty after the other is being surmounted.

When Mustafa Kemal elevated Angora to the status of a capital, it was an appalling, fever-infested hole, surrounded by the steppe and the Anatolian desert.

The name was then Turkicized. The world's most modern capital received the name " Ankara." Mustafa Kemal himself drew up the general plan of construction. Town-planners were then brought over from Germany, and at Kemalist pace the work began. The fever swamps were drained, and in their place there rose a modern municipal park. Millions of roses filled the air with their aroma. A planetarium was then erected.

Mustafa Kemal had millions of trees planted. Skyscrapers and wide thoroughfares next appeared. All were constructed according to the most modern methods of technology. The whole was constructed on the vast, typically American scale. Mansions, villas, hotels, schools and hospitals rapidly appeared.

The great architect made no attempt to imitate an oriental style. Everything was constructed on the straight-line, practical system : massiveness was the goal aimed at.

For the first time the Turks had built a city. Formerly they had merely occupied cities which they gained in conquests and which they subsequently extended, or left untouched, as the case might be.

From the windows of his simple country house at Chankaya Mustafa Kemal could see Ankara growing, growing according to his will and his ideas. It was like a return to the oldest times of the Turkish nomads and the Arabian caliphs : out of rough army camps there grew splendid cities. Ankara was the army camp of the Nationalist Revolution. There they slept under the stars, in the streets and public squares. Newspapers were printed in goats' sheds. Now the warlike chaos was being transformed into an ultra-modern city—a monumental stone memorial to one great ruling will.

Constantinople was also included in the general plan of reconstruction. The old Imperial City on the Bosporus is to have a new harbour, which most probably will be built on the Sea of Marmora. A *conservatoire*, a modern theatre and many other large and important buildings have been projected.

The Saint Sophia has been turned into a museum. The costly Byzantine mosaics, which a century ago were white-washed, have been restored and are now available for the whole world to inspect.

Electricity is being carried even to the remotest parts of the country. Main water supplies are obtainable everywhere.

There is one shadow which darkens the work of progress : the illiteracy of the nation.

The great work of reformation threatens to collapse before this greatest of all obstacles. Nine-tenths of the people are unable to read and write.

Schools and still more schools are needed. In Turkey there were several high schools. They were foreign. Mustafa Kemal decided to close some of them. The rest had to give an undertaking only to employ the Turkish language and in addition to engage a certain percentage of Turkish teachers.

For the great mass of the people Mustafa has created new schools. But the Turks have no money to buy their children the requisite school books. They are granted credit for this purpose.

Mustafa Kemal is a sort of Inspector-General of Schools. He pays surprise visits to the various institutions, tests the teachers, examines the children, makes enquiries about their progress, their state of health and their home life, and then takes his place at one of the desks and listens to the lessons. In whatever sphere of life he may be employed each Turk is made to feel the Ghazi's presence.

Just as frequent are his surprise visits to the different administrative offices—and woe to the clerk or official who fails to pass the tests which he applies ! Regularly every year, during the Parliamentary vacation, Ismet leaves on an incognito tour of the country. During this time there are many unpleasant shocks in store, not infrequently for high provincial officials.

Kemalism, the Nationalist Revolution *Weltanschauung* of New Turkey, will not be able to take its full effect on the present generation. Accordingly, it is the rising generation which merits the greatest part of the care and attention of Mustafa Kemal and his helpers.

He has helped to organize boy scout associations and national youth societies; he encourages sport and games and physical training.

Progress is much too slow to satisfy his fiery spirit. While illiteracy lasts the great mass of the people can get very little further.

The chief root of evil was the complicated Turkish alphabet. It made it practically impossible for the ordinary man in the street to learn to read and write. Moreover, these difficult signs were an intolerable burden on international relations.

Turkey was to have a modern script, resembling that used by the European nations. A language congress assembled and famous experts from all over the world wrestled for weeks in a vain endeavour to reproduce the Turkish alphabet in Latin script.

This was more than the Ghazi could stand. These scholarly gentlemen might go on debating about this or that letter till doomsday, and still fail to arrive at a decision.

One evening Mustafa Kemal took a pencil and paper and got to work. When dawn rose over Anatolia, and the sun tinted the rocks in all hues from bright yellow to dark mauve, the alphabet was ready. It was practical and simple, in fact so much so, that the experts almost certainly would never have thought of it.

Now began the big fight against illiteracy.

Mustafa Kemal went to Constantinople and gave a big reception in the former sultan's palace. On rows of chairs placed in the ballroom sat deputies, leading members of the priesthood, Press representatives, authors, State officials, school-teachers and members of important commercial concerns. The ladies were dressed in the latest fashion. It was frightfully hot.

At the end of the room there was a platform, on which Ismet and Kiazim Pasha, the President of the Great National Assembly, had taken their seats. Standing near them was the President of State. On one side of the platform was a big school blackboard.

Mustafa Kemal stood by the blackboard and explained why the whole Turkish nation, without distinction of class or age, must return to school.

Knowledge brought power, prosperity, progress. A mastery

of the Latin script as used in all parts of the civilized world was the key to knowledge.

He then explained the alphabet, and wrote it on the blackboard. Then, better to illustrate its practical uses, he invited several of his audience, ladies as well as men, to come to the board and write their names in the new script. This was the cause of many humorous incidents and much amusement at the expense of awkward pupils.

Ismet, laughing, said that the head of the Army had turned himself into headmaster.

Then the deputies were invited to spend their holidays at the Ghazi's country house and learn the new script—as homework.

You cannot compel civilization to come to a country. First the need for it must be impressed on the people, and the people themselves must be induced to welcome it voluntarily.

Mustafa Kemal and his colleagues again skilfully mobilized the forces which helped them to victory in the War of Independence: propaganda and influenced public opinion.

A giant national campaign was opened to arouse public hunger for civilization. Mustafa Kemal controlled the campaign. The President copied the methods of those huge American firms who invent innumerable cunning means of attracting a demand for their goods through advertisement and other ways.

Presently the inhabitants of all the cities and villages were expressing a hope that the Ghazi would visit them and instruct them in the new script. That was just what the Grey Wolf had wanted. Armed with a blackboard and chalk, he travelled the length and breadth of Anatolia. He gave instruction on the open market-square, and from far and near the peasants gathered to hear and learn. Everyone wanted to see what was the magic gateway to success. Everyone wanted to master the new script. This systematically-created hunger for knowledge knew no bounds. It was impossible to see a Turk who was not practising self-education. At the corners of the mosques, in the streets and bazaars and in the cafés people could be seen sitting over a slate exercising themselves in the new script. Writing became a sport.

Prices were offered for the best writers. No longer could anyone feel secure. There was no knowing when the Ghazi would come along, pounce on some unsuspecting wretch and ask him to provide a specimen of his proficiency in the new art.

Finally the new script was made official by Act of Parliament. So-called National Schools were opened, in which special courses in writing were held. All Turks under the age of forty had to attend one of these annual courses.

In the Act it was stated that " The First Teacher in the National Schools is the President of the Republic, His Excellency Ghazi Mustafa Kemal."

Calculations proved to be shrewd. Who, especially among the women, were willing to admit that they had passed forty and were rapidly becoming old iron? They all wanted to learn. Shirkers were punished, just as at other schools. Further, no convict was allowed to leave prison until he had mastered the Latin script! Agents of the Kemalist police combed the country for illiterates who showed an unwillingness to play the game.

Haidar Rushti, Deputy for Denesli, composed a four-line stanza:

" When the Ghazi was Commander and the nation in arms,
We snatched victory from the enemy.
So when the Ghazi is master and the nation pupil,
Ignorance shall be chased from the field."

Mustafa Kemal then gave the signal for the next phase of the battle. A renaissance of the Turkish language was to be brought about. This was not a matter of picking out all the foreign words and substituting new ones for the old, but a long and gradual process in which the whole nation was to be called upon to help.

The President drew up a plan.

He created a Turkish Language Academy, whose task was to study the Turkish language and history. Part of its work was to trace old original Turkish words. In this sphere of its activities the whole nation was called to help it. Those who knew any of the old folk-songs, sayings or expressions were asked to communicate them to the society. The latter sifted the material thus acquired, published the results of its work in magazines, and did everything possible to popularize the new words. Great care was taken to ensure that the pace was not too fast for the people, and that reintroduced words had been properly absorbed before more new words were brought along.

The Arabic tongue was prohibited for religious use. The muezzins now summoned the people to prayer in the mosques in the Turkish language. For technical and scientific purposes the expressions in normal international usage were adopted without hesitation.

The ultimate goal was the removal of discord between the language of the simple man and that of the educated man.

. . . . . .

A truly royal architect, Mustafa Kemal not only adorned the country with splendid, modern buildings, he also had many monuments erected. In 1927 Ankara was presented with a fine Victory Memorial, the work of the Viennese sculptor, Krippel.

Not less impressive is the huge memorial, "Public Security," which has been erected in the park in the Government quarter of the capital.

The first monuments and statues were the work of foreign artists. In order to encourage a Turkish national art, a Fine Arts Academy has been opened in Constantinople, and already an imposing number of Turkish painters and sculptors are producing successful work.

Many of the statues of the Ghazi which may be seen in Anatolian cities are the work of Turkish artists.

If plastic art, that stepchild of old Islam, has received special attention from the Ghazi, he is no less eager to encourage another art, in which, up till now, the East has not excelled—music.

In the early days of the battle to reconstruct the new State, he made several remarks which tended to show that he wished to adopt European music.

In August, 1928, Mustafa Kemal was in Constantinople. It was the occasion of the unveiling of the Victory Memorial. On the following day an enthusiastic audience of many thousand people assembled in the park at the Seraglio Head to listen to a concert.

Tremendous applause filled the air. The Ghazi had arrived. It was at the time when the great crusade against the old script was being conducted. Mustafa Kemal wished to address the audience.

He explained his musical creed and appealed to the Turkish people to follow him and help in the creation of a new music constructed on the principles of the European branch of the art.

Previously in Turkey, apart from the military bands, there had only been so-called " Orchestras of Fine Stringed Instruments," which were employed to accompany the national folk-songs. They performed a typical Oriental music, whose effect was rather monotonous and whose scope was limited.

This ancient folk music was to be kept, provided that it was of genuine Turkish origin. But occupying a far more important place, there was to be created a new music, which although employing European forms would at the same time preserve a distinctive Turkish character. A glance at Europe showed that although, generally speaking, the classic and romantic forms had much in common, there were definite distinctions between German, Italian, Russian and French music. And so a Turkish music could be created modern in form, which expressed the Turkish character.

When music was neglected, said Mustafa Kemal, the national character lacked something important.

His appeal was not left unanswered. A High School of Music and a Conservatoire were established in Constantinople, and a musical life of the German pattern came into being. The State helped in every way possible, and with financial assistance enabled talented young people to receive a musical training. Many were sent to foreign academies of music, and on their return were installed as teachers to train the growing generation. Here again foreign advisers and organisers were employed to help over the transition stage and enable the nation to stand on its own feet.

The Conservatoire Orchestra, under the direction of two Turkish conductors, gives in the winter season a regular series of symphony concerts, at which the best works of European composers (including some of the modern writers) are performed.

In the schools children are tested for musical talent, and the State is constantly on the look-out for promising material. Musicians who employ their time in composing original works receive every encouragement from the Government. Free concerts are held with the object of popularizing music with the general public.

To-day Turkey has several instrumentalists who have performed with credit in European concert-halls, among others Jemal Reshid (pianist) and Seyfettin Azaf ('cellist).

The theatre is also being pushed ahead. In the House of the People in Ankara a small but technically perfect theatre has been built.

In other cities new theatres have been projected. Until they are ready performances will be given in public halls and cinemas.

Constantinople is now to have a new State Theatre. In addition to Turkish works, those of European playwrights are to be performed. Nowadays Goethe's *Faust* is played in the old Municipal Theatre in Constantinople. The typically Teutonic philosophy of this work may be a little incomprehensible to the audiences, but the *Gretchen* tragedy is enthusiastically received.

The progress which has so far been made in theatrical art is satisfactory and has encouraged further ventures.

Opera and the operetta are also considerably patronized.

Literature has experienced a tremendous impetus.

· · · · · ·

In 1929 disturbances again broke out in East Anatolia. Far beyond the frontier, in Afghanistan, the Reaction had defeated Progress. The Reaction in the Near East saw in this their last chance. Deported Dervishes secretly made their way back to Turkey and began to work up a hostile feeling. Here and there they found numbers of malcontents and enemies of law and order, who followed their call.

Revolt again flamed up in the wild mountains of Kurdistan. The sheikhs again summoned their followers to fight against the *sheitan* incarnate, the Ghazi of Ankara.

The Kurds had not ceased to be a source of trouble and anxiety to the Government. They were the last remaining parasitic body in the National State, and a factor of danger at that, for on the other side of the frontier, in Iran and Iraq, related tribes were seeking union with them. Hostile Powers had in the Kurds a convenient means of causing the Government difficulties.

This time, too, there were grounds for believing that foreign influences were behind the revolt. The rebels were very well armed and adequately supplied with money.

There had been no other choice—the Kurds had had to submit to a process of nationalization in order for the reform policy of the Government to be achieved. There could have been no question of denationalization, because the semi-savage nomads were in any case completely devoid of feelings of patriotism. The task of the Government was to treat them as though they were unruly children and force them, whether they liked it or not, to be useful members of the community.

These untamed sons of the mountains, very naturally, resisted with every means at their disposal.

A rude shock was in store for the agitators. They knew that there was no joking with the Ankara people when it was a matter of keeping law and order in the State, but they were hardly prepared for such swift action as took place on this occasion.

Before the insurgent forces had made up their minds what was to be their next goal, Turkish troops stormed the Ararat, the headquarters of the rebellion, combed the valleys and ravines, and cleaned up the whole district.

The authorities attempted to solve the Kurdish problem in a different way. Whole tribes were driven from their mountain home and settled in cultivated areas on the Mediterranean coast. The Government hoped that, there, they would grow like the local, civilized population.

But now there were also disturbances in the Western Provinces. Everywhere the concealed hand of the Nakishbendi, the Enemies of Laughter, was apparent. Evidently they were deluded enough to believe that the Grey Wolf could be driven to a similar fate to that which overtook King Amanullah.

In the general confusion which prevailed Communist agents suddenly estimated that the time had come for the introduction in Turkey of the totally unfamiliar doctrine of class warfare.

They approached the Smyrna dock workers and tried to induce them to join in a general strike. To their acute disappointment they received precious little support. In Anatolia there had never been class differences. Each Turk, be he rich or poor, considered himself a gentleman, an *osmanli*. Even in the old Ottoman Empire many of the men occupying the highest positions in the State were of the humblest origin.

MODERN TURKEY IS ATHLETIC

The Government proceeded against the Communists with their accustomed rigour. The general strike came to nothing.

At this time, at Menemen, a little place on the outskirts of Smyrna, there appeared a religious fanatic, a Dervish of the Order of Nakishbendi, who preached the re-establishment of the realm of Allah.

An officer of the Reserve, Lieutenant Kublay, who was passing on one occasion, intervened, and dragged the man from his platform. Immediately he was set upon by a horde of ruffians and beaten to death. His head was then severed and borne in triumph through the streets by Dervishes.

The inhabitants of Menemen were appalled. In the depths of their hearts there still remained something of the old, superstitious awe of the Enemies of Laughter, that once so powerful and respected order. No one dared to raise a hand against these fanatical monks, whose yells could be heard for miles.

They proposed to gather round them all good Moslems in the district, assemble them under the green banner of the Prophet and then advance on Constantinople, where numerous sharers of their views would welcome them with open arms. From there it would be a relatively simple matter to march on Ankara.—So argued the Dervishes in their rapture. They were dreaming in the future, having for the present lost all sight of reality.

It was not long before a convoy of lorries drove up to the city tightly packed with the Ghazi's soldiers with fixed bayonets.

A few hours later silence had returned to Menemen. Somewhere, handcuffed, the Dervish was being marched to prison between tall gendarmes in patent boots and white breeches.

Tranquillity had been restored. In no other part of the country did the Menemen incident produce an echo.

Mustafa Kemal ordered that the culprits were to receive exemplary punishment.

The whole may only have been an apparition, an hallucination, but it at all events proved one thing: namely, that a certain amount of discontent existed. Discontent which ventilated itself in such violent fashion did not arise without cause.

Mustafa Kemal travelled up and down the country by special

train and by car. It was high time that he studied matters for himself, at close quarters.

A big reshuffle in the Party and the State now took place. A general election was announced, in which old deputies were dropped and their places taken by younger men from the artisan and craftsman classes. The Party was completely reorganized. From an instrument of supervision it was transformed into an instrument of education. The Party commissioner in his allotted district was the big confidant of his people.

The time had now come for the dictatorship to be somewhat relaxed. Discontent was to be provided with a means of voicing itself. Mustafa Kemal, in fact, had decided to create an opposition party, however a party whose " opposition " would not be allowed to take a form likely to cause harm to the State.

Mustafa Kemal dropped a hint to his old friend, Fethi. Fethi left his post as Minister in London, returned to Ankara, and founded an " Independent Republican Party," which in the National Assembly was to represent the opposition.

A number of seats were to be set aside for it in the new National Assembly.

Had Mustafa Kemal adopted Western Democracy ? Not at all. The principal of absolutism remained unaltered. The Ghazi meant to take care that the opposition did not overstep the mark, but adhered to the purpose for which it had been created : the service of the State. It was to perform the function of a logical antithesis.

The leaders and supporters of the old People's Party sternly disapproved of the new decision. But Mustafa Kemal would not be persuaded to change his mind. He had come to the conclusion that a freer exchange of views would be helpful. On propaganda grounds, too, it seemed a wise move. No one was to be given cause to accuse the Kemalist system of being an obstinate dictatorship and thus have a weapon with which to inflame public opinion.

The electioneering campaign opened. In all parts of the country candidates of the new opposition party canvassed for votes.

The people set themselves up as judges.

What does this mean, they asked themselves ? Here are men who ask us to vote for a party which is not the Ghazi's. They announce positively that they intend being loyal to the State, that their only ambition is to serve the nation as a whole and to echo the voice of the Ghazi.

The Republican Progress Party in its day had also promised many things, but they had transpired to be a base deception, had led to serious national crises and to that abominable plot against the life of the Head of the State.

The appearance of the new party was bitterly resented, and in many places the people assumed a menacing attitude.

In view of this the opposition candidates were obliged without delay to seek protection under the wing of the People's Party. Fethi handed in his resignation to the Ghazi—of a position which he had never held.

The experiment had been a failure. The one-party system was kept.

The voices of sceptics throughout the world ceased one by one. Even the fiercest opponents of the Kemalist system had no option but to acknowledge that the incredible had become fact and that what had seemed impossible had been achieved.

General Kemal Pasha's wretched, revolution-born State, that strange product of a frightful collapse and a surprise victory, had proved its ability to survive. And not only had it survived, it had gone ahead in a manner, and at a pace, which should have caused several nations in old Europe to turn green with envy.

No one could deny that tremendous strides had been taken in all branches of civilization. Buildings, dams, schools, hospitals, institutes and industrial undertakings had been created; the new cities were extending, the old ones were being rejuvenated; railways connected all parts of the land; the fields produced fine crops; culture was gradually advancing into the virgin steppe, winning from it fertile soil to create more wealth for the country; the banks functioned accurately, speedily and in a manner which might well serve as a pattern for many similar institutions in Europe; the machinery of administration ran smoothly; corruption had been rooted out and destroyed, and a strict, Spartan sense of honour regulated life. All this had been achieved without foreign money!

The Revolution State became a factor of power such as the old

Ottoman Empire had not been for centuries. The Ghazi continued to strive to elevate his State to the position of a Great Power.

While civil construction had been proceeding at this pace, the Army had not been neglected. The Turkish nation sacrificed more than half its income for the maintenance of the Forces. They were organized on the basis of general conscription and possessed the latest equipment. Work is proceeding energetically to extend the national armaments industry and so make the country independent even in this respect.

The size of the Air Force is being constantly added to. In their modern, Anglo-Saxon-style uniforms, and with their smart bearing, the members of the three branches of the Forces make an exceedingly favourable impression. The standard of training, both for officers and the other ranks, is a very high one.

The Fleet in tonnage is still small, but its armament and equipment are good and the organization is very thorough. It, in any case, represents an efficient weapon.

What has become of those prophets who, a good decade ago, imagined that they could see the shadow of a new Genghis Khan darkening Anatolia, who saw in the mysterious man of Angora a first-class mischief-maker in what has been for many years one of the stormiest corners in world politics, and who could not issue loud-enough warnings?

The world had still to recover from the days of the dictated Peace Treaties. Treaties drawn up with malicious intent were almost certain to produce bad blood, and bad blood they did produce! But in one corner of the world there is to-day an astonishing degree of tranquillity and security—in South-East Europe and in Asia Minor.

Who to-day fears those eternal, immeasurable complications and frictions and those interminable squabbles whose pole and source were the old Ottoman Empire?

Mustafa Kemal has wiped out all old accounts, or has simply torn them up and consigned them to the waste-paper basket of history. The old Ottoman Empire was weak, had no will of its own, was defenceless and represented an open invitation to foreign powers to intervene in its affairs. The rival interests of the different governments became a source of international strife, and so the notorious, complex Oriental Question arose—that nightmare of the pre-War world.

What is left of those times? It only needed one great man—and international diplomacy evacuated Asia Minor, and the Balkans into the bargain.

Mustafa Kemal has badly deceived all the romanticists and prophets of evil. The power of the new State has been cast in the scales on the side of peace.

The Grey Wolf has demonstrated that although politics may be conducted with wisdom, only human greatness can make history.

The echoes of the Anatolian War and its aftermath had hardly died away when he extended the hand of permanent reconciliation to the arch-enemy who had inflicted such terrible wounds.

He resumed feeling with the Greek Government for the purpose of establishing an understanding between the two nations. It was to be a difficult task. The old hatred still sat deep in the hearts of the former foes, and memories were still fresh. Undeterred, the Ghazi set to work. At home he was the great civilizer, abroad the peacemaker.

The power of speech, of propaganda, which had already accomplished so much, would also pave the way to friendly feelings between Turks and Greeks.

This task, also, was achieved. The feelings of hostility steadily vanished; mutual dislike became less pronounced; feelings of sympathy made their appearance and developed finally into friendship. The terms of the Treaty of Lausanne, with its many bitter features to Greece, afforded many possibilities of friction. But of recent years the desire for a strong, authoritative State has been steadily gaining ground in Athens, and that desire has done much to make a *rapprochement*, an agreement, easier.

Turkey for the Turks! that is the principle of Kemalist policy. In accordance with the same principle, Kemalism respects the vital interests of the other nations. A State whose aims are of a pronounced national character very naturally is anxious to avoid being drawn into any kind of international complications. Domestically the State had been freed from the fetters of foreign interests, and in its foreign policy it is determined to remain equally free.

Mustafa Kemal strictly avoided being drawn into any sort of " Group of Powers."

In order to exclude the rival European Powers from the Balkans, he did his utmost to expedite the Balkan Federation, the strongest member of which was Turkey. The Balkan States in all probability have many points to settle among themselves. But in future these things are to be a purely Balkan affair, whereby there are to be none of those fatal interventions of the past. Moreover, the various differences are to be settled by friendly collaboration and discussion. Turkey desires a consolidation of the *status quo*. And it is that interest which determines her foreign policy.

Kemalist policy has in a large measure contributed to the relative calm and security which now obtain in South-East Europe, which is one of the few bright spots in the general gloom of the world situation to-day.

Ankara continues to exercise an increasing influence on European affairs. Turkey's entry to the League of Nations has been partly responsible for this. Increased interest in Europe has again brought Constantinople and the Straits into the foreground. More and more voices were raised demanding a revision of the Lausanne Straits Pact.

Friendship and non-aggression pacts were concluded with all States. In Western Asia, Persia and Afghanistan showed a strong disposition to close friendship with Turkey, whom they had taken as their pattern in the work of modernizing.

On principle a strictly neutral attitude is displayed towards Arab nationalism and, in fact, all Arab questions. Sentimentally, the Arab betrayal in the Great War has rendered a *rapprochement* extremely difficult, and in any case Mustafa Kemal has no desire to bring himself into conflict with England and France.

The Arabs have secured their independence from the old Ottoman Empire. What they do in future is their affair.

The process of weeding out Arab words and Arab customs was continued and culminated in a decree published on 26 November, 1934, which prohibited the further use of all titles and descriptions of rank which were employed in Arab and Ottoman circles.

The titles of *aga*, *muchtar*, *pasha* and *bey* disappeared. In the Army the old ranks of *mushir* and *liva* were substituted with *mareschal* and *general*.

A woman is no longer addressed as *hanum*. Each male Turk is a gentleman, a *bay*; each woman is a lady, *bayan*. No distinction is made between a married and an unmarried woman.

As the first to comply with this decree, Mustafa Kemal laid aside his two names. They were of Arabic origin. But as luck would have it, there is an old Turkish word which has a very similar sound to the name Kemal, a name that has earned world renown : it is *kamal*, meaning the " strong," the " armed." And so the President of State is now known as Kamal, and his system of government the Kamalist.

He also dropped the Arab title Ghazi.

Finally the last step towards complete harmony with European custom was taken. At the commencement of 1935 a decree was published concerning family names. Formerly in Turkey there were no fixed surnames. Now every Turk must by 1937 decide upon a fixed surname.

On 24 November, 1934, the Great National Assembly, at a special session, bestowed upon their President of State his new name.

As an expression of gratitude and admiration for their greatest and most-deserving son, the nation had decided in future to call him Kamal Ataturk, " Father of the Turks."

In the spring of 1935 the Turkish nation elected for the fourth time a new National Assembly. It was the President's wish that, in addition to the deputies of the People's Party, there should be a small number of independent deputies elected. They were to be persons of high character, with a strong sense of responsibility, and with known national and republican convictions. These deputies, through impartial criticism and control of Government measures, were to contribute towards increased national efficiency.

Thirteen independent deputies were elected to the new National Assembly. When Kamal Ataturk opened the new session of Parliament—the men according to the recently-introduced custom were in evening dress—he welcomed for the first time seventeen women to the House.

One of his oldest wishes had been fulfilled : at last the Turkish woman had achieved full equality of status. She now took an active part in the government of the country.

Meanwhile, Italian troop-transports were ploughing their way through the Suez Canal. The Ethiopian conflict loomed on the horizon.

Six months later the Damocles sword of war flashed above the blue waves of the Mediterranean.

The League of Nations was completely unable to master the affair.

In the case of warlike developments, who was going to guarantee the security of the Straits and Constantinople? Not with resolutions, but in actual fact?—so the people of Ankara asked.

Turkey freely acknowledged the existing position at Lausanne— said the opponents of revision.

That's true—replied the Turks—but since then the world situation has undergone a substantial change. Proof had been obtained that the League of Nations was unable to provide security. It would be an irresponsible act, were the Turkish Government to renounce any longer its right to defend itself at one of the country's most susceptible points.

In the last ten years the Kamalist Government had given proof that it had a positive contribution to make to the severe task of stabilisation and pacification.

England, as the Power principally interested, was not blind to the correctness of these arguments. When England began her sounding operations along the Eastern Mediterranean to discover who was her friend, she was able to confirm that Kamalist Turkey honourably and completely recognized British Empire interests.

But not all the obstacles in the path of settlement had been removed. Mussolini had meanwhile confronted the world with a *fait accompli* and assured Turkey that he entertained no aggressive intentions. Italy, having gained her African Empire, was satisfied.

The Turkish Press began to hint that, if necessary, sovereignty of the Straits would simply be seized. The means for doing that were available.

In order to forestall this possibility it was decided to open negotiations. Ankara officially demanded revision. The Straits Conference met at Montreux. The main question did not need long discussion. Turkey recovered complete sovereignty over a territory which rightly belonged to her.

Rushti Aras, as host of the Conference, handed a gold fountain-pen in the name of his Government to all signatories of the Pact. They were used in signing the new treaty.

Waiting on the frontiers of the former neutral zone were the troops. Then, to the cheers of an enthusiastic populace, they made their entry to the old, ruined forts, which two decades ago were the scene of heroic fighting.

The work was complete. The ring had closed. The renaissance of the Turkish people was continued on Gallipoli. Gallipoli was the splendid last brick in the building of Turkish freedom and independence.

A little later, when the whole civilized world was concentrating its attentions on the Olympic Games, and when the pick of the world's athletes were competing in Berlin, his former Majesty King Edward VIII was inspecting the military cemeteries on Gallipoli.

King and President met in Constantinople. They stood face to face, both in simple lounge suits, men of action, both filled with a new, live spirit, free from all prejudices and burdens and obsolete conceptions. Both were soldiers and servants of their peoples, who had been through the school of the most terrible of all wars.

They shook hands in the spirit of genuine, soldierly friendship. That handshake meant that in future there should be peace and friendship between the two nations.

One could almost imagine that the hot, aromatic breeze bore from nearby Gallipoli the greetings and blessings of the hundred thousand who fell in battle.

· · · · · ·

Annually, on 29 October, the Turkish nation celebrates its national holiday, on the anniversary of the proclamation of the Republic.

In 1936 it was celebrated with the proud feeling that Great Power status had been gained. Flags were flown; the streets were thronged with jubilant people; a brilliant blue decked the sky; the sounds of music were to be heard everywhere.

In Ankara there was a parade of the famous Nationalist Army. Loud-speakers carried the President's words to the remotest village.

An erect, soldierly figure in morning dress, his cool, sharp wolves' eyes looked out over the heads of the people. Behind him were his leading colleagues, the Ministers of State, the untiring Ismet Inoneu, Dr. Rushti Aras, the man with the big horn-rimmed spectacles, the herculean Fevzi....

In the world the coming year will be a period of big preparations. The Turkish People's Republic stands fast and unshakable. The Turkish nation can face the future with calm. The economic position is good. Construction proceeds smoothly. The Forces are equipped with the latest arms, and are competent to discharge any duties which they may be called upon to perform.

The voice of its President dies away over the vast Anatolian high plateau. The military bands strike up the " Sakaria March." The whole country joins in the anthem of a liberated nation:

" Fear Not . . ."

INDEX

A

Abdul Hamid, 26, 50, 51, 53, 56, 60, 65, 83, 112, 133, 224
Achmed Nessimi, 68
Adana (Kilikia), 142, 143, 144, 152
Adrianople, 65
Aegean, 11, 12, 13, 16, 17, 18
Afiun Kara Hissar, 159, 160, 167, 168
Aidan, 155, 159, 190
Ali Fuad, 150, 156, 225, 246, 252
Ali Galib, Governor of Malatia, 113, 124, 127, 129, 130
Ali Riza. *See* Chapter II
Allenby, 79
Amery, 243
Angora (Ankara). *See* Chapter IX, 131, 132, 159, 160, 161, 163, 167, 170, 171, 174, 175, 180, 182, 183, 184, 187, 193, 195, 196, 202, 203, 208, 211, 212, 213, 214, 215, 218, 219, 225, 229, 230, 233, 234, 235, 240, 244, 245, 246, 250, 251, 256, 264, 271, 273, 276, 281
Ariburnu, 20, 21, 24, 27, 29, 92
Arif, Colonel, 96, 97, 98, 99, 105, 106, 107, 110, 111, 117, 118, 119, 127, 128, 129, 150, 151, 152, 160, 161, 169, 171, 177, 178, 220, 221, 222, 233, 247, 248, 250, 252, 253, 254, 255
Ataturk, 279

B

Bald Ali, 238, 246, 251, 252, 253, 254, 255
Baldwin, 243
Bismarck, 50
Bonar Law, 257

C

Caliphate Army, 148, 151, 153
Calthorpe, Admiral, 84
Chalkoi, 189

Chamberlain, Sir Austen, 241
Chanak, 11, 14, 15, 193
Chankaya, 136, 183, 184, 212, 229, 234, 242, 255, 256, 264
Chatalja, 64
Chemsi, 38, 40
Chunuk Bair, 32
Churchill, 18
Clemenceau, 121, 122, 123
Committee of Union and Progress, 60, 61, 62, 69, 79, 96, 122, 149, 156, 219, 247, 248
Constantine, King of Greece, 159, 163, 174, 257
Curzon, 198, 199, 200, 201, 202, 203, 204, 205, 207, 209

D

Damad Ferid Pasha, 94, 102, 103, 104, 105, 111, 112, 113, 121, 122, 130, 131, 132, 133, 134, 138, 148, 154, 183
Dardanelles. *See* Chapter I, 201
Derna, 63
Diarbekr, 131, 132, 235
Dumlu Punar, 162, 183. *See* Chapter XII, 208

E

Edward VIII, 281
Enver Pasha, 12, 26, 60, 62, 63, 64, 66, 67, 69, 70, 71, 74, 75, 78, 81, 83, 92, 96, 103, 122, 125, 187, 239, 257
Erzerum. *See* Chapter V, 131, 178, 227, 233
Eski Shehir, 141, 162, 167, 168, 170, 173, 177, 188, 189, 220

283

INDEX

F

Falkenhayn, 74, 75
Feisal, 73, 229
Fethi, 54, 66, 212, 232, 234, 274
Fevzi Pasha, 78, 107, 144, 150, 171, 178, 191, 220, 282
Franklin Bouillon, 194

G

Gallipoli. See Chapter I, 193, 201, 281
Genghis Khan, 184, 191, 204, 215, 276
German Asia Corps, 74, 82
Gouraud, General, 144, 154

H

Hadyanesti, General, 188, 257
Hafis, 43, 44
Hague Tribunal, 243
Hakkiari, 229, 230, 242
Hamidie, Fort, 15, 16
Hamilton, Sir Ian, 19, 29
Harington, Sir Charles, 194, 196
Hedjaz, 73
Hilmi, Dr., 70, 71
Hindenburg, 77, 78
Hussein, King, 72

I

Independent Republican Party, 274
In Eunu, 158, 159, 160
Irak, 203, 205, 229, 242, 243, 271
Ismail Pasha, 53, 54, 55, 56
Ismet Pasha, 97, 107, 144, 149, 150, 156, 158, 178, 187, 191, 195, 198, 199, 200, 201, 202, 203, 204, 205, 206, 207, 208, 209, 210, 212, 213, 220, 234, 240, 244, 267
Italian Penal Code, 240
Izzet Pasha, 84, 94

J

Javid, 219, 221, 231, 247, 255, 257
Jemal, 61, 65, 75, 80
Jevad, Colonel, 13

K

Kadri, Major, 44
Kamal Ataturk, 279
Kannengiesser, Lieutenant-Colonel, 31
Kemaleddin Sami, 189, 212
Kiazim Karabekir Pasha, 114, 115, 116, 117, 118, 119, 134, 149, 178, 213, 219, 221, 225, 228, 232, 235, 236, 246, 250, 251, 252
Kiazim Pasha, 212, 220
Konia, 131, 132, 186, 229

L

Latifeh, 216, 217
Lausanne, 195. See Chapter XIII, 225, 233, 240, 277, 280
Lawrence, Colonel, 73, 74, 76, 79, 81, 82
Liman von Sanders, 12, 19, 22, 28, 29, 33, 34, 66, 67, 69, 74, 75, 76, 80, 81, 84, 85, 92
Lloyd George, 121, 155, 183, 194, 257
Ludendorff, 77, 78

INDEX

M

Mackensen, 34
Mahmud Shevket, 65
Marash, 140, 231
Mecca, 72
Medina, 73
Mohammed V, 12, 27, 65, 78
Mohammed VI. *See* Vahideddin
Monastir, 47, 52, 53
Monastirli Hamdi, 145
Mosul, 203, 204, 209, and *see* Chapter XIV
Mudania, 194, 198, 207, 257
Mussolini, 245, 280

N

Nakishbendi Order, 230, 272, 273
Narrows. *See* Straits
National Pact, 128, 138
Nazim, 65, 221, 231, 247, 255
Nestorians, 230
Nureddin Pasha, 237

O

Osman the Lame, 228, 229

P

Papulas, General, 181, 182
Paris and Peace Conference. *See* Chapter VII
People's Party, 246, 274, 275
Poincaré, 198, 209, 210

R

Rauf, 118, 221, 247
Refat, Colonel, 97, 107, 110, 118, 119, 120, 150, 160, 177, 195, 213, 219, 221, 225, 246
Republican Progress Party, 227, 231, 232, 235, 275
Rumbold, Sir Horace, 209
Rushti Aras, 281, 282

S

Sakaria. *See* Chapter XI, 208, 257
Salonika, 36-46, 57, 60, 62, 216, 248, 255
Sari Bair, 30, 31, 32
Sedd-el-Bahr, 20
Sèvres. *See* Chapter X, 184, 198, 242
Sforza, Count, 121
Sheikh Said, 230, 231, 233, 234, 235, 252
Sheikh-ul-Islam, 148
Sheria Legal Code, 239, 240
Sivas. *See* Chapter VIII, 136
Smyrna, 108, 109, 110, 152, 155, 163, 186, 188, 189, 190, 191, 192, 193, 215, 216, 248, 249, 251, 272, 273
Sofia, 21, 25, 27, 66, 67
Soviet Russia, 202, 203, 244
Straits, 13, 14, 15, 17, 18, 153, 193, 201, 202, 203, 209, 244, 259, 280
Suvla Bay, 29, 30
Swiss Civil Code, 240

T

Talaat, 66, 92, 103, 122
Tewfik Rushti, 242, 243
Tchitcherin, 201
Townshend, General, 84
Trebizond, 227
Tribunal of Independence, 233, 235, 238, 246, 251
Trikupis, General, 188, 189, 191

INDEX

U

Uif, 191
Urfa, 140, 143
Ushak, 190

V

Vahideddin, Crown Prince and Sultan, 77, 78, 83, 84, 93, 94, 95, 100, 111, 112, 113, 131, 132, 133, 134, 135, 138, 144, 145, 148, 152, 154, 155, 156, 158, 183, 195, 196, 197, 218, 257
Vatan, 53, 54
Venizelos, 109, 155

W

Wehrle, Colonel, 13
William II, 77
Wilson and " 14 Points," 122

Y

Yakub Jemil, 70, 71, 158
Yildiz Kiosk, 56, 98, 132, 183, 195, 211

Z

Zubeida, 38–45, 52, 53, 55, 57, 58–60, 64, 75, 76, 106, 148, 150, 185, 215, 217

INDEX

U

Uif, 191
Urfa, 140, 143
Ushak, 190

V

Vahideddin, Crown Prince and Sultan, 77, 78, 83, 84, 93, 94, 95, 100, 111, 112, 113, 131, 132, 133, 134, 135, 138, 144, 145, 148, 152, 154, 155, 156, 158, 183, 195, 196, 197, 218, 257
Vatan, 53, 54
Venizelos, 109, 155

W

Wehrle, Colonel, 13
William II, 77
Wilson and " 14 Points," 122

Y

Yakub Jemil, 70, 71, 158
Yildiz Kiosk, 56, 98, 132, 183, 195, 211

Z

Zubeida, 38–45, 52, 53, 55, 57, 58–60, 64, 75, 76, 106, 148, 150, 185, 215, 217

INDEX

M

Mackensen, 34
Mahmud Shevket, 65
Marash, 140, 231
Mecca, 72
Medina, 73
Mohammed V, 12, 27, 65, 78
Mohammed VI. See Vahideddin
Monastir, 47, 52, 53
Monastirli Hamdi, 145
Mosul, 203, 204, 209, and see Chapter XIV
Mudania, 194, 198, 207, 257
Mussolini, 245, 280

N

Nakishbendi Order, 230, 272, 273
Narrows. See Straits
National Pact, 128, 138
Nazim, 65, 221, 231, 247, 255
Nestorians, 230
Nureddin Pasha, 237

O

Osman the Lame, 228, 229

P

Papulas, General, 181, 182
Paris and Peace Conference. See Chapter VII
People's Party, 246, 274, 275
Poincaré, 198, 209, 210

R

Rauf, 118, 221, 247
Refat, Colonel, 97, 107, 110, 118, 119, 120, 150, 160, 177, 195, 213, 219, 221, 225, 246
Republican Progress Party, 227, 231, 232, 235, 275
Rumbold, Sir Horace, 209
Rushti Aras, 281, 282

S

Sakaria. See Chapter XI, 208, 257
Salonika, 36–46, 57, 60, 62, 216, 248, 255
Sari Bair, 30, 31, 32
Sedd-el-Bahr, 20
Sèvres. See Chapter X, 184, 198, 242
Sforza, Count, 121
Sheikh Said, 230, 231, 233, 234, 235, 252
Sheikh-ul-Islam, 148
Sheria Legal Code, 239, 240
Sivas. See Chapter VIII, 136
Smyrna, 108, 109, 110, 152, 155, 163, 186, 188, 189, 190, 191, 192, 193, 215, 216, 248, 249, 251, 272, 273
Sofia, 21, 25, 27, 66, 67
Soviet Russia, 202, 203, 244
Straits, 13, 14, 15, 17, 18, 153, 193, 201, 202, 203, 209, 244, 259, 280
Suvla Bay, 29, 30
Swiss Civil Code, 240

T

Talaat, 66, 92, 103, 122
Tewfik Rushti, 242, 243
Tchitcherin, 201
Townshend, General, 84
Trebizond, 227
Tribunal of Independence, 233, 235, 238, 246, 251
Trikupis, General, 188, 189, 191